Torah and Nondualism

Torah and Nondualism

DIVERSITY, CONFLICT AND SYNTHESIS

James H. Cumming

IBIS PRESS
Lake Worth, FL

Published in 2019 by Ibis Press
A division of Nicolas-Hays, Inc.
P. O. Box 540206
Lake Worth, FL 33454-0206
www.ibispress.net

Distributed to the trade by
Red Wheel/Weiser, LLC
65 Parker St. • Ste. 7
Newburyport, MA 01950
www.redwheelweiser.com

ISBN: 978-0-89254-187-4
Ebook ISBN: 978-0-89254-683-1

Library of Congress Cataloging-in-Publication Data

Names: Cumming, James H.
Title: Torah and nondualism : diversity, conflict, and synthesis /
by James H. Cumming.
Description: 1st Edition. | Lake Worth, FL : Ibis Press, 2019. |
Includes bibliographical references.
Identifiers: LCCN 2019009846 | ISBN 9780892541874 (hc : alk. paper)
Subjects: LCSH: Bible. Pentateuch--Criticism, interpretation, etc. | Bible.
Pentateuch--Hermeneutics. | Zohar. | Mythology, Egyptian. | Mythology,
Canaanite.
Classification: LCC BS1225.52 .C86 2019 | DDC 222/.106--dc23
LC record available at https://lccn.loc.gov/2019009846

Book design and production by Studio 31
www.studio31.com

Printed in the U.S.A. [MV]

This book is dedicated to the memory of

DONALD WEISER

זכר צדיק לברכה

"The memory of a righteous person is for a blessing."

(Prov 10:7)

"Woe to the person who says that Torah intended to present a mere story and ordinary words! For if so, we could compose a Torah right now with ordinary words, and more laudable than all of them [in the existing Torah]!... Concerning Torah, one should look only at what is beneath the garment. So all these words and all these stories are garments."

(*Zohar* 3:152a)

Table of Contents

"An Egyptian man saved us"

Who was Moses?

If we take the biblical account at face value, Moses was the scion of a distinguished Israelite family residing in Egypt in about the 13th century B.C.E. Due to Egyptian persecution, Moses' mother hid him after his birth and later placed him, still an infant, in a tarred basket floating among the reeds on the bank of the Nile. Moses was then found and adopted by the pharaoh's daughter, and he was reared in the royal household. This endearing story serves to confirm Moses' great favor with God, his powerful influence in the Egyptian royal court, and his impeccable Israelite pedigree. Suspiciously, however, this much-loved tale of Moses' birth runs in close parallel to the birth story of Sargon of Akkad, a powerful king who conquered Mesopotamia a thousand years *before* the time of Moses. Sargon, like Moses, was left on the riverbank in a basket woven from reeds and sealed with tar, and Sargon, like Moses, was rescued and reared in the royal household.

Obviously, the Sargon birth story raises questions about the historicity of the Moses story. And then, too, there is the story from the *Mahabharata* of Karna's birth. Karna is the son of the sun god, conceived in the womb of noble Kunti, the future mother of the Pandava kings. Kunti, who remains a virgin, feels shame about the birth of Karna and places the child in the river in a basket. Eventually, Karna becomes a king and also a leading warrior in the army of the Pandavas' enemy, Duryodhana. With this third rendition of the Moses-in-the-bulrushes tale, again describing an infant king set adrift on a river in a basket, we begin to wonder if we are dealing less with history than with archetype.

Whatever we might conclude about the historicity of Moses'

birth story, the biblical account makes clear that at least from his third birthday, when he was weaned (see Exod 2:7–10; 2 Macc 7:27), he was reared in the pharaoh's palace, essentially as a son of the pharaoh. Therefore, Moses would have spoken Egyptian, not Hebrew, as his primary language. Moreover, as a son of the pharaoh, Moses would have been trained in the esoteric wisdom of the Egyptian religion, for each successive pharaoh was considered to be an incarnation of the Egyptian god Horus, and the pharaoh's sons and grandsons were all trained for that role.[1] Thus, we can conclude from the biblical account that Moses' first religion—the religion of his childhood associations—was the Egyptian religion, not the Israelite religion.

Moses, the Egyptian prince, reached adulthood, and according to the Jewish historian Flavius Josephus (1st century C.E.), he led a successful military campaign to Ethiopia and married an Ethiopian princess.[2] What Josephus calls "Ethiopia" is a reference to ancient Nubia, the Nile kingdom just south of Egypt. Archaeological, linguistic, and genetic evidence demonstrates that the Nubian people were ethnic Dravidians (South Asians) who migrated to the Nile region during prehistoric times from what is now south and west India.[3] It was relatively common for Egyptian pharaohs to wage military campaigns against the Nubians, and it would not be surprising for a son or grandson of the pharaoh to lead such a campaign, but an interesting detail

---

[1] On Moses' mastery of Egyptian esoteric wisdom, see Acts 7:22.

[2] See Josephus, *Jewish Antiquities II*, chapter 10. Moses' "Ethiopian" wife is mentioned in chapter 12 of the book of Numbers, where Miriam and Aaron criticize Moses on her account.

[3] See Lal, "The Only Asian Expedition in threatened Nubia," pp. 579–581 [archaeological findings connecting the Nubians to the prehistoric people of southwest India]; Tuttle, "Dravidian and Nubian," pp. 133–144 [linguistic similarities between these two groups]; Gonzalez et al., "Mitochondrial Lineage M1 Traces an Early Human Backflow to Africa," 8:223 [DNA analysis showing that these two groups are genetically related].

appears in the story of Moses' Nubian campaign as it is related by Josephus.

Josephus says that Moses led the army by way of Egypt's interior, instead of leading it south along the Nile. This interior route offered a tactical advantage, but it also required the army to cross an area infested with poisonous "winged serpents." According to Josephus, Moses instructed his soldiers to carry ibises in baskets and to release the ibises when the army reached the infested area. The ibises killed the serpents, and the army was able to proceed without harm. Thus, Moses' name became associated, in legend at least, with the ibis, a sacred emblem of the Egyptian god Thoth. That connection between Moses and Thoth is important, as this book will show.

According to the biblical account, the pharaoh's daughter who adopted Moses gave him the name Moses (Hebrew: *MoSHeH*) because, as she put it, "I drew him" (Hebrew: *MeSHITiHU*) from the water. (Exod 2:10.) But the pharaoh's daughter would have spoken Egyptian, not Hebrew. Not surprisingly, then, the name Moses is an *Egyptian* name. In fact, many Egyptian names end with forms of the Egyptian word *mose*, which means "born from" or "drawn from." Ramesses II, who may have been the pharaoh during Moses' time (see hint in Exod 1:11), provides a good example. His name (*Re-mose*) translates as "Born from Re"—Re being the Egyptian sun god. Considering Moses' legendary association with ibises, and thus with the Egyptian god Thoth, we might suppose that Moses' full Egyptian name was Thutmose, meaning "Drawn from Thoth." In fact, at the approximate time of Moses' life, several Egyptian pharaohs bore the name Thutmose.

Another Jewish historian, Artapanus of Alexandria (2nd century B.C.E.), relates a slightly different history of Moses.[4] Artapanus describes Moses as a sage who taught practical sciences to the Egyptians—particularly the priestly sciences asso-

[4] See Eusebius, *Preparatio Evangelicum* 9:27:3–20.

ciated with the god Thoth. According to Artapanus, Moses was highly respected by the Egyptian priests, who called him by Thoth's name. Artapanus thus confirms that Moses' full name was Thutmose. The Torah records Moses' role as a leading priest and sage of ancient Egypt, saying that "Moses was very great in the land of Egypt, in the eyes of Pharaoh's servants and in the eyes of the people." (Exod 11:3; see also Acts 7:22.) Artapanus's account fills in some of the details of Moses' revered status.

Artapanus records that during Moses' military campaign against the Nubians, he consecrated his military camp to the ibis, Thoth's emblem. Also, Moses' military camp was located in Hermopolis, Thoth's primary city. Artapanus further relates that the husband of the Egyptian princess who adopted Moses was bitterly envious of Moses' talents and successes, and he tried several times to have Moses killed, perhaps viewing Moses as a rival for the throne of Egypt. Moses escaped these plots, and—according to Artapanus—Moses' rival died from elephantiasis.

The Torah only hints at the latter events. It states that Moses killed a man, and Jewish legend adds that this was achieved by the utterance of divine names. Specifically, the Torah states: "And [Moses] saw an Egyptian man striking a Hebrew man—from his brothers.... And he struck down the Egyptian man...." (Exod 2:11–12.) The phrase "from his brothers" might be describing either the Egyptian man or the Hebrew man, and the Torah is delightfully ambiguous in this regard. The phrase is usually read as a description of the Hebrew man (the Hebrews being Moses' ethnic "brothers"), but that reading makes the phrase redundant. If we read the phrase more literally, it might be a description of the Egyptian man, and the word "brothers" might then refer to one of the sons of the pharaoh, with whom Moses grew up as an adopted brother.[5]

---

[5] In translating the Bible's Hebrew text, the author of the present book has erred on the side of literalism, and therefore the translations may sometimes seem unfamiliar or awkwardly phrased. The literal translations,

In other words, Moses saw a violent injustice being done to a Hebrew slave by a son of the reigning pharaoh, and he responded by striking down the violent prince. This reading finds support a few verses later when the Torah states that the pharaoh heard about the incident and sought to kill Moses. (Exod 2:15.) Would the pharaoh have sought to kill Moses—a prince of Egypt—if Moses had merely struck down a petty officer who was abusing a Hebrew slave? Not likely. Under Torah law (and, more generally, under ancient Near Eastern law), the reigning pharaoh would only be the "avenger of the blood," with the legal right to kill Moses, if Moses had killed a member of the pharaoh's own household. (See Num 35:9–28; Deut 19:1–13; Josh 20.) It appears, then, that Moses' victim must have been some prominent member of the Egyptian royal family.

The Torah next describes Moses fleeing to Midian. There, he encounters seven sisters (daughters of the chief priest of Midian), and he defends them against a group of shepherds. When the sisters return to their father, they do not say, "A Hebrew man saved us," nor do they say, "An Israelite man saved us"; rather, they say, "An Egyptian man saved us." (Exod 2:19.) In other words, Moses dresses, looks, and speaks *like an Egyptian.*

Many other biblical hints suggest that Moses was essentially a foreigner to the Israelites. For example, when Moses' god—referred to in the Bible by the name YHVH—instructs Moses to lead the Israelites to freedom, Moses objects that he does not speak well (Exod 4:10), although we later find that he speaks quite beautifully (see Deut 1–11). Perhaps, the meaning of

---

however, often reveal subtleties of meaning that are lost in more idiomatic renderings. In addition, the author has occasionally italicized portions of the biblical text to add emphasis. The original text, of course, has no emphasized portions. Finally, careful readers who might choose to look up biblical citations should note that the author has worked from publications of the Bible's Hebrew text, and therefore verse numbering may vary slightly from verse numbering in Christian translations of the Bible.

Moses' objection is that he does not speak *Hebrew* well, explaining why ʏʜᴠʜ then instructs Moses to use Aaron as a translator. (Exod 4:16.) In addition, in describing the relationship between the Israelite people and the god ʏʜᴠʜ, the Torah uses covenantal language that closely parallels contemporaneous Near Eastern peace treaties, suggesting that the relationship was one of submission to a foreign god and king.[6]

Was then Moses more Egyptian than Israelite? Was the charming Moses-in-the-bulrushes story added to the Torah as a contrivance to transform Moses into a native son of Israel? Was the greatest prophet of the Israelite people really an Egyptian prince and priest named Thutmose?[7]

For some Jews, ancient Egypt evokes memories of slavery and genocide, and the Hebrew term for ancient Egypt (*Mitzrayim*) functions as a metaphor for irreligion. Can it be, then, that many of the greatest secrets of the Torah are revealed in the study of the ancient Egyptian religion? Of course, it can be.

Aegyptus...., diuinitatis amantissima,
deorum in terras suae religionis merito sola deductio,
sanctitatis et pietatis magistra....

---

[6] See Kugel, *How to Read the Bible*, pp. 243–247; Coogan, *The Old Testament*, pp. 116–125; Hayes, *Introduction to the Bible*, pp. 119–121; see also Wright, *Inventing God's Law*, p. 350.

[7] See Exod 32:9–13 [suggesting that the descendants of the Israelite patriarchs would not be abundant if God annihilated the Israelites and built up a new nation from Moses]; Deut 33:9 [suggesting that Moses did not know his parents, brothers, or sons]; 1 Chron 23:14 [stating that Moses' sons were "called upon" the tribe of Levi (implying adoption into that tribe)]. On the thesis that Moses was an Egyptian and that the repressed memory—the intentional forgetting (see Deut 25:19)—of ancient Egypt has a strong influence on present-day Western culture, see Assmann, *Moses the Egyptian*.

Egypt..., most loving of divinity,
by reason of her reverence the only land on earth where the
gods settled,
she who taught holiness and fidelity....

— The Latin *Asclepius* [25][8]

The Torah (the first five books of the Hebrew Bible) is sacred
scripture for more than half the world's population. But even as
religious fundamentalists cite chapter and verse in support of
their competing doctrinal claims, modern critical scholarship has
uncovered a radically new biblical narrative, revolutionizing our
understanding of the Torah. These modern scholars, however,
too often focus on the plain meaning of the biblical text, ignor-
ing the ancient hermeneutical tradition that explains the methods
by which that text is encoded. The *Zohar* (13th century C.E.),
the leading work of the Jewish mystical tradition, describes this
encoding of the Torah in this way:

> Woe to the person who says that Torah intended to present a
> mere story and ordinary words! For if so, we could compose a
> Torah right now with ordinary words, and more laudable than
> all of them [in the existing Torah]!... Therefore, concerning
> Torah, one should look only at what is beneath the garment.
> So all these words and all these stories are garments.[9]

So, how then does one remove the "garments" of the Torah,
gaining access to the story behind the story? The present book
explains in plain language some of the complex hermeneutical

---

[8] Translated in Copenhaver, *Hermetica*, pp. 81–82. A Coptic version of
Asclepius 25 appears in the eighth tractate of Codex VI of the Nag Ham-
madi library, dating to roughly the 3rd century C.E.

[9] *Zohar* 3:152a, translated in Matt, *The Zohar: Pritzker Edition*, vol. VIII,
pp. 518–521.

techniques recorded in ancient biblical commentaries, persuasively demonstrating that the Torah is encoded and revealing how to pierce that code. The book then combines those ancient hermeneutical techniques with the methods of modern critical scholarship to unlock the Torah as never before, revealing a hidden subtext previously known only to a few experts and hinted about in obscure Hebrew and Aramaic manuscripts. The basic theme of that subtext is the synthesis of both diversity and conflict in a world in which God is understood to be the one power at the source of all things, whether familiar or foreign, good or evil.

The analysis is divided into five parts. Part One is a commentary on the book of Genesis. As we explore the rich motifs of Genesis, we will see that the Torah has its roots in two religious cultures (Egyptian and Canaanite) and that this subtle ideological division within the Torah reflects the complex history of two rival kingdoms (Judah and Israel). Part One begins by exploring the many areas of correspondence between Genesis and ancient Egyptian mythology. It then turns to the Canaanite religion and demonstrates the many ways in which the Torah integrates Egyptian and Canaanite religious ideas.

Part Two is a commentary on the book of Exodus. The primary focus of Part Two is the divine name YHVH, the most sacred name of God in Judaism. YHVH is the divine name used by Moses, the Egyptian prince, and Part Two demonstrates, by scribal hermeneutics and by a close reading of the Torah's own text, that the name YHVH is an encoded reference to the Egyptian god Thoth. Thus, Part Two offers scholars of Hebrew scripture access to the single most significant secret of the Torah, known among Jewish mystics as "the great secret of the name" (*ha-sod ha-godol ha-shem*). This secret demonstrates that the Torah is fundamentally a syncretistic text aimed at harmonizing Egypt's venerable Thoth cult with Canaan's rival El cult.

Part Three, which concerns the book of Leviticus, takes the reader on an intellectual excursion to South Asia, presenting a brief introduction to Vedic thought. Leviticus focuses, among other things, on ritual fire sacrifice, a once ubiquitous form of worship that continues today primarily in South Asia. South Asia thus functions as a time capsule of sorts, preserving ancient ideas about sacrificial worship, and therefore Part Three seeks to deepen our understanding of ancient Jewish sacrificial ritual by comparing it to its Vedic counterpart, analyzing the common modes of thought that make both ritual systems comprehensible. In particular, Part Three shows that the Jewish fire sacrifice operated as an *enacted metaphor* that unified diverse human experiences, thus enabling a person to repair, through ritual actions, the way he or she viewed and engaged the external world.

Part Four, an essay on the book of Numbers, introduces a thesis that is even more provocative than the assertion that YHVH is the Egyptian god Thoth. Part Four argues that after a deadly confrontation with a band of Israelite rebels, Moses and Aaron were arrested, charged with capital offenses, tried, convicted, and Aaron was executed, dying as a martyr. That, of course, is a huge interpretive claim, but it is one that finds undeniable support in the Torah's encoded text and also in the esoteric Jewish tradition, as Part Four shows.

Part Five, an explication of Deuteronomy, carries the provocative thesis of Part Four a step further. The book of Deuteronomy introduces a new set of chauvinistic values to the Torah, supplanting the Egypt-Canaan syncretism of Genesis and Exodus with a denunciation of Canaan's religious culture in favor of a centralized, pro-Jerusalem, pro-YHVH religious model. Deuteronomy achieves this ideological shift through the guise of relating Moses' last words to the Israelites. But the revisionist content of Deuteronomy suggests that the book was composed at a relatively late date, when Judah and Israel were established kingdoms with an agrarian, not a pastoral, economy. Deuteronomy was probably put into semifinal form shortly after the fall of the Kingdom of Israel (the Northern Kingdom), when the Kingdom of Judah (the Southern Kingdom) was struggling to absorb Ba'al-worshiping refugees from its northern neighbor, and when Judean kings were seeking to consolidate political and cultic authority in Jerusalem, where YHVH, not Ba'al, was worshiped. Deuteronomy not coincidentally reflects those concerns—concerns that prevailed in the 7th century B.C.E., which just happens to be the time when the book of Deuteronomy was rather conveniently "found" in the Jerusalem temple. The effort to assimilate refugees from the Kingdom of Israel into the YHVH-worshiping Southern Kingdom explains the famous declaration of faith set forth in Deuteronomy: "Hear, O Israel; YHVH is our god; YHVH is one and only." (Deut 6:4.) In short, Deuteronomy modifies the Torah in ways that serve the interests of a particular political regime, and it corresponds to the historical reality of a particular time.

Nonetheless, Deuteronomy's recapitulation and revision of the Torah also includes a beautiful and compelling justification by Moses of his own actions while leading the Israelites. When the latter point is considered in light of the hidden subtext of the book of Numbers, we see that Deuteronomy—even if composed long after Moses' death—takes the literary form of Moses' defense at his own trial, ending in a description of his martyrdom. Deuteronomy is, thus, a powerful Hebrew analog to Plato's *Apologia Socratis*.

PART ONE

Myths, Gods, and Syncretism
A Commentary on Genesis

The road is long
With many a winding turn
That leads us to who knows where,
Who knows where.
But I'm strong,
Strong enough to carry him.
He ain't heavy, he's my brother.

—Bob Russell (1914–1970 C.E.)

1. "And Jacob said to Joseph, 'El Shaddai appeared to me in Luz, in the land of Canaan, and He blessed me' "

In the second millennium B.C.E., people from the Levant—which includes the region the Bible calls "Canaan"—began migrating to the Nile Delta in northern Egypt.[10] Some came as traders or refugees from famine; others came as prisoners of war, or as slaves offered as tribute. The Egyptians called these people "*hyksos*," which means (roughly) "foreign rulers," reflecting the fact that some of these migrants eventually rose to political power in northern Egypt, ruling there as pharaohs for more than a century. The Torah relates the story of one clan among these Asiatic immigrants—Jacob's clan—and the Torah asserts that Jacob's clan was the specific clan that assumed political power. Jacob's son Joseph, for example, asserted that God had made him "father to Pharaoh" (Gen 45:8), indicating that Joseph's descendants were Egyptian pharaohs.

According to the historical evidence, the Hyksos were worshipers of the Egyptian storm god Set. More accurately, the Egyptian storm god Set was the "translation" into Egyptian culture of their Canaanite storm god Ba'al, although the respective mythologies of these gods differed in their details.

In ancient times, "gods" were sacred images located in specific temples, but "gods" also represented archetypes that were not place specific, and just as the name for "water" could be translated from one language to another, so too the name for the "mother goddess" or the "storm god" could be "translated" from one pantheon to another. According to this logic of ancient

---

[10] On the political and social history of ancient Egypt, see Grimal, *A History of Ancient Egypt*; Shaw (ed.), *The Oxford History of Ancient Egypt*. On the historical evidence of Israelites sojourning in Egypt, see Hoffmeier, *Israel and Egypt*.

religion, the Egyptian storm god Set was the "translation" of the Canaanite storm god Ba'al, and historical records tell us that the Hyksos who migrated to northern Egypt from the Levant (Canaan) worshiped Ba'al/Set. But is that true specifically of Jacob's clan, the progenitors of the Israelite people? Did Jacob's clan worship Ba'al/Set?

The Torah relates that the god of the Israelite patriarchs was El Shaddai, a god that the Torah expressly connects to the land of Canaan. For example, when the patriarch Jacob was near the end of his life, and his son Joseph came to see him, Jacob said: "El Shaddai appeared to me in Luz, in the land of Canaan, and He blessed me." Likewise, God told Moses: "I appeared to Abraham, to Isaac, and to Jacob [(that is, to the patriarchs)] as El Shaddai, and with my name YHVH, I was not known to them." (Exod 6:2–3.) What, then, does history tell us about the god named El Shaddai, and what if any connection is there between El Shaddai and Ba'al/Set?

The biblical word *El* is often translated as if it meant "God" in the modern generic sense, but archaeological records confirm that El was the *proper name* of a specific god, the divine "father" of Canaan's seventy gods and thus the chief God of the Canaanite pantheon. As the progenitor of the gods, however, El's name was sometimes used to indicate divinity in the more generic sense. Hence, the name El Shaddai might refer to "El in the aspect of Shaddai." But who or what was Shaddai?

The Hebrew word *shad* means "breast," but in ancient Hebrew, the word *shaddai* may have meant "mountain" (from the Akkadian word *shaddu*). Therefore, El Shaddai might have been "God of the Mountain." The name Shaddai, however, might also have been related to the Hebrew word *shadad*, which means "to plunder," "to ravage," or "to despoil." In a few places, Hebrew scripture refers to a divine being called "Shodeid" ("the Despoiler") (see Isa 16:4, 21:2; Jer 6:26, 15:8, 48:8, 48:18, 48:32, 51:56; Job 15:21), and the name Shodeid might be a variation of the name Shaddai. The latter conclusion is supported by an examination of Shaddai's character. Shaddai almost always appears in Hebrew scripture as the fierce aspect of God—the aspect that sets limits or metes out punishment. (See, e.g., Isa 13:6; Joel 1:15; Job (*passim*); Ruth 1:20–21.) For this reason, English-language Bibles sometimes translate the name Shaddai as "the Almighty."

In Hebrew scripture, Shaddai is also a divine name that is widely invoked by *non-Israelites*. Excepting the patriarchal narratives, the primary places in the Hebrew Bible where the name Shaddai appears as a reference to God are the "Bala'am passages" of the book of Numbers (Num 22–24), the book of Job, and the book of Ruth, all of which quote the words of non-Israelite prophets. In Job, moreover, Shaddai appears to be the same as the divine being called "Satan" (the "adversary" or the "accuser"), a being who is presented in later texts as a demonic enemy of God but who in earlier, less dualistic texts lacks the characteristics of an anti-god.

The book of Job includes a main section, written in a distinctive poetic style, and a prose prologue that may have been written at a different time. The prologue tells us that the "sons of God" (*i.e.*, the seventy gods) were assembled before YHVH, and Satan was also present. (Job 1:6.) Thus, Satan is presented in Job as one of the gods included in the divine assembly. This same divine assembly is described in the book of Psalms: "God stands in the assembly of El; in the midst of the gods he judges." (Ps 82:1.) In the prologue to the book of Job, however, YHVH (not El) is the name used for the presiding deity of the divine assembly, and Satan is presented *as a member* of the divine court.

Nonetheless, Satan acts as YHVH's arm of justice; he is the divine force that YHVH uses to inflict punishment. Hebrew theology is thus radically nondual. Satan is presented as a divine being that is subordinate to YHVH (God), which makes YHVH the ultimate author of both good and evil, both mercy and punishment. According to this theology, there is no independent second power in competition with God, responsible for the things a per-

son might dislike. Many examples from Hebrew scripture illus-
trating this nondual theology are cited in the footnote below,[11]
but one of the most explicit is from the book of Isaiah, where
YHVH declares: "I make peace, and I create evil; I, YHVH, do all
these things." (Isa 45:7.)

In the prologue to the book of Job, Satan acts as YHVH's agent
of affliction sent by YHVH to test Job. (Job 1:12, 2:6.) Significantly, however, the main section of the book refers to this same
divine afflicter as "Shaddai." By implication, then, Shaddai is
Satan, the fierce and punitive aspect of the nondual Godhead,
which of course is consistent with Shaddai's role elsewhere in
scripture as the aspect of God that metes out punishment.

The foregoing conclusions are confirmed by an important
extrabiblical source, the Deir 'Alla inscription, which dates to
about 800 B.C.E., earlier than any known manuscript of the Bible.
This plaster inscription was discovered in 1967 during archaeological excavations at Deir 'Alla, in western Jordan, near the
Jordan River. The plaster fragments had fallen from the wall of
a building (perhaps a sanctuary) that had been destroyed by an
earthquake. Pieced together, the text describes a time when the
social order, including even the natural hierarchy of the animal
world, had somehow become subverted, and in response, "the
gods gathered together; the *shaddai-in* [(plural of 'Shaddai')]

---

[11] On YHVH as the author of evil, see Exod 4:21, 7:3, 9:12, 10:1, 10:20,
10:27, 11:10, 14:4, 14:8, 14:17 [YHVH hardens Pharaoh's heart]; Num
22:22, 22:32 [an "angel of YHVH" appears "for a *Satan*" (*i.e.*, "for an adversary")]; Deut 2:30 [YHVH hardens enemy's heart]; Josh 11:20 [same]; Judg
9:23 [an evil spirit from God]; 1 Sam 16:14–23 [an evil spirit from YHVH];
1 Kings 22:19–23 [YHVH put a lying spirit in the mouths of the prophets];
Isa 10:5–6 [Assyria is YHVH's rod of anger], 36:10 [same], 45:7 [YHVH creates evil]; Jer 25:9 [Nebuchadnezzar is YHVH's servant], 27:6 [same]; Job
1:12 [YHVH permits Satan to afflict Job], 2:6 [same], 38–41 [Job, who suffered, has no right to question YHVH's actions]; see also Exod 3:14 [God
says: "I will be what I will be."]; and compare 2 Sam 24:1 with 1 Chron
21:1 [Satan = YHVH].

took their places as the assembly."[12] The gathering of the divine assembly and the arrival, too, of the *shaddai-in* is strikingly similar to the scene depicted in the prologue to the book of Job: "And the sons of the gods came,... and also the Satan came in their midst." (Job 1:6.) The Deir 'Alla inscription thus supports the apparent identity between Satan and Shaddai. The use of the plural form of Shaddai (*i.e.*, the "*shaddai-in*") in the Deir 'Alla text is of no moment; it merely suggests that Shaddai acted through a host of divine minions. We find similar plural forms of Shaddai's name in some biblical passages, particularly in older passages written in poetic form. (See Deut 32:17; Ps 106:37.)

The Deir 'Alla inscription also gives an account of "Bala'am son of B'eor," a non-Israelite prophet who appears in Hebrew scripture as an enemy of the Israelites (see Num 22–24). The biblical Bala'am and the Bala'am of the Deir 'Alla inscription are both called "Bala'am son of B'eor," and both refer to God by the name "Shaddai." In addition, their manner of prophecy is strikingly similar.[13] Thus, the two sources clearly refer to the same person, making Bala'am the only major figure in the Torah whose historical existence and role is confirmed by a contemporaneous extrabiblical source.

After describing the convening of the divine assembly, the Deir 'Alla inscription relates the gods' response to the subversion of the social order that has overtaken the earth: "And they [(*i.e.*, the *shaddai-in*)] said to *sh[agar]*: 'Sew up, bolt up the heavens in your cloud, ordaining darkness instead of eternal light!'" Here, assuming the reconstruction of the text is correct,

---

[12] This and other quotations from the Deir 'Alla inscription are taken from the translation appearing in Hackett, *The Balaam Text from Deir 'Allā*.

[13] Compare Deir 'Alla Inscription, Comb. I, vv. 1–3 ["The gods came to him in the night, and he saw a vision like an oracle of El.... And Bala'am arose the next day...."] with Num 22:20–21 ["And the god(s) came to Bala'am at night.... And Bala'am rose in the morning...."], and also with Num 24:4, 24:16 ["The hearer of the words of El...."].

the *shaddai-in* (plural of "Shaddai") are clearly presented as gods who have directory power over storms and who act as a divine disciplinary force, not unlike the disciplinary role Satan/ Shaddai plays in the book of Job (see, e.g., Job 37).

One more detail from the Deir 'Alla text merits attention. Although the text is fragmented, and its translation is the subject of continuing debate, it appears to describe a grim ritual by which El (and, indirectly, the *shaddai-in*) is placated through child sacrifice, thus restoring order to the world. Archaeological and epigraphic evidence confirms that child sacrifice was practiced by Near Eastern peoples in ancient times,[14] and there are several references to it in the Bible (all condemning the practice).[15] In the book of Jeremiah, for example, YHVH decries the worship offered by the inhabitants of Jerusalem to the Canaanite god Ba'al, saying: "They built the high places of Ba'al to burn their sons in fire as whole offerings to Ba'al, which I never commanded, nor spoke, nor even thought in My heart." (Jer 19:5.)

The Deir 'Alla inscription seems to refer in broken fragments to a similar ritual. These fragments include the following: (1) "his boy, full of love [   ]"; (2) "Why are the scion and the firepit containing foliage [   ]?"; (3) "El will be satisfied. Let him cross over to the House of Eternity [   ]"; (4) "I will put [   ] under your head. You will lie down on your eternal bed to perish."; (5) "The scion sighs in his heart."; (6) "Death will take the newborn child, the suckling [   ]"; and (7) "The heart of the scion is weak for he goes to [   ]." In short, the Deir 'Alla inscription suggests a connection between the biblical prophet

---

[14] See, e.g., Brown, *Late Carthaginian Child Sacrifice, passim*; Levenson, *The Death and Resurrection*, pp. 20–21; Smith, *The Early History of God*, pp. 132–138.

[15] See Lev 18:21, 20:1–5; Deut 12:31; Judg 11:30–40; 2 Kings 16:3, 17:16–17, 21:6, 23:10; Jer 3:20–25, 7:31, 19:5, 32:35; Ezek 16:20–21, 20:26, 20:31, 23:37–39; Hosea 13:2; Mic 6:7; Ps 106:28–38; cf. Exod 22:28; see generally Levenson, *The Death and Resurrection*, pp. 3–17.

Bala'am son of B'eor, the fierce aspect of God called "Shaddai," and the practice of child sacrifice.

The possibility that Bala'am was associated with child sacrifice explains the episode immediately following the Bible's Bala'am passages. The book of Numbers relates in chapter 25 that, at Bala'am's instigation, the Israelites sinned by way of attachment to Ba'al P'eor,[16] and Psalm 106 makes clear that the episode involved worship of Shaddai with child sacrifices, stating that the Israelites "joined themselves to Ba'al P'eor and ate the sacrifices of the dead; . . . they sacrificed their sons and their daughters to *shaddai-im* [(plural of 'Shaddai')]." (Ps 106: 28–38.)

The Deir 'Alla text and Psalm 106, read together, strongly suggest that child sacrifice was somehow associated with both Bala'am and the cult of Shaddai. In this light, the passage in the book of Exodus stating that the patriarchs worshiped God as "El Shaddai" (Exod 6:3) takes on a new significance, putting into context Abraham's faithful conviction that God wanted him to sacrifice his son Isaac (Gen 22). Abraham's aborted act of child sacrifice took place in a society in which that form of worship was at least conceivable, and the point of the Abraham story seems to be to reject the practice and to encourage the sacrifice of animals as surrogates.

As noted, Egyptian historical records assert that the Hyksos worshiped the Egyptian storm god Set, or more accurately, they worshiped the Canaanite storm god Ba'al, who corresponded to Set in the Egyptian pantheon. The Deir 'Alla inscription makes clear, however, that the "*shaddai-in*" (plural of "Shaddai") were in charge of storms, rain, and clouds, and their fierce role as the divine disciplinary force that could be placated through child

---

[16] Ba'al P'eor is an encoded reference to Bala'am himself. By a scribal trick, the word "P'eor" is the same as the word "B'eor," making the phrase "Ba'al P'eor" the rough equivalent of Bala'am's epithet, "son of B'eor." See p. 280, below.

sacrifices (Ps 106:28–38) is much like that of Ba'al. Moreover, as we have seen, the Deir 'Alla inscription supports the conclusion, already implicit in the book of Job, that Satan is an alternative name for Shaddai, God's punitive aspect. Thus, Shaddai, the god of the Israelite patriarchs, appears to be a variant of Ba'al, the Canaanite storm god, and Shaddai, Ba'al, Satan, and Set appear to be four different ways of referring to essentially the same fierce, limit-setting aspect of the indivisible nondual Godhead.

In this light, it is worthwhile considering how the names Satan and Set might be written in Hebrew, using the name Sutekh for Set since Sutekh was Set's name in the Egyptian language:

| kaf | tet | shin | | nun | tet | shin |
| KH | T | S | | N | T | S |

←←←←*direction of reading*←←←←

"SuTeKH"   "SaTaN"

The first two letters of both names are identical, and the final letter of the name SaTaN (a *nun*) is almost identical to the final letter of the name SuTeKH (a *kaf*), the principal difference being the length of the horizontal crossbar at the top of the letter. Moreover, this similarity between the *nun* and the *kaf* was even closer in the paleo-Hebrew script of ancient times. Thus, in a handwritten text, the name of the Egyptian storm god SuTeKH (*i.e.*, Set) might easily have been miscopied as SaTaN. Perhaps, then, the name Satan found its way into Hebrew texts as a misinscription (or even an intentional occultation) of the name Sutekh.

In summary, the historical record confirms, at least in broad outline, the Torah's account of the Israelites' sojourn in Egypt and their ascent to political power, and it adds the detail that the Israelites' fierce god Shaddai corresponded to the Canaanite storm god Ba'al and also to the Egyptian storm god Set. The worship of Ba'al was, of course, strongly denounced by the later Israelite prophets, but prophets speak to the need of the time and place in which they live, and as we have seen, the worship of Ba'al was linked to extreme ritual practices that Hebrew scripture strongly denounces (see Deut 12:31). Thus, while the early prophets chose to assimilate YHVH to Shaddai/Ba'al, the later prophets chose to present YHVH and Ba'al in sharp contrast. That fact suggests that the worship of Moses' god, YHVH, became more acceptable with the passage of time, allowing the later prophets to present YHVH as a superior alternative, rather than as a syncretistic twin, to Ba'al. We will consider this point in much more detail below, when we analyze the Canaanite religion more closely.

What then does our brief examination of the historical record suggest about Israelite culture and religion? Because the Israelites came originally from Canaan and because they worshiped Shaddai, a variant of the fierce Canaanite storm god Ba'al, we would expect Israelite culture and religion to parallel that of Canaan in many ways. Conversely, because the Israelites sojourned for several generations in Egypt, even ascending to political power in that land, and because Moses, the prophet who led the Israelites out of Egypt, was reared more or less as a son of the pharaoh, we would expect to find many Egyptian ideas absorbed into the culture and religion of the Israelites.

Part One of the present book is a commentary on the book of Genesis. We will proceed by exploring two areas of correspondence between Genesis and the ancient Egyptian religion. First, Part One will consider the striking similarity between the Egyptian creation myths and those of Genesis, focusing in particular on the similarity between the Heliopolitan pantheon and the ten *sefirot* that Jewish mystics find symbolically represented in

Genesis. Next, we will analyze the motifs underlying the Egyptian Osiris myth, finding those same motifs at the heart of the many sibling rivalry stories of Genesis.

After examining those two areas of correspondence between Genesis and the ancient Egyptian religion, Part One will turn its focus to the Canaanite religion, and it will consider the possibility that ancient Judaism was essentially an integration of Egyptian and Canaanite religious ideas. Part One will then close with a philosophical meditation on monotheism. Monotheism can express itself as the chauvinistic assertion that one's own national god is the only true God—an idea that we encounter in Deuteronomy and the later books of the Bible. But monotheism can also express itself as a syncretistic principle that unites disparate cultures and theologies and that ultimately implies a radical nondualism—an idea that can be discerned from a careful reading of the oldest parts of the Torah.

2. Egyptian Creation and Biblical Creation

Ancient Egypt comprised several important cultural centers, each having its own economy and political structure, its own temples and deities, and its own mythology.[17] Thebes was the religious, economic, and political capital of "Upper Egypt" (*i.e.*, southern Egypt). It was dedicated to the god Amun, who was eventually identified with Egypt's sun god Re. In modern

---

[17] On ancient Egyptian religion and culture, see Redford (ed.), *The Ancient Gods Speak*; Assmann, *The Search for God in Ancient Egypt*; Baines et al., *Religion in Ancient Egypt*; Meeks and Favard-Meeks, *Daily Life of the Egyptian Gods*; Sauneron, *The Priests of Ancient Egypt*; Horning, *Conceptions of God in Ancient Egypt*; Hare, *ReMembering Osiris*; Frankfort, *Kingship and the Gods*. For a translation of *The Book of the Dead*, see Faulkner (trans.), *The Egyptian Book of the Dead*. For a compilation of ancient Egyptian literature, see Lichtheim (trans. and ed.), *Ancient Egyptian Literature* (three volumes).

times, Thebes is called "Luxor." Hermopolis lay near the border between Upper Egypt and "Lower Egypt" (*i.e.*, northern Egypt). It was dedicated to the Egyptian god Thoth, whom the Greeks called "Hermes." The Greek name Hermopolis means "City of Hermes." In modern times, Hermopolis is called "El Ashmunein." Memphis, which was the capital city of Lower Egypt, was dedicated to the god Ptah, the god of builders and craftsmen. Its ruins are located near modern-day Mit Rahinah, about ten miles south of Cairo. Finally, Heliopolis was another important city of Lower Egypt. It was dedicated to the god Atum, who (like Amun in Thebes) was eventually identified with Egypt's sun god Re. Because of Atum's association with the sun, the Greeks named Atum's city Heliopolis, meaning "City of the Sun." In modern times, Heliopolis is a district of Cairo called "Ain Shams."

The Hyksos, including the Israelite patriarch Jacob and his family, settled in Lower Egypt (*i.e.*, northern Egypt), and therefore Heliopolis holds a prominent place in the story of the Israelites. The Torah calls Heliopolis by the name On, and it is the city where Potiphar, the man who purchased Jacob's son Joseph as a slave, once served as the chief priest. It is also worth noting that according to the Torah, Joseph was not just Potiphar's slave but also his son-in-law, Joseph having eventually redeemed himself from slavery and married Potiphar's daughter. (Gen 41:45.) Because of his position as the son-in-law of the chief priest, Joseph would have been familiar with all the esoteric details of the Heliopolitan religious cult.

Each of the major Egyptian cities—Thebes, Hermopolis, Memphis, and Heliopolis—was associated with a distinct creation myth. As noted, Thebes was dedicated to Amun, a god that was identified with Re, the sun god, and also with Min, the god of creation and fertility. Amun was the leader of a triad of gods that included Amun's consort (Mut) and their son (Khonsu). His name, Amun, means "hidden," and Amun was the invisible and hidden source from which everything arose, including the gods and mankind. He is still widely invoked today by way of the word "Amen" that Jews, Christians, and Muslims use in blessing or solemn affirmation. (See Isa 65:16 ["The one who blesses in the land, he will bless by the god of AMuN [(Egyptian: 'hidden')], and the one who swears in the land, he will swear by the god of AMuN, because the initial troubles are forgotten and because they are hidden from my eyes."]).)

Hermopolis was dedicated to the god Thoth, and according to the creation myth linked to Hermopolis, Thoth was the first being to emerge upon the primordial mound. This "mound" represents a withdrawal of the infinite waters of dissolution, which according to Egyptian thought, stand just outside Creation, pressing to rush back in and reabsorb the created world. Thoth next created eight reptilian deities, but these eight were really four dyads, where each dyad was named using the male and female grammatical forms of a single name. One could therefore say that the first entities of Hermopolitan Creation were four divine couples, or perhaps four androgynous beings. Their names were Amun-Amaunet, Kuk-Kauket, Huh-Hauhet, Nun-Naunet, which translate as (male-female) "hiddenness," "darkness," "endlessness," and "waters of dissolution." Amun ("hiddenness") is the same Amun that became the chief god of Thebes—the hiddenness from which, according to Theban mythology, everything arose.

Memphis was dedicated to the god Ptah, who represented the ability of a builder or craftsman to form a mental conception of the thing to be constructed. Ptah was said to have created the world by imagining it (forming it, that is, as a mental conception) and then by speaking it into existence.

Heliopolis was dedicated to Atum. The Heliopolitan creation myth, like other creation myths, tells of a primordial mound that provides the stage on which the Creation drama will unfold. Atum arose upon the mound and then created other gods. According to one model, the four divine dyads of Hermopolitan Creation represented a sort of pre-Creation in relation to Heliopolitan Creation; the four died, and what followed was the emergence of Atum upon the mound. Similarly, the god Ptah of Memphian Creation was said to be a precursor to Heliopolitan

Creation. It was Ptah's creative thought and speech that caused Atum to form upon the primordial mound.

Atum created other gods, but when Atum first arose upon the primordial mound, he was alone, and therefore sexual creation was not possible. In other words, there was no second god who could contain Atum's creative emission. Atum therefore had to be the vessel of his own creative act. Atum emitted his generative seed into his mouth, and Atum's mouth thus became the womb that gestated Creation.

We should not take this description too literally. Mythologically, we are at the level of the androgynous One from whom Creation unfolds, and terms such as "seed," "mouth," and "womb" are all metaphors. At this mythological beginning, there is no gender; there is only *emanation* and *reception*, and Atum comprised both. The Egyptian texts call Atum a "he-she." Atum emanated the seed, and Atum also received the seed, and after gestating the seed, Atum spoke the gods into being, Atum's mouth having become generative by reason of the seed.

Atum's creative act eventually gave rise to a set of ten deities, among whom Atum was the first. The names of these ten deities are Atum, Shu, Tefnut, Geb, Nut, Osiris, Set, Isis, Nephthys, and Horus,[18] with the first nine referred to collectively as the "Heliopolitan Ennead." The tenth, Horus, was the living pharaoh of each generation—the divine king.

Among other things, the ten gods of the Heliopolitan pantheon signified the ten days that separate the lunar year (about 355 days) and the solar year (about 365 days). The focus of many ancient religions was to rectify that rift in astrological time, and priests and prophets carefully constructed their ritual calendars to that end. In ancient Egypt, the ten-day gap between the lunar and solar years corresponded to the ten gods of Heliopolitan Creation, and in Judaism, this same ten-day gap was (and still

---

[18] The names are written here as they generally appear in English scholarly texts, with spellings derived from Greek.

is) recognized in the ten days of penitence and austerity that run
from Rosh ha-Shanah (when the lunar year ends)[19] to sundown
on Yom Kippur (when the solar year ends, bringing cosmic rec-
tification).

The ten gods of Heliopolitan Creation are actually members of an extended family comprising several generations. By
speech, Atum created Shu and Tefnut. According to one telling,
Atum exhaled Shu (breath) from his nose, and he spat Tefnut
(moisture) from his mouth. With the emergence of Shu and Tefnut, sexual creation becomes possible. Shu and Tefnut produced
Geb (earth) and Nut (sky), and Geb and Nut produced Osiris,
Set, Isis, and Nephthys. Finally, Osiris and Isis produced Horus.

As noted, Horus was an *incarnate* god. He was the living
pharaoh of each generation. The gods desired that civil order,
compassion for the weak, and social justice would prevail on
earth, and the king who maintained those values was therefore
their earthly manifestation and representative. According to the
Heliopolitan myth, the divine mantle of kingship passed from
Atum to Shu, from Shu to Geb, from Geb to Osiris, and from
Osiris to Horus, and by a secret rite, each successor to the throne
of Egypt received that mantle of kingship, being ritually transformed from an ordinary person into the Horus of his or her
generation.

Let us now turn, by way of comparison, to the creation myths
of the Bible. The Hermopolitan creation myth is reflected in the
Torah's opening sentence: "In the beginning, God created the
heavens and the earth, and the earth was *Tohu veVohu* ('obscu-
rity'), and *Choshekh* ('darkness') was upon the face of *Tehom*
('bottomlessness'), and the spirit of God hovered upon the face
of the *Mayim* ('waters')." (Gen 1:1–2.) Here, we encounter the
same four primordial elements ("hiddenness," "darkness," "end-

---

[19] The numeric value of the word *SHaNaH* ("year") is 355, which corresponds to the approximate number of days in a lunar year.

lessness," "waters") that were the four divine dyads of Hermopolitan Creation.[20]

After describing those four primordial elements, the Torah presents Creation as a series of seven creative episodes—or, more accurately, six plus one, because the Torah seems to assert the completeness and perfection of any set of six by making the seventh in a series distinct.[21] The Torah speaks of "Light" (day one); a "Firmament" to separate the upper and lower waters (day two); the primordial mound called "Dry Land" (day three); celestial "Luminaries" to mete out time (day four); nautical and aeronautical "Creatures" (day five); terrestrial "Creatures," including "Adam" (day six); and finally, "Repose" (day seven), which—as the absence of creation—seals the sixfold Creation sequence. (Gen 1:3–2:3.) About each of these "days," God says that it was "good," except that God does not say about day two that it was "good," and God says about day six that it was "very good." (Gen 1:6–8, 1:31.) As we shall see, the Torah does not like the polarity implied by the number two: Two are always really one.

Significantly, the first six days pair up neatly, giving rise to two corresponding sets of three. Day one (light) corresponds to day four (luminaries); day two (separation of upper and lower waters) corresponds to day five (nautical and aeronautical creatures); and day three (dry land) corresponds to day six (terrestrial

---

[20] On this correspondence, see Kilian, "Gen. I 2 und die Urgötter von Hermopolis"; see also Sayce, "The Egyptian Background of Genesis 1."

[21] Six is highly divisible—what the mathematician Srinivasa Ramanujan (1887–1920 C.E.) called a "superior highly composite number"—and it is also the sum of its proper divisors. It can be represented by two opposing and interlocking triangles, and therefore it signifies stability, union, and completion. It is also associated with balance and beauty (consider, for example, snowflakes and six-petal flowers). There are, of course, six directions in three-dimensional space, and a regular hexagon comprises exactly six equilateral triangles, which means that six circles of equal size will fit perfectly around a seventh circle of the same size.

creatures). Thus, the first three days focus on the physical environment, and the next three days focus on the *agents of action* within that environment.

Note also that God creates by speaking and that the Torah's telling of the seven days of Creation happens to include exactly ten repetitions of the phrase "and God said" (*vayomer elohim*), implying ten distinct acts of creation. The Jewish mystical tradition—the Kabbalah—focuses special attention on these ten creative utterances, describing them as the source of ten divine "potencies" (*sefirot*) and dividing them into "configurations" (*partzufim*) that include the seven "days" noted above.

Having described Creation as a series of seven creative episodes ("days") and ten creative utterances (the phrase "and God said"), the book of Genesis abruptly shifts direction, relating a different creation myth—one that gives God a new name (YHVH) and Adam a more central role. ADaM is, of course, ATuM of the Heliopolitan creation sequence, reflecting the linguistic shift from *t* to *d* that occurred in many ancient languages. The book of Genesis states:

> These are the offspring of the heavens and the earth… on the day YHVH-God made earth and heavens. Now, all the shrubs of the field were not yet in the land, and all the herb of the field had not yet sprouted, for YHVH-God had not sent rain upon the land, and there was no Adam to work the soil. And a mist ascended from the land and watered all the face of the soil, and YHVH-God formed the ADaM (*i.e.*, ATuM) with dust from the soil, and He blew into his brow Living Spirit, and the Adam became a living creature. And YHVH-God planted a garden in Eden, in the east, and emplaced there the Adam he had formed. And YHVH-God caused to sprout from the soil all the Trees pleasing for appearance and good for nourishment, and the Tree of Life in the midst of the garden, and the Tree of Knowledge of Good and Evil.[22]

---

[22] Gen 2:4–9.

What follows is the well-known story of how YHVH tested Adam, a story in which Adam is instructed not to consume from the Tree of Knowledge of Good and Evil (*i.e.*, the Tree of Dualism), does so at the urging of an upright serpent, and then is banished from Eden. (Gen 2:15–3:24.)[23]

As noted, the story of God creating Adam from the soil is a retelling of Heliopolitan Creation in which Atum arises upon the primordial mound. The "Trees" of the Garden of Eden, like the ten creative utterances (the *sefirot*), represent the ten gods of the Heliopolitan pantheon, and Adam himself is one of those "Trees." The Torah later hints at this point when it asserts that "Adam is a Tree of the field." (Deut 20:19.) As we learn more about the Heliopolitan gods, we will be able to identify the "Tree of Life" and "Tree of Knowledge" in that group. The ten gods of the Heliopolitan pantheon are also subtly alluded to in the

---

[23] We are led to assume that YHVH gave the correct instruction (which Adam ignored) and that the serpent gave the incorrect instruction (which Adam followed), but alternative interpretations are possible. The story presents an interesting contrast to the Mesopotamian myth of Adapa. The sage Adapa is directed by the god Ea to ascend to heaven to meet Anu, the king of the gods. Ea instructs that when Adapa confronts the gatekeepers of Anu, he must not eat the "Bread of Death." Adapa then ascends to heaven. He confronts the gatekeepers of Anu, and Anu speaks to him, urging him to eat what Anu calls the "Bread of Life." Adapa refuses to eat, assuming that the "Bread of Life" is Anu's deceptive term for the "Bread of Death," which Ea warned him not to eat. Anu then laughs at Adapa, asking him why he did not eat, and Anu dismissively sends Adapa back to the world of mortals. See Dalley (trans.), *Myths from Mesopotamia*, pp. 182–188.

In the Mesopotamian myth, (1) a god tells the protagonist not to eat, (2) the protagonist follows that instruction, rejecting the instruction of a different god, and (3) he thus misses out on immortality. In the biblical myth, (1) a god again tells the protagonist not to eat, (2) this time the protagonist *rejects* that instruction, following the instruction of a different god (the serpent), and (3) again the protagonist misses out on immortality. The biblical myth is thus an inversion of the Mesopotamian myth.

ten generations between Adam and Noah (Gen 5) and in the ten generations between Noah and Abraham (Gen 10–11).

With the story of Noah and the Flood (Gen 5–9), the Torah begins yet another creation myth, this one based on the ancient Mesopotamian myth of Atrahasis, which dates to approximately 1700 B.C.E. and is retold as part of the Gilgamesh Epic. Because our focus here is on Egyptian and Canaanite influences on Israelite culture and religion, we will not delve deeply into the Mesopotamian roots of the Noah story. In brief, the "descended ones" (Hebrew: *nephilim*), who are also called the "sons of the gods," intermarry with human women, giving rise to the "heroes of eternity past, men of name." (Gen 6:4.) The terrestrial world then becomes corrupt, and YHVH uses a flood (*i.e.*, the waters of dissolution) to destroy both the terrestrial world and its creatures. But when the flood is about to begin, God warns one man, Noah, who builds a boat, seals it with tar, and places on board his family and male-female pairs of each species of animal (seven pairs in the case of sacrificial animals). The rains then come and submerge the land. As the waters recede, Noah sends forth a dove and a raven, and when the waters have fully receded, Noah worships YHVH with sacrifices. YHVH smells the fragrance of the sacrifices and is appeased. What follows is a new Creation, with new instructions from God. (Gen 6:11–9:17.)

Many scholars have noted that the Flood story as it appears in the Torah is an interweaving of two separate accounts, one in which the Flood lasts forty days and is directed by YHVH and another in which the Flood lasts a year and is directed by Elohim ("God").[24] The same pattern can be traced throughout the Torah, which often interweaves Yahwist and Elohist versions of the same events. Clearly, the redactors of the Torah hoped to heal an ideological and spiritual divide by integrating the sacred stories of two distinct but closely related groups. That point will become critical below, when we examine the long and some-

---

[24] See, e.g., Friedman, *Who Wrote the Bible?*, pp. 54–60.

times bitter rivalry between Judah (the Southern Kingdom) and Israel (the Northern Kingdom).

As noted, the Flood story originates in the ancient Mesopotamian myth of Atrahasis, and each of its details—God's warning to one man, the boat made to specifications and sealed with tar, the animals of every type, the man's family, the terrifying rains, the submerged earth, the receding waters, the dove, the raven, the sacrifice, and the fragrance that appeases God—appears in the Mesopotamian version of the story.[25]

The story of the Flood also marks an important transition in the Torah from myth to legend. Antediluvian events in the Torah are purely archetypal, with the leaders of each generation enjoying extraordinarily long lifespans that are symbolic, not literal[26]; postdiluvian events are quasi-historical, with the leaders of each generation having more realistic lifespans. Legends often represent the mythologization of history—that is, the recognition of mythological archetypes in historical events. Thus, the Bible's creation stories, including the Flood story, present us with the mythological schematic through which the Bible will interpret and rationalize the diverse events of history.

3. The Ten Divine Aspects

According to the Heliopolitan myth, Atum exhaled Shu (breath) from his nose, and he spat Tefnut (moisture) from his mouth. Then, by sexual union, Shu and Tefnut produced Geb (earth) and Nut (sky), and Geb and Nut produced Osiris, Set, Isis, and

---

[25] For a translation of the relevant portions of the Atrahasis myth, see Dalley (trans.), *Myths from Mesopotamia*, pp. 4–8, 28–35, 109–116.

[26] Lamech, for example, lives 777 years. Gen 5:31. When the same name, Lamech, appears in a different story, we learn that Lamech's vengeance is 77 (Gen 4:24), suggesting that, for Lamech, the number "seven" has a purely symbolic significance.

Nephthys. Finally, Osiris and Isis produced Horus. Thus, the family relationships among the members of the Heliopolitan pantheon can be depicted as follows:

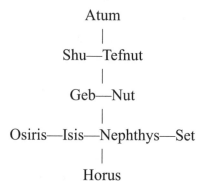

Atum
|
Shu—Tefnut
|
Geb—Nut
|
Osiris—Isis—Nephthys—Set
|
Horus

These same ten gods can also be listed in terms of their archetypal roles:

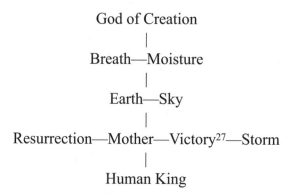

God of Creation
|
Breath—Moisture
|
Earth—Sky
|
Resurrection—Mother—Victory[27]—Storm
|
Human King

---

[27] Isis's role as a mother goddess follows logically from her close association with Hathor (depicted as a cow) and her nurturing of Horus in his youth. The connection between Nephthys and victory is less certain, although Plutarch (1st century C.E.) associated Nephthys with the Greek goddesses Nike (victory in war) and Aphrodite (love, pleasure, and sensuality).

Anyone familiar with the *sefirot* of the Jewish mystical tradition will recognize the similarity between the *sefirot* and the Heliopolitan pantheon. According to the Kabbalah, the original Adam (*Adam Kadmon*) comprised ten divine potencies called "*sefirot*" (literally: "enumerations"), corresponding to the ten repetitions of the phrase "and God said" in Genesis 1. These *sefirot* constituted Adam's external form, but they also emerged out of Adam. Thus, the *sefirot* represent Adam's self-revelation. They are usually depicted hierarchically as follows[28]:

Keter ("Crown")
|
Binah ("Understanding")—*Chokhmah* ("Wisdom")
|
Gevurah ("Strength")—*Chesed* ("Kindness")
|
Tiferet ("Beauty")
|
Hod ("Splendor")—*Netzach* ("Victory")
|
Yesod ("Foundation")
|
Malkhut ("Kingship")

The ten *sefirot*, like the ten gods of the Heliopolitan pantheon, are interrelated to one another in family-like relationships, and they emanate from ADaM, much as the deities of the Heliopolitan pantheon emanate from ATuM. Also, both systems culminate with divine kingship. The close affinity between the two systems is further reinforced when we look at the first stage of the creative work. The *Zohar* (13th century C.E.), the leading text of the Jewish mystical tradition, describes this first stage as

---

[28] The names of the *sefirot* derive in part from Prov 9:10 and 1 Chron 29:11.

an act of self-generation by Adam, similar to Atum's act of self-generation:

> [I]n what place [(*i.e.*, in what womb)] was this seed fashioned
> and engraved, becoming an engraving of the image of *Adam*?
> [¶] Well, this mystery of Primordial Adam was formed and
> engraved without a Female. The second was engraved and
> formed from the potency and seed of this one within a Female.
> [¶] Primordial Adam—engraving of form and image of the
> body was not within a Female and was entirely without form.
> He was formed and engraved... without Female or Male.[29]

Although the *Zohar*'s prose is difficult to follow, it clearly describes Adam's first creative emission as being "without a Female," thus paralleling Heliopolitan mythology.

But despite the striking similarities between the two systems, there are also clear distinctions, particularly when we look at the intermediate members of the two lists. Let us therefore consider what might account for those distinctions.

4. The Shattering of the Vessels

Isaac Luria (1534–1572 C.E.) was a giant among Kabbalists, although his period of active teaching was quite short. His most famous teachings stem from the two years he spent in the town of Safed in the hills west of the Sea of Galilee.

Luria incorporated the ten *sefirot* into a powerful creation myth. Luria's myth begins with the infinite presence of divinity, and he describes the first creative act as a retraction of that divinity, giving rise to a space wherein Creation can occur. Here, Luria's myth already parallels the Heliopolitan creation myth,

---

[29] *Zohar* 2:167b, translated in Matt, *The Zohar: Pritzker Edition*, vol. V, p. 471.

which describes the withdrawal of the infinite waters of dissolution and the emergence of the primordial mound.

Luria next describes the emanation of a ray of divinity back into the space created by the earlier retraction of divinity. That emanation takes the form of the "Primordial Adam" (*Adam Kadmon*), a being that is distinct from, though related to, the Adam of the Garden of Eden. The Primordial Adam then produced the ten *sefirot*. As Luria describes it, "Light" emanated from Adam's nose, mouth, ears, and eyes, forming into ten divine emanations. Here again, Luria's creation myth parallels the Heliopolitan creation myth, which asserts that Atum arose upon the primordial mound, after which "breath" and "moisture" emanated from Atum's nose and mouth, giving rise to ten deities. Thus, Luria's creation myth is apparently a retelling of the Heliopolitan myth, using—in place of Egyptian gods—the abstract divine qualities that constitute the ten *sefirot*.

Luria explains that the divine Light that emanated from the Primordial Adam's face filled ten vessels. But Luria then takes the Heliopolitan creation myth to a new level, describing a cosmic cataclysm that is not part of the Heliopolitan myth. According to Luria, the vessels that received the divine Light were too weak. Due to a lack of integration and unity among them, the vessels were unable to hold the emanated Light. They *shattered*, and the broken fragments of the vessels fell, containing within them disconnected sparks of the Light. In short, Luria presents a Creation that is marred by disaster, a universe broken in the making. Or, did perhaps God *intend* the vessels to break?

Luria relates that, after the shattering of the vessels, more Light emanated from the Primordial Adam, this time from Adam's forehead, and the new Light began the work of cosmic repair. The fallen sparks of divine Light rose from the fragments of the shattered vessels, and the sparks arranged themselves into new configurations (*partzufim*)—five in all. They are: (1) *Arikh Anpin*, (2) *Abba*, (3) *Imma*, (4) *Zeir Anpin*, and (5) *Malkhut*.

These five configurations comprise all ten of the *sefirot*. The first three configurations (*Arikh Anpin, Abba,* and *Imma*) correspond among the *sefirot* to *Keter, Chokhmah,* and *Binah.* The fourth configuration (*Zeir Anpin*) corresponds to the hexad (the set of six) from *Chesed* through *Yesod.* And the last configuration corresponds to *Malkhut,* the last of the *sefirot.* Moreover, based on the six-plus-one pattern of Torah's seven-day creation myth, *Zeir Anpin* (comprising six) and *Malkhut* (comprising one) are described as being in a special relationship to one another, a relationship that is sometimes referred to metaphorically as a sexual union.

With the shattering of the vessels, the emanation of more Light, and the arrangement of the Light into new configurations, Luria has taken us well beyond Heliopolitan Creation and into new mythological territory. But what, by way of allegory, does Luria's creation myth tell us about the history of world religions?

The Heliopolitan pantheon constituted the central core of the religion that Jacob's clan encountered when it migrated to ancient Egypt. But the "vessels" (*i.e.,* the gods of the Heliopolitan pantheon) were not strong enough to hold the divine Light, and they shattered. In other words, Luria used myth and symbol to relate the "fall" of the Egyptian pantheon and its reorganization as the ten *sefirot* of the Kabbalah.

Joseph Gikatilla, the great 13th century Kabbalist, makes the same point. He asserted that "the gods of Egypt" (*i.e.,* the Heliopolitan pantheon) were "like *the firstborn* in regard to the rest of the gods."[30] But as the Torah instructs, the firstborn must be either sacrificed or redeemed. Hence, the ancient Egyptian religion failed, and its gods fell from favor. In Luria's terms, the "vessels" could not hold the "Light." The Torah employs a different metaphor, stating that "all the Trees of the field shattered" (Exod 9:25), which can be read as a veiled reference to the Heliopolitan pantheon.

The Torah tells us, moreover, that YHVH brought about this

---

[30] Weinstein (trans.), *Gates of Light*, p. 42, italics added.

spiritual cataclysm. In the Passover story, we learn that YHVH brought ten plagues upon Egypt, after which Pharaoh permitted the Israelites to leave. By one reading of the text,[31] YHVH has this to say about the last plague:

> I will traverse in the land of Egypt in this night, and I will strike all the firstborn [gods] of the land of Egypt, from ATuM onward. Among them and among all the gods of Egypt, I will execute judgments—I am YHVH.[32]

By this reading, the last of the ten plagues was not the death of all the firstborn children of Egypt; rather, it was the destruction of the Heliopolitan pantheon, including Horus, the pharaoh's heir: ten plagues for ten gods.

According to Luria's allegorical critique of the Egyptian religion, the flaw in the Heliopolitan pantheon was a lack of integration and unity among its diverse members. The book of Psalms hints at this point, saying: "Your eyes saw my protean self, and upon your scroll all of them were inscribed; *yomim* were formed, but no unity among them." (Ps 139:16.[33]) Here, the word *yomim*, which means "days," might refer to the seven

---

[31] Scriptural Hebrew has no punctuation and very few vowels, and therefore the text supports several readings simultaneously. Most English translations of the Hebrew Bible rely on the traditional way of pronouncing the text in the synagogue as a guide to meaning, but in some cases this traditional vowelization of the letters was adopted *to conceal* the secrets of scripture.

[32] Exod 12:12 [the Hebrew phrase *MeiADaM Ve'AD BeHeiMaH, UVeKHoL ELoHaY MiTZRaYiM* (which means "from man to animal, and against all the gods of Egypt") can be vowelized instead as *MeiADuM Va'AeD, Ba-HeiMaH UVeKHoL ELoHaY MiTZRaYiM* (which means "from Atum onward, among them and among all the gods of Egypt")]; see also Num 33:4.

[33] The text contains a homophonic ambiguity, and therefore it can also be translated: "Your eyes saw my protean self, and upon your scroll all

"days" of Creation, ending with the Sabbath. But the seven days of Creation correspond, according to Lurianic Kabbalah, to the last seven of the *sefirot* (the hexad from *Chesed* through *Yesod*, plus *Malkhut*). Therefore, in Kabbalistic terms, the psalm is saying that the original configuration of these last seven *sefirot* (called "days") was unstable due to a lack of unity among the divine forces, and as a result, the original configuration—*i.e.*, the Heliopolitan pantheon—shattered.

In further support of his theology of spiritual cataclysm, Luria cites the following obscure verse from the Torah: "These are the kings who reigned in the land of Adom before a king reigned over the descendants of Israel." (Gen 36:31.) According to Luria, the phrase "kings who reigned in the land of Adom" is an allegorical reference to the "broken vessels," the vessels that were too weak to contain the divine Light that emanated from Adam, and because the "broken vessels" are Luria's veiled reference to the Heliopolitan pantheon, the term "Adom" must be a reference to Heliopolis's chief god Atum.

Consider also what YHVH says by the mouth of the prophet Ezekiel, words which superficially are addressed to the king of Tyre, but which can be read as an allegorical reference to the downfall of Atum and the Heliopolitan pantheon:

> You were the prototype, full of wisdom, perfect in beauty. You were in Eden, the garden of the gods [(*i.e.*, Egypt[34])]; all the precious stones were your canopy: *Adam, pitedah* and *yahalom, tarshish, shoham,* and *yashfeh, sapir, nophekh* and *barkas* and *zahav* ("gold") [(*i.e.*, a set of ten that begins with Adam/Atum and culminates in royal gold)].... You were on

---

of them were inscribed; *yomim* were formed, one among them was His." According to the Kabbalah, both translations are meaningful.

[34] The Torah hints that Egypt was the earthly garden of Eden, saying: "Lot... saw the entire plain of the Jordan that it was well watered... like the garden of YHVH, like the land of Egypt." Gen 13:10.

the holy mountain of the gods; you walked among fiery stones [(*i.e.*, among the gods)]. Perfect were you in your ways from the day of your creation, until wrongdoing was found in you. In your great commerce, your midst filled with injustice and you sinned. So I desecrated you from the mountain of the gods and destroyed you, O sheltering *cheruv*, from among the fiery stones [(*i.e.*, the gods)].... Thus, I made you into ashes upon the earth in the eyes of all who see you. All who knew you among the peoples were astonished over you; you were a terror, but you shall be no more, forever.[35]

Thus, drawing from several scriptural sources, Luria's creation myth describes a cosmic and spiritual cataclysm, but according to Luria, sparks of the original Light remained among the broken fragments of the shattered "vessels." In other words, bits of the true religion remained among the broken pieces of the failed religion, and it only took a new emanation of divine Light—Moses perhaps?—to gather up those sparks of the true religion from the debris of the failed religion and to arrange the "vessels" into new, stronger configurations that would be capable of holding the Light.

The *Zohar* describes this reconfiguration of the Heliopolitan pantheon, using the Torah's "Tree" metaphor to refer to the individual gods. The *Zohar* explains that the "Trees" of the Garden of Eden had to be uprooted and transplanted, and only in that new arrangement were they able to endure.[36] Likewise, the dramatic and well-known story of Moses shattering the first set of tablets at Mount Sinai can be interpreted as an allegorical reference to this reconfiguration of the Heliopolitan pantheon. (See Exod 32:19.) With regard to the second set of tablets, YHVH promises to write upon the tablets the same "ten words" (*i.e.*,

---

[35] Ezek 28:12–19.

[36] *Zohar* 1:35a–35b, translated in Matt, *The Zohar: Pritzker Edition*, vol. I, pp. 220–222.

the same ten gods) that were on the first set of tablets (see Exod 34:1, 34:28), but the Kabbalah adds that YHVH wrote those words in a new sequence.

In summary, Isaac Luria's mythology of cosmic cataclysm and repair accounts for all the distinctions that we see between the ten-member Heliopolitan pantheon and the ten *sefirot* of the Kabbalah. The "vessels" as originally configured (the Heliopolitan pantheon) were not strong enough to contain the divine Light, but the new configuration of the vessels (the ten *sefirot* of the Kabbalah) can do so.

The *sefirot* of the Kabbalah, then, are not merely an echo of the Heliopolitan pantheon; rather, they constitute a more sustainable theological construct. Nonetheless, the *sefirot* retain many key characteristics of the system on which they were modeled. Luria taught that the first three "vessels" did not break at the time of the cosmic cataclysm, and the last "vessel" (divine "Kingship") only cracked—it did not shatter. The reconfiguration thus occurred within the hexad of *sefirot* that, in Kabbalistic thought, constitutes the body of *Zeir Anpin*, and that reconfiguration is evident when the hierarchical depiction of these six *sefirot* is compared to the successive generations of the Heliopolitan pantheon.

Like Heliopolis's theology of ten gods, the Kabbalah's theology of ten *sefirot* culminates in divine kingship, a ruler who draws down or reveals the presence of God in our world. This idea of divine kingship is widespread in Near Eastern mythology. A cynic might argue that it was merely a convenient way for the kings of ancient times to aggrandize themselves and maintain the loyalty of their subjects, but we might also consider that in ancient times, civilization itself was considered to be a gift of the gods, and the one who maintained civil order, who showed compassion toward the weak, and who upheld justice in society was, by reason of so doing, manifesting or revealing divinity.

Heliopolitan theology used the name Horus for this quality of divine kingship, and the Kabbalah calls the same principle *Malkhut* ("Kingship"), associating it with the messianic hope of a king who will inaugurate an era of righteousness. And although "king" is a masculine term, the Kabbalah often refers to this last of the *sefirot*—the sexual partner of *Zeir Anpin*— in female terms, as "Shekhinah,"[37] "Bride," "Sabbath Queen," and "Daughter." Moreover, we can rightly include the feminine in this role because Egypt had a female pharaoh (Hatshepsut, 1508–1458 B.C.E.) who was recognized to be the Horus of her generation.

5. The King is Dead; Long Live the King

Thus far, we have seen that biblical creation mythology is rooted in other Near Eastern creation myths, and we have detailed the close parallel between the Heliopolitan pantheon and the *sefirot* of the Kabbalah. Next, we will compare the Egyptian Osiris myth with the sibling rivalry stories of Genesis. Egyptian texts do not present the Osiris myth as a connected and internally consistent mythological narrative; instead, we find isolated scenes scattered throughout the Egyptian literary record. What follows here is a summary of the myth's primary episodes.

Shu inherits the mantle of kingship from his father Atum, and Geb later inherits it from Shu. But after Geb, the succession is less clear. Which of Geb's two sons—Osiris or Set—should inherit? According to one legend, Geb (or perhaps Shu) slays Osiris, but Geb later revives him, restoring him to his original status and leaving the question of the royal succession unresolved. Therefore, the two brothers, Osiris and Set, contend with one another. Although Set is an unruly troublemaker and although Osiris appears to have the better claim, the succession remains disputed.

---

[37] The Hebrew word *shekhinah* ("presence," from the root for "dwell") is grammatically feminine.

Egyptologists surmise that this mythological contest between two heirs to the mantle of kingship is rooted in an actual historical power struggle. Egypt, which the ancient Egyptians called the "Two Lands," was formed by the unification of "Upper Egypt" and "Lower Egypt," and this unification of the two lands is celebrated in many of the dual symbols associated with Egyptian royalty. Thus, it is likely that the mythological contest between Osiris and Set is a cultural memory of a political contest that took place in the hoary past between Egypt's two lands.

But Set's battle against his more civilized brother Osiris may represent cultural and economic factors, too. Lower Egypt, which included the fertile land of the Nile Delta, was a settled agricultural community, and Osiris was the god of agriculture. Upper Egypt, which had less arable land, was necessarily more austere and individualistic, reflecting Set's roguish character. Set was associated with Upper Egypt, and his jurisdiction included the wilderness areas outside the settled encampment. But despite Set's role as an outcast and his reputation for instigating chaos and disaster, he was a god that ancient Egyptians held in great esteem.

Set eventually accuses Osiris of having sex with Nephthys (Set's consort), and he murders Osiris. Some texts refer to Set's dismembering of Osiris, with the severed limbs of Osiris being strewn across Egypt. Other texts refer to Osiris being drowned in the Nile. Either way, Osiris is dead, and he has no heir. Therefore, Isis and Nephthys come to his aid. They gather the parts of Osiris's dismembered body, wrap him back together, and Thoth teaches them the sacred spells they can use to revive him. Their song of lament becomes an incantation of life. Thus, they revive Osiris, and Isis conceives a child by him. Her child is Horus, the rightful heir to the mantle of kingship that descended from Atum. The mummified Osiris descends to the netherworld, and his soul sails the "Nile of the Sky" (*i.e.*, the Milky Way) in the barque of Re (*i.e.*, the sun). Thus, Osiris becomes the god who suffered death and overcame death.

The popularity of this part of the Osiris myth might explain the spread of Christianity in the first centuries of the Common Era. Jesus could be the god who died and overcame death because Osiris was the god who died and overcame death. Jesus could be resurrected to eternal life by the two Marys who visited his tomb because Osiris was resurrected to eternal life by Isis and Nephthys who visited his tomb. Jesus could be the judge of the living and the dead because Osiris presides as chief judge of the divine assembly when a deceased person's soul is weighed against the feather of Truth.

After Isis conceives Horus, thereby producing an heir for the slain Osiris, she flees to the Nile Delta's marshes to rear the child. In that role, she assumes the iconographic form of the cow-headed Hathor, the goddess who suckles the newborn ruler and hides him from Set, who is still jealously contending for the mantle of kingship. As Horus grows to maturity, Set does not relent in his attacks. Nor should he, for he is the archetypal antagonist, and the antagonist plays a critical role in prodding the hero toward spiritual maturity.

In the course of the ongoing rivalry, Horus castrates Set, and Set damages Horus's eye. According to Egyptian lore, the sun and moon are the right and left eyes of the sky, but because Set damaged Horus's left eye, the moon waxes and wanes, its light periodically diminished. The phases of the moon, however, also represent the slain and resurrected Osiris, whose body is severed by Set into fourteen pieces during the waning fortnight and then reassembled by Isis and Nephthys during the waxing fortnight. The full moon, therefore, signifies Osiris's victory over death and his and Horus's victory over Set.

The story of Set damaging Horus's eye is particularly rich in symbolic meaning for it is said to describe the central problem of the human condition. Our dualistic perception of the world is rooted mythologically in the poverty of one of our two eyes, a poverty that resulted from Set's mischief. With this imbalance in our scales of perception, we weigh all experiences. But Thoth is the god who "fills the eye," and when the damaged eye is restored to wholeness, the poverty of our vision is removed, and the divine unity of Creation becomes apparent.

Set's rivalry with Horus finally culminates in a trial before the divine court—in other words, before the gods of the Heliopolitan pantheon. In light of Set's uncivilized attacks, first against Horus's father and later against Horus himself, we naturally favor Horus in this archetypal litigation, but from the divine perspective, the correct outcome is not so obvious. Was Set an unjustified aggressor, or was he vigorously defending an honest claim? There is uncertainty, and the gods debate the merits of the case. But after hearing Thoth's persuasive defense of Horus, the gods rule in Horus's favor. He is "true of speech," meaning that his claim to the throne of Geb is the valid claim, and Thoth, the scribe of the gods, records the "verdict" (from Latin for "true speech"). The same court also hears Set's charges against Osiris. Thoth advocates on behalf of Osiris, and the divine court rules that Osiris is "justified" and declares him king of the dead. Among the living, Horus assumes the throne, and Set is banished to the desert.[38]

Of course, the myth of Osiris is not mere myth. Osiris's victory over death and Set's subsequent rivalry with Horus prefigure a drama that is regularly reenacted in historical time, for civil government, too, must transcend the danger of generational succession. The living pharaoh of each generation is Horus, and his predecessor—the deceased pharaoh—is Osiris. In the world of myth, Set contends against Horus for the divine mantle of kingship, and in the real world, a similar crisis of succession occurs each time the pharaoh dies. One contender, for example, might be the son of the deceased pharaoh's daughter; another might be the deceased pharaoh's son-in-law. Whose claim to the

---

[38] In older variants of the myth, Thoth reconciles Horus and Set, and Set is assigned Upper Egypt. Thus, Thoth acts as mediator and peacemaker regarding the political and cultural rivalry between the two Egypts.

throne is true? Who should bear the mantle of divine kingship that descended from Atum to Shu to Geb to Osiris?

In this way, Osiris dies once again in every generation, and in every generation, he overcomes death and is resurrected as Horus, the new pharaoh. And by way of a secret ritual that mimics the actions of Isis and Nephthys, the new pharaoh receives the divine mantle of kingship that descended from Atum.

The king is dead; long live the king.

6. Osiris in the Book of Genesis

Recall that the Egyptians did not record the Osiris myth as a single narrative; rather, they recorded it in pieces, as disconnected scenes, and for purposes of the present book, the significance of these scenes is that almost all of them are echoed in the sibling rivalry stories of Genesis.

Adam is a victim of the serpent's manipulations, just as Osiris was a victim of Set's manipulations. As a result, Adam "dies" (*i.e.*, he becomes mortal—Gen 2:17), after which he conceives two sons: Cain and Abel. Adam's sons, however, are bitter rivals. Abel is described as a seminomadic herdsman, and Cain as a settled cultivator of the soil, and the Torah's apparent preference for Abel implies an admiration for the untamed world that lies beyond the city walls. (See Gen 4:1–16.) The early Israelites were a seminomadic pastoral people like Abel; they settled and became cultivators of the soil only in later times. Thus, their myths favor Abel, the herdsman, reflecting a cultural memory of their rugged seminomadic past.

Cain kills Abel, just as Set killed Osiris, but Abel is resurrected as Adam's third son, Seth, just as Osiris was resurrected as Horus. Meanwhile, the blood that Cain spilled prevents the ground from yielding its fruit to Cain, and so Cain, like Set, is banished to a lonely life as a wanderer in the wilderness. By making Cain (the cultivator of the soil) into the antagonist, the

Torah seems to invert the roles of Osiris and Set—for Osiris, not Set, is associated with agriculture. But by banishing Cain to a life of wandering, the Torah casts Cain in Set's traditional role as outsider.

In this way, the scenes of the Osiris myth are echoed in the stories of Adam and his immediate descendants, and if we fast-forward several generations, we find that the same pattern continues. Abraham has two sons who contend with one another for the mantle of kingship that passed through the generations from Adam to Abraham. One of Abraham's sons—Ishmael—is a "wild man." (Gen 16:12.) Thus, Ishmael is now in the role of Set, and his brother Isaac is playing Osiris. Isaac, the son of Abraham's old age,[39] is the favored son, and Ishmael poses a threat to Isaac's inheritance. So, like Set, he is driven into the wilderness. (Gen 21:9–21.)

Interestingly, like Geb, who killed his son Osiris but later revived him, Abraham offers his son Isaac as a sacrifice (Gen 22:1–10), but Isaac, like Osiris, survives (Gen 24:62). Was Isaac actually slain and then revived? The Torah is ambiguous. The text says that Abraham offered a ram as a fire offering "*tachat beno*." (Gen 22:13.) The phrase *tachat beno* can be translated "instead of his son," but an equally valid translation for *tachat* is "beneath." Perhaps, then, Abraham offered a ram as a fire offering "*beneath* his son," which would explain why the Torah describes Abraham returning from the sacrifice without Isaac. (Gen 22:19.)

Of course, the standard reading of the story is that Abraham, having been interrupted by an angel of YHVH, did *not* sacrifice Isaac. Thus, the story serves to validate substitution sacrifices (animals in place of sons). The Babylonian Talmud, however,

---

[39] The miracle of Sarah's octogenarian fertility might be explained by the fact that there were more than one Sarah. See Gen 23:1 ["And the lives [(plural)] of Sarah were a hundred years and twenty years and seven years."].

hints at Isaac's actual death, stating that Isaac's ashes upon the altar are what protect the Jewish people from the Angel of Destruction. (See *Berachot* 62b.)[40] Likewise, the Jewish mystical tradition asserts that Isaac's soul actually departed his body but then returned to it, implying a sort of death and resurrection.

Whether or not Isaac was actually slain, he somehow survives his encounter with violent death. He then marries and has two sons. Again, we are presented with rivals for the mantle of kingship, and again, one of the rivals is more civilized than the other.

Jacob "dwelled in tents." (Gen 25:27.) In other words, he dwelled in a community encampment. Esau, by contrast, emerged from the womb "red" (Gen 25:25) and was called "Red" (Gen 25:30), implying the ruddiness of a man who lives in the wilderness. Also, Esau was a hunter, "a man of the field." (Gen 25:27.) Thus, Esau is the one who is now playing the role of Set, contending against Jacob, his more domesticated brother, for the mantle of kingship.

Esau's claim appears to be the superior one; he is, after all, Isaac's firstborn son. But a power struggle nonetheless ensues. Does Esau truly have the superior claim? Was perhaps Jacob the more worthy brother? Moreover, did not Esau sell his birthright to Jacob, thus forfeiting his claim? (See Gen 25:31, 25:33.) But was that sale a fair one? The succession remains disputed until Jacob tricks his father, thereby obtaining the royal blessing intended for Esau. (Gen 27:1–29.)

Esau then seeks to kill Jacob (Gen 27:41), just as Set sought to kill Osiris, but Jacob flees to the home of his maternal uncle, Laban, where he marries two sisters, Leah and Rachel. Hebrew legend tells us that Leah was actually intended to be *Esau's* wife, not Jacob's wife, for Esau was the elder brother, and Leah, the elder sister. (See Gen 29:26.) But because Jacob usurped Esau's position as firstborn, Jacob had to marry Leah. A snide taunt

---

[40] See also Levenson, *The Death and Resurrection*, pp. 173–199.

by Laban drives that point home: "It is not done in our place to give the younger before the firstborn." (Gen 29:26.) On the surface, Laban is merely explaining to Jacob why he gave his elder daughter in marriage rather than his younger daughter, but more subtly Laban is mocking Jacob for supplanting is elder brother.

Leah and Rachel correspond, of course, to Isis and Nephthys. Recall that after Osiris's death, Nephthys abandons Set and joins forces with Isis in her effort to resurrect Osiris and to conceive, by him, Horus. Similarly, Rachel and Leah become joint wives to Jacob.

Jacob next encounters his rival Esau at the Ford of Jabbok. (Gen 32:23–33.) The Torah's text does not mention Esau by name, referring only to "a man" wrestling Jacob (Exod 32:25), but the book of Hosea identifies this "man" as the "angel" Esau. (Hosea 12:3–5.)[41] Jacob's battle with Esau continues throughout the night. Jacob eventually prevails, but Esau injures the "socket of [Jacob's] thigh" (Gen 32:26)—he injures, in other words, Jacob's *testicles*, for the Hebrew word *yoreikh* means both "thigh" and "testicles."[42]

Here, we have another apparent inversion of the Osiris myth. In the Egyptian myth, Horus damaged Set's testicles, and Set damaged Horus's eye. In the Torah, Esau (who is in the role of Set) damages the testicles of Jacob (who is in the role of Osiris), and it is Isaac (the father of Esau and Jacob) whose eyes are weak (Gen 27:1). Perhaps the Torah is subtly reminding us that Jacob (Osiris) seized the mantle of kingship by trickery, usurping the place of Esau (Set), and therefore Jacob suffers the injury associated in Egyptian mythology with Set.

At the end of the nightlong wrestling match, Esau gives Jacob the new name Israel, saying, "for you strived with God

---

[41] See also Ginzberg, *The Legends of the Jews, Volume 5*, p. 305.

[42] Gen 46:26 makes clear that the word *yoreikh*, which is usually translated as "thigh," has the alternative meaning of "testicles."

(*elohim*)... and prevailed." (Gen 32:29.)[43] In several places, Hebrew scripture presents Esau as a god, not a mere man. For example, Jacob declares about his encounter with Esau at the Ford of Jabbok: "I have seen the gods (*elohim*), face to face, and preserved my life." (Gen 32:31.) And the next day, when Jacob again meets Esau, he bows to him, calling him "Lord" (Gen 32:5–6, 32:19, 33:8, 33:13–15), and he says: "I have seen your face like seeing the faces of the gods (*elohim*)" (Gen 33:10). Likewise, in the book of Hosea, we read this about Jacob: "In the womb he seized his brother's heel, and with his strength he struggled with the gods (*elohim*)." (Hosea 12:4.) In this way, the Torah makes clear that its leading figures are meant to represent archetypes of the divine.

In the generation after Jacob, the pattern of the Osiris myth repeats itself once again, with Jacob's many sons rivaling one another for the mantle of kingship. The rivalry focuses primarily on Judah (Hebrew: *Yehudah*) and Joseph (Hebrew: *Yosef*). Which of these two sons, born of different mothers, should bear the mantle of kingship that descended through the generations from Adam (Atum)?

At first, the Torah seems to prefer Joseph. Jacob even gives young Joseph a royal coat, suggesting symbolically that Jacob has chosen Joseph as his heir. (Gen 37:3.) Moreover, Joseph has prophetic dreams in which all his half brothers bow to him, acknowledging his leadership. (Gen 37:5–11.) But Joseph's brothers respond to Joseph's arrogance by abandoning him in a pit where he is likely to die. The brothers then take Joseph's royal coat and smear it with goat's blood, thus making it appear to Jacob, their father, that Joseph has been ravaged by wild animals. (Gen 37:18–35.)

Joseph, however, is rescued from the pit by some traveling traders, and he ends up in Egypt as a slave to Potiphar, the chief priest of Heliopolis. At that point in the story, the Torah again

---

[43] The name Israel means "he will strive with El (God)."

hints that the mantle of kingship belongs to Joseph, for Joseph rises out of slavery to become Egypt's viceroy (Gen 41:40–46) and the "father to pharaoh" (Gen 45:8). The story of Joseph's seduction by Potiphar's wife, his imprisonment, and his subsequent rise to royal power is clearly derived, at least in part, from the Egyptian tale of *The Two Brothers*. The latter story includes all the major motifs from the Joseph story, including sibling rivalry and reconciliation, the rebuffed seductress, her accusation against the man she unsuccessfully seduced, the man's punishment, and his eventual rise to the position of pharaoh.[44]

Joseph becomes viceroy of Egypt, and then his half brothers, facing famine in Canaan, travel to Egypt to purchase grain from Joseph, not recognizing him to be the brother they had earlier abandoned in a pit to die. (Gen 43:1–26.) Joseph then tests his half brothers by arranging for young Benjamin's arrest. (Gen 44:1–17.)

Benjamin, like Joseph, is a son of Jacob's second wife, Rachel, and therefore he stands in Joseph's place in relation to the sons of Leah. Thus, Joseph wants to see if his half brothers will abandon Benjamin or if they will fight for him. Will the brothers repeat the moral error they committed when they left Joseph to die in a pit, or will they redeem themselves by facing the same situation a second time and doing the right thing? The story reaches its dramatic climax, when Judah openly subjugates himself to Joseph, calling Joseph "Lord" (Gen 44:16) and asking Joseph to take him (Judah) as a prisoner in place of Benjamin (Gen 44:18–34). Thus, Judah seems to acknowledge Joseph's royal status, and he proves that he has repented for his error in mistreating Joseph. Joseph's heart is moved. He reveals his identity to his half brothers, forgives them, and the entire family migrates to Egypt to live in comfort, with Joseph as de facto king. (Gen 45–47.) Joseph later openly declares his Horus-like

---

[44] Lichtheim (trans. and ed.), *Ancient Egyptian Literature: Volume II*, pp. 203–211.

status, saying to his half brothers: "Do not fear, for I am the stand-in of the gods"—that is, he is the representative of the gods on earth. (Gen 50:19.)

Jacob also seems to confirm that Joseph is his rightful heir by bestowing the double portion of his estate on Joseph. (Gen 48:5, 48:22.) The double portion is an indication that Joseph has gained the status of "firstborn." Later, however, the Torah hints that Jacob erred in doing so (Deut 21:15–17), and at the time of Jacob's final blessing to his twelve sons, he asserts that it is Judah, not Joseph, who has inherited the mantle of kingship, saying: "The scepter [of kingship] shall not depart from Judah." (Gen 49:8–12.) According to the Kabbalah, Judah proved that he merited the mantle of kingship when he freely offered himself as a sacrifice in Benjamin's place.

But irrespective of Jacob's blessing to Judah, the rivalry between Judah and Joseph continues, generations later, between the two halves of a painfully divided kingdom. King David, a descendant of Judah, was able to unite the tribes, and David's son, Solomon, was able to maintain that unity. But after the reign of Solomon, the Davidic kingdom split in two, with Rehoboam, a descendant of Judah, reigning as King of Judah (the Southern Kingdom), and Jeroboam, a descendant of Joseph, reigning as King of Israel (the Northern Kingdom). (See 1 Kings 11:26–39, 12:1–24; Ezek 37:15–28.) According to Egyptian lore, Upper and Lower Egypt competed as rival kingdoms until they were united by a single pharaoh, who was an incarnation of Horus. Similarly, Judah and Israel compete as rival kingdoms yearning to be united by a single king, the rightful heir to Adam's mantle of kingship.

The myth of Osiris tells an awesome tale, and it keeps being retold, again and again, with each turn of the wheels of time. Ancient Egypt's mythological drama is retold in Genesis, and it is retold throughout history, for according to Jewish thought, the events of historical time are like shadows cast by the dance of these timeless mythological archetypes.

7. The Religion of the Canaanites

The foregoing discussion shows the significant influence of Egyptian myths and religious ideas in the book of Genesis. Let us turn next to Canaanite myths and religious ideas to see if they, too, are reflected in Genesis.

(a) El, the Magnificent, Father of the Seventy Gods

In 1928 c.e., a farmer was plowing a field near the Mediterranean coast in what is modern-day Syria, and he unearthed ancient ruins that were later found to be part of a buried city called "Ugarit." Archaeologists eventually excavated thousands of clay tablets, many dating to roughly the time of Moses, relating the primary myths of the Canaanite people. For the first time, Bible scholars were able to piece together details about the religion that the biblical Abraham encountered when he migrated from Mesopotamia to Canaan—a religion that he and his descendants more or less adopted. These Canaanite myths provide scholars with a cultural background that contextualizes many of the obscure passages of Hebrew scripture, and they confirm that the biblical term "El," when standing alone, is not, as it is usually translated, a generic word for "God," but rather the proper name of a *particular* god, the foremost god of the Canaanite pantheon.

Consider, for example, the story of Melchizedek in the book of Genesis. The Bible relates that Melchizedek, the King of Salem (*i.e.*, Jerusalem), was a "priest to highest El." (Gen 14:18.) This text is often translated as "priest of the Most High God," but considering that Melchizedek was a Canaanite king and that El was the chief god of the Canaanite pantheon, the text could not possibly be referring to God in the modern generic sense. Rather, the text is clearly referring to a particular god, the Canaanite god named El, the father of the seventy gods.

Moreover, Hebrew scripture makes clear that just as much as the ancient Israelites revered Shaddai, a variant of the Canaanite storm god Ba'al, so also they revered El, the mythological father of Ba'al. For example, Genesis describes Melchizedek as an ally and friend to Abraham, and it depicts the two participating together in a religious rite dedicated to El, stating that Melchizedek brought out bread and wine and announced: "Blessed is Abram to highest El, creator of heavens and earth." (Gen 14:19.)

Likewise, the personal names of the ancient Israelites, recorded in the numerous genealogical lists of the Torah, frequently use "El" as their theophoric element, including names such as Isra-El, Eli-Tzur, Shelumi-El, Nethan-El, Eli-Av, Eli-Shama, Gamli-El, Pagi-El, Deu-El, El-Yasaf. (See, e.g., Num 1:5–15.) The name one chooses for one's child certainly reveals something about what is most dear to one's heart, and these names indicate that, irrespective of the Torah's narrative assertions, the Israelites whom Moses led out of Egypt were devoted to the Canaanite god El, not to YHVH. In fact, relatively few names in the Torah suggest reverence for Moses' god, YHVH, although in the *later* books of the Bible, the element *yahu* (a reference to YHVH) becomes prevalent in personal names, especially in the Kingdom of Judah, where YHVH was the deity of the local ruling family.

Aside from the patriarchal narratives, biblical references to the Canaanite god El are most frequent in the Bala'am passages of the book of Numbers (Num 22–24), the book of Job, and the book of Psalms, the same places where we also encounter the name Shaddai. El is usually praised as the supreme deity, abundantly merciful and generous, and also trustworthy to protect his devotees. Significantly, the book of Job frequently refers to El and Shaddai in parallel statements, reinforcing the idea that Shaddai (Job's afflicter) was a specific aspect of El.[45]

There are also several scriptural passages that unambiguously identify YHVH with El, suggesting that syncretism was a

---

[45] Examples include Job 8:3, 8:5, 13:3, 15:25, 22:17, 23:16, 27:2, 27:11, 27:13, 33:4, 34:10, 34:12, 35:13.

leading value of the Bible's redactors. One particularly explicit example occurs in the book of Psalms where we read: "For YHVH is El the Great and great king over all the gods." (Ps 95:3.) Among the Israelite patriarchs, Abraham in particular emphasizes the syncretistic equivalence between YHVH and El, calling YHVH "Highest El" (Gen 14:22) and "Eternal El" (Gen 21:33). And Moses, too, in his final speech to the Israelites, emphasizes the unity between YHVH and El, saying: "And you will know that YHVH, your God, He is the gods (*hua ha-elohim*), the faithful El...." (Deut 7:9.) Similarly, King David asks: "Who is El besides YHVH?" (2 Sam 22:32.)[46] Finally, the Jewish prayer book includes many beautiful passages associating El with YHVH and praising El in the same reverent terms used for YHVH.

The Ugaritic tablets establish that these statements are not, as they are usually translated, abstract assertions that YHVH is "God"; rather, they are specific assertions assimilating YHVH to the chief god of the Canaanite pantheon, the beloved god of the Israelites. That, of course, leaves one to wonder about the identity and origins of Moses' god, YHVH, a god that Hebrew scripture so insistently equates with El. Canaanite mythology does not make any references to a god named YHVH. Therefore, the frequent assertions in Hebrew scripture that YHVH is El can have no purpose except to link the leading deities of two distinct cultures. We will consider this point in Part Two.

From an ancient Phoenician source (Sanchuniathon), we learn that the Canaanite El was called "Kronos" by the Greeks, that he sacrificed his beloved son, and that he was linked with the planet Saturn, the highest of the visible planets and thus the overlord of the astrological powers. In astrological speculation, Saturn is sometimes described as the chief malefic, the source, among the astrological powers, of difficulty, confusion, and

---

[46] Other examples include Gen 16:13; Exod 20:5, 34:14; Deut 4:24, 4:31, 5:9, 6:15, 7:21; 1 Sam 2:3; Isa 43:12; Pss 10:12, 29:3, 84:3, 118:27–28; Dan 9:4; Neh 1:5.

obstacles. But Saturn also has a benefic aspect, goading individuals to spiritual maturity.

The connection between El and the planet Saturn is confirmed in several classical sources,[47] and this same connection is asserted in the book of Job, in which Eliphaz says:

> Is not *eloah* ("god") the highpoint of the heavens, and see *the highest of the planets that are aloft?* And [so] you say, "What does El know? He will judge [from] behind darkness. Thick clouds hide him, and he will not see, and he will traipse the compass of the heavens." Will you [thus] observe the eternal way that the people of iniquity traveled…, those who say to El, "Turn aside from us," and, "What will Shaddai do to them?"[48]

In this passage, Eliphaz unambiguously equates El with Saturn, "the highest of the planets that are aloft," but in his role as punisher of iniquity, the passage also associates El with Shaddai, a variant of the Canaanite god Ba'al. The identity between the god of the Israelites and the planet Saturn is made even more explicit in the book of Amos, where we read: "In the wilderness for forty years, O House of Israel, you carried… your images of Saturn—the star of your god—that you made for yourselves." (Amos 5:25–26.) The Hebrew text uses the phrase "your images of Chiun," but the Septuagint—a Greek translation of Hebrew scripture prepared in Alexandria in the 2nd or 3rd century B.C.E.—translates "Chiun" as "Remphan," and "Remphan" was an Egyptian name for Saturn.[49]

---

[47] See Brown, *Late Carthaginian Child Sacrifice*, pp. 21–26; Levenson, *The Death and Resurrection*, pp. 22, 25–27; Cross, *Canaanite Myth and Hebrew Epic*, p. 25.

[48] Job 22:12–17.

[49] The connection between the God of Israel and Saturn is also attested in medieval Jewish literature. See, e.g., Idel, *Saturn's Jews*, pp. 5–38;

We have already noted that the book of Job uses the name Shaddai to describe El's role as the punisher of iniquity. The many gods can thus be thought of as *names* given to various functions of El, not as indpendent gods. The Ugaritic texts describe El as the "father" of seventy such "gods." Significantly, a version of the Torah found among the Dead Sea Scrolls likewise refers to precisely seventy "sons of God," thus confirming that the word "El" in the Torah invokes the Canaanite El and also confirming the polytheistic foundation of biblical monotheism.[50]

Although El as described in the Ugaritic texts was a remote deity, acting through seventy lesser gods, he was also a compassionate deity, and he could be supplicated directly. Nonetheless, the Ugaritic texts place special emphasis on the redemptive role of El's son Ba'al.

(b) Ba'al Hadad, the Lord of the Earth

Ba'al was the fierce, storm god that we have previously likened to Shaddai, and based on his fierceness and his power over the weather, he was considered the sovereign of the terrestrial world. But as we shall see, fierceness and power were not Ba'al's only traits; like Osiris, he was also the god who overcame death and who thus could redeem his devotees from death, and like Horus, Ba'al was incarnate in the living Canaanite king of each generation.

In Hebrew scripture—and particularly in Elijah's challenge to the "prophets of Ba'al" (1 Kings 18:18–40)—Ba'al appears as YHVH's chief rival for the devotion of the Israelites. Scripture

---

Sela, *Abraham ibn Ezra and the Rise of Medieval Hebrew Science*, pp. 151–158; Ginsburg (trans. and ed.), *Sod ha-Shabbat*, pp. 54–55, 163–167.

[50] See Smith, *The Origins of Biblical Monotheism*, pp. 48–49. The interested reader can compare the Dead Sea Scrolls version of Deut 32:8 (which states that the number of nations is equal to the number of the "sons of God") with Gen 10 (which lists seventy nations).

refers to Baʻal as "Boshet,"[51] a term that came to mean "shame," and the prophets of YHVH spare no ink in condemning Baʻal worship. Significantly, the passages from Leviticus that forbid child sacrifice (Lev 18:21, 20:2–5) specifically forbid sacrifice to MoLeKH, a god whose name is written in Hebrew with the same letters as the Hebrew word for "king" (*MeLeKH*) but inserting the *vowels* of the name Boshet. Encryption through vowel substitution is one of the techniques of the Hebrew scribes, and here it would seem that the intent is a veiled polemic against *Melekh Boshet* ("King Boshet"), the god-king of the Canaanite religion.

Nevertheless, the appearance of several individuals in Hebrew scripture whose names include "Baʻal" or "Boshet" as their theophoric element proves that, at one time at least, Baʻal/Boshet was not perceived by the Israelites to be such a menace. Likewise, Baʻal's mythological home—a mountain called "Tzafon," which means "North"—might be a variant of Mount Tzion ("Mount Zion") (see Ps 48:3 ["Mount Tzion, utmost place of Tzafon"]), and Mount Tzion is a place revered in Hebrew scripture as the preferred dwelling of YHVH (Pss 2:6, 87:2, 132:13). In addition, the term "Baʻal Tzafon" appears in the book of Exodus as a place name (Exod 14:2), and Moses had a cousin named El-Tzafon (Exod 6:22; see also Num 34:25), apparently a reference to Baʻal. Finally, Baʻal was sometimes depicted iconographically as a bull, suggesting a connection to the golden calf cult that the Israelites practiced in the wilderness (Exod 32:1–6) and that they continued to practice in the Northern Kingdom (1 Kings 12:28–29).

The Ugaritic texts, which are contemporaneous with the Israelites' departure from Egypt, give us a favorable view of Baʻal,

---

[51] Compare Judg 6–9 [Jeru-Baʻal] with 2 Sam 11:21 [Jeru-Boshet]; compare 2 Sam 2–21 [Ish-Boshet and Mephi-Boshet] with 1 Chron 8–9 [Ish-Baʻal and Merib-Baʻal]; see also Jer 3:24 [child sacrifices to Boshet], 11:13 [altars to Boshet]; Hosea 9:10 [Israelites dedicated themselves to Boshet at Baʻal Pʻeor; here "Boshet" may be a reference to Balaʻam].

revealing details of this Canaanite deity that the early Israelites embraced, but the later prophets condemned.[52] Ba'al (or Ba'al Hadad[53]) is presented in the Ugaritic texts as the son of El and Asherah. In Hebrew scripture, Asherah often takes the form of an "Asherah tree"—a holy tree near which people gathered and worshiped, sometimes a tree located near the altar of YHVH. (See, e.g., Gen 35:4; Exod 34:13; Deut 16:21.) Asherah also appears to be the deity called "Wisdom" in Solomon's "Ode to Wisdom" (Prov 1–9), a hidden identity that the author reveals in code: "Happy ('ASHRei) is the man who has found Wisdom.... Length of days are in her right hand; in her left are wealth and glory. Her ways are the ways of pleasantness, and all her paths are peace. She is a Tree of Life (eitz chayim hi) to those who seize hold of her, and those who grasp her are happy (m'AuSHaR)." (Prov 3:13–18.) This famous passage begins and ends with words that have the letters of the name Asherah, and it expressly refers to Wisdom as a "Tree," which, as noted, was the primary form in which Asherah was worshiped.[54]

In the Ugaritic texts, Ba'al's chief rivals are Yam ("Sea")

---

[52] For translations of the Ugaritic texts, see Coogan (trans. and ed.), *Stories from Ancient Canaan*, pp. 75–115.

[53] The term *ba'al* (meaning "lord" or "master") was sometimes used generically to refer to any localized deity. The specific Ba'al that was a leading member of the Canaanite pantheon was Ba'al Hadad. The Ba'al that Elijah opposed in his confrontation with the "priests of Ba'al" was apparently Ba'al of Sidon. See 1 Kings 16:31.

[54] Consider also this passage from the book of Hosea, which seems to include another encoded reference to Asherah: "Ephraim [will say]: 'What is [the need] to me anymore for idols?' I [God] will answer and look at him ('ASHuRenu). I am like a fresh cypress Tree. From me, your fruit will be found. Who is wise and comprehends these things ('ELaH)?" Hosea 14:9–10. This passage, like the passage from Proverbs, uses the letters of the name Asherah and refers to god as a "Tree." It also uses the word *'elah*, which can be read as a feminine grammatical form of the name El.

and Mot ("Death"), two gods that, like Ba'al, are sons of El. Yam appears in Hebrew scripture as the Sea of Reeds (*Yam Suf*) and also as the Jordan River, and Mot also plays an important part in Hebrew scripture—for example, in the myth of Adam's fall from grace, in which Adam becomes subject to Death (*Mot*) (Gen 2:17).

The god Yam represents the destructive power of water, and he is particularly associated with the waters of dissolution that threaten to reabsorb Creation. According to the Canaanite myth, Yam sends his messengers to El, demanding the inheritance that has been designated for Ba'al, and Ba'al responds by urging the gods not to fear. El then surrenders Ba'al into the hands of Yam. Kothar-and-Hasis (a god of temple crafts) next rallies Ba'al to eternal kingship and makes for Ba'al two weapons with which Ba'al can combat Yam. These weapons are "Driver" and "Chaser." With Chaser, Ba'al is able to defeat Yam, and Astarte, the goddess of love and sexuality, hails Ba'al's victory. Astarte is mentioned in several passages of Hebrew scripture, all of which condemn Canaanite forms of worship.

After Ba'al's victory over Yam, Ba'al assumes the title of "Lord of the Earth," and a feast is held in his honor. But despite the victory, Ba'al's messengers approach the warrior goddess Anat—Ba'al's sister—praying for peace. Anat appears in Hebrew scripture primarily as a place name ("Temple of Anat"). (See Josh 19:38; Judg 1:33.[55]) In response to Ba'al's emissaries, Anat recounts her many victories on behalf of Ba'al, including his victory over Yam, and she wonders what new enemy might be threatening Ba'al. As we shall see, this new enemy is Death.

Anat accepts the messengers' invitation to go to Ba'al, and Ba'al holds a feast in her honor. Anat then goes to El ("Father of Time"), demanding that El give Ba'al a "house" like those of the other gods. In other words, she demands for Ba'al a temple, priests, and a cult. Anat insists on Ba'al's greatness above all

---

[55] But consider also Judg 3:31; 2 Sam 22:36.

the gods. Ba'al and Anat also approach Asherah, but Asherah hesitates to intervene, deferring to "El the Compassionate," the "Creator of All." Anat nonetheless bestows gifts on Asherah, and Asherah is thus enlisted into the cause of helping Ba'al to obtain a "house."

Asherah travels to El, with Anat following. Standing before El, Asherah declares the supremacy of Ba'al and demands that El give Ba'al a house like those of the other gods. El agrees, and Asherah is pleased. Ba'al—who is described as the "Rider on the Clouds"—will have a house made of cedar, bricks, silver, gold, and lapis lazuli. Gratified by daily offerings, he will release rain, thunder, and lightning. Anat too is pleased, and she travels to Ba'al's celestial residence in Tzafon. Ba'al then sends for Kothar-and-Hasis, the god of temple crafts.

Kothar-and-Hasis constructs Ba'al's house, using the cedars of Lebanon as building materials. In Hebrew scripture, the "cedars of Lebanon" are used in the construction of the Jerusalem temple. (See 1 Kings 5:6.) On the seventh day, Ba'al's house is complete, and Ba'al gives a feast, inviting Asherah's "seventy sons" (*i.e.*, all the gods). With the completion of his house, Ba'al declares his lordship over the terrestrial world. No other king will rule on earth, and no more tribute will be sent to El's son Mot ("Death"). In other words, Ba'al's status as "Lord of the Earth" will redeem the earth's mortal inhabitants, depriving Death of his tribute. Ba'al next sends messengers to the underworld to warn Death.

But Ba'al's messengers return with Death's grim response: Death is hungry. Death thus insists on receiving the tribute that is his due. To overcome Death, therefore, Ba'al himself must be consumed by Death, thus satisfying the debt. Ba'al, like Osiris, will be the god who suffers human mortality and thereby breaks the power of Death.

Ba'al descends to the underworld. He is dead, and El sits upon the ground, mourning Ba'al's demise. El puts dust on his head; he dons sackcloth; he cuts his cheeks and chin. Then, he summons Asherah to choose a replacement god who will sit on Ba'al's throne in Tzafon and assume Ba'al's role as Lord of the Earth. But no suitable replacement is found.

Anat, the goddess of war, also mourns Ba'al's death. But the gods declare that Anat will defeat Death, for she defeated Leviathan and demolished the Twisting Serpent. The Bible refers to Leviathan as a multiheaded, fire-breathing sea monster and also as a "twisting serpent" (Isa 27:1; Pss 74:13–14, 104:25–26; Job 41:1–26). Thus, the statement in the Canaanite myth that Anat defeated Leviathan and the Twisting Serpent appears to be a reference to Anat's role in helping Ba'al overcome Yam ("Sea"). Note that in the Bible, it is YHVH, not Anat, who defeats Leviathan and tames Yam (see Isa 27:1, 51:9–10; Pss 77:17–20, 89:10–11, 104:3–13; Job 38:8–11, 26:10–14, 40:25–32), reflecting the tendency of the Bible to attribute the actions of lesser Canaanite gods to either YHVH or El.

After Anat is rallied by the gods, she summons the sun, and with the sun, she descends to the underworld. With the sun's help, Anat carries Ba'al's lifeless body back to Tzafon, where she buries him with honor. Anat then approaches Death, pleading on behalf of Ba'al. Death responds that he was hungry, that he found Ba'al on Death's shore, and that he ate him. Months pass, and Anat continues to mourn for Ba'al. Then, finally, she takes action, seizing Death and defeating him. Death is so thoroughly overcome that the birds will not eat Death's remains. Anat splits, burns, grinds, winnows, scatters, and sows Death's body. And El then has a dream in which the heavens rain oil and the seasonal riverbeds run with honey. El's dream signifies the restoration of Ba'al to life.

Ba'al returns to his throne and displays his authority over both Yam and Mot, but in the seventh year, Death challenges Ba'al to a rematch, complaining that, because of Ba'al, he (Death) was split, burned, ground, winnowed, scattered, and sown. Death demands one of Ba'al's divine brothers as compensation. At last, Death and Ba'al engage in direct battle, but the Sun warns Death not to fight Ba'al, because El will always ensure that Ba'al prevails.

This fascinating myth, describing Ba'al's victory over Yam and Mot, is obviously a precursor to Christian theology, with God assuming mortality as a way of paying the debt mankind owes to Death. But the Ba'al myth also has parallels in the *Enûma Eliš,* a Babylonian creation myth that dates to the first half of the 2nd millennium B.C.E.[56] The *Enûma Eliš* tells of how the storm god Marduk agrees to fight the goddess Tiamat (seawater) provided he is made king of the gods, sovereign of the universe, and master over death and resurrection. Tiamat, in the form of a huge sea monster, then engages Marduk in direct battle, but Marduk prevails. After his victory, Marduk establishes the astrological forces, and he creates the moon to mark four seven-day periods (new moon, waxing half-moon, full moon, waning half-moon).

Clearly, Marduk corresponds to the Canaanite Ba'al, and Tiamat corresponds to Ba'al's enemy Yam. As already noted, the giant sea creature, which is the form Tiamat assumes in her battle against Marduk, appears in numerous Bible verses. For example, in Psalm 74 we read: "You broke with your strength Yam, shattered the heads of the sea monsters upon the waters. You crushed the heads of Leviathan." (Ps 74:13–14.) In Psalm 89, it is King David who is given credit for this victory over Yam, thus assimilating David to both Marduk and Ba'al. (Ps 89:26.)

The Canaanite myth describing Ba'al's victory over Yam and Mot has deep roots in the mythology of the ancient Near East, and the archetypes of that mythology are echoed in the Hebrew Bible's text and theology and also in Christian theology. The biblical distinction lies in the rigorous monotheistic nondualism that the Bible constructs from these polytheistic roots, making

---

[56] For a translation of the *Enûma Eliš*, see Dalley (trans.), *Myths from Mesopotamia,* pp. 228–277.

artful use of the idea that the one God functions in the world through diverse names, roles, and derivative powers.

8. The Plurality of the Singular God

The Egyptian word for "god" is *netjer*. The English word "god," however, does not quite capture the broad semantic range of the word *netjer*, a word that can encompass such diverse things as a genie or tree spirit, a demon, a household god, the soul of a departed ancestor, a local deity with a thriving cult, and the supreme god of one of Egypt's capital cities. Thus, we might more accurately translate *netjer* as "spirit," having in mind that "spirit" describes a continuum that includes the beatified dead, minor gods, major gods, and God. In ancient Egyptian texts, the word *netjer* often appears in the plural, as *netjeru*, but sometimes the plural form *netjeru* is used in a collective sense, as in the English expressions "May the gods protect you" and "May the gods grant you long life."

In ancient Semitic languages, the words used for "god" and "gods" have the same broad semantic range as their Egyptian counterparts. That point is confirmed by Hebrew scripture. In Hebrew, the word for "god" is *eloah*, and its plural form is *elohim*. The word *eloah* is relatively rare in Hebrew scripture, but the plural word *elohim* is ubiquitous, and it is used to refer to spirit forces, minor deities, household deities, deceased souls, angelic or celestial powers, and also the gods of other nations. But Hebrew scripture also uses the same plural word (*elohim*) as a collective noun to refer to the gods acting together as a single corpus, and when used in this collective sense, the plural word "gods" (*elohim*) takes a singular pronoun and verb form.

The same grammatical irregularity occurs in English with collective nouns such as "agenda," "mathematics," and "United States." In each case, the term is plural in form, but it is used to refer to an indivisible group, and therefore it generally takes a singular pronoun and verb form. Interestingly, when the United States of America was first established, politicians typically spoke of "*these* United States" and they said "the United States *are*...." It was after the Civil War that singular pronouns and verb forms became the norm in this context, implying an intention to emphasize the unity of the states rather than their diversity.

When the plural Hebrew word *elohim* is used as a collective noun to refer to the gods acting together as a single corpus, it is generally translated into English as "God" (singular, with an uppercase *G*), and it generally refers to the all-powerful God of biblical monotheism. And although "God" is a suitable translation of the collective noun *elohim*, the phrase "Divine Council" (indicating both plurality and unity) might be a more accurate rendering. We have encountered this "Divine Council" in Egyptian and Canaanite mythology, and we have noted that Hebrew scripture adopts the same metaphor to describe the gods acting in concert. (See Exod 21:6, 22:7–8; Isa 6:8; Jer 23:18–22; Ps 82:1; Job 1:6.)

Thus, Hebrew scripture does not categorically deny polytheism; quite the opposite, it validates the plurality of God, but it equates all those divine forces with YHVH, saying: "You were shown to know that YHVH is the gods; [*there is*] *nothing else besides him....* [I]n the heavens above and upon the earth below, [*there is*] *nothing else.*" (Deut 4:35–39; see also Deut 7:9.) In other words, scripture emphasizes the essential unity of the gods, using the name YHVH (and sometimes El) to express that unity.[57] In the view of Hebrew scripture, the "gods" of ancient myth and

---

[57] The Torah also urges the Israelites not to serve "*later* gods that you did not know, you nor your ancestors" (Deut 13:7; see also Deut 11:28, 13:3, 13:14, 28:64, 29:25, 32:17; Jer 19:4), and of course the Torah tells the Israelites to worship only YHVH (Deut 6:13, 10:12–17, 13:5). As we shall see in Part Five, the book of Deuteronomy's more chauvinistic conception of monotheism is quite different from that of older parts of the Torah.

epic are quite real, but their purpose is not their individual activity; rather, their purpose is the collective resultant of all their activities and interactions. Thus, for example, it is critically important that kindness (*Chesed*) and strength (*Gevurah*)—mercy and justice—be in holistic balance, with no single divine principle dominating another. The gods of myth and epic are the powers and forces (including astrological forces) through which YHVH governs Creation, but as aspects of that one God, they are perfectly integrated.

Consider, for example, the following selection of verses from Hebrew scripture, all of which expressly validate polytheism while stressing the supremacy of YHVH:

- "And Abraham said: '…[T]he gods made me wander [(plural verb)] from the house of my father.…'" (Gen 20:11–13.)
- "And [Jacob] called to the place 'El Beit-El' for there the gods were revealed [(plural verb)] to him.…" (Gen 35:7.)
- "Who is like you among the Els [(*i.e.*, the diverse aspects of El)], O YHVH?" (Exod 15:11.)
- "Now I know that YHVH is greater than all the gods." (Exod 18:11.)
- "YHVH, your God, he is God of the gods and Lord of the lords, the great, mighty, and awesome El.…" (Deut 10:17.)
- "When the Most High gave inheritance to the peoples and divided the sons of man, he stood the borders of the [seventy] nations according to the number of the gods." (Deut 32:8 [Dead Sea Scrolls version of the text].)
- "Surely there are gods, judges of the earth." (Ps 58:11.)
- "God stands in the assembly of El; in the midst of the gods he judges." (Ps 82:1; see also Ps 82:6–7.)
- "There is none like you among the gods, my Lord." (Ps 86:8.)
- "For who in the skies can be compared to YHVH; [who can be] likened to YHVH among the sons of the gods?" (Ps 89:7.)
- "For YHVH is El the Great and great king over all the gods." (Ps 95:3.)

- "YHVH is great and exceedingly praised; He is awesome over all the gods." (Ps 96:4.)
- "Mountains melted like wax before YHVH, before the Lord of the earth; ... all the gods bow to him.... For you, YHVH, are most supreme upon all the earth and elevated over all the gods." (Ps 97:5–9.)
- "Know that YHVH is the gods, he made us, and we are his...." (Ps 100:3.)
- "I know that YHVH is greater—our Lord—than all the gods." (Ps 135:5.)
- "Give thanks to YHVH...; give thanks to God of the gods...; give thanks to Lord of the lords...." (Ps 136:1–3.)

According to these scriptural passages and many others, the gods (*elohim*) are actors in a drama that YHVH is authoring. They are the enforcers of natural and moral laws, upholding order in the universe, but YHVH is that which *preexists* the natural and moral order of the universe.

9. The Sweetening of Boshet

The Ugaritic texts may be relatively new to scholars of the Bible, but the stories they record were well known to the Israelites who followed Moses out of Egypt, and they reveal a lot to us about the Israelite conception of divinity. El was the God of Abrahamic monotheism, but Ba'al was the specific aspect of El that functioned as sovereign of the terrestrial world—the divine archetype of kingship—and it was through the ritual reenactment of Ba'al's mythological victory over Death that ancient Semitic society was able to transcend the periodic death of the human king.[58]

---

[58] The funerary ritual for deceased Ugaritic kings incorporated several elements from the Ba'al myth. See Smith, *The Origins of Biblical Monotheism*, pp. 31, 120–128.

But as we have seen, Ba'al was also a storm god similar to the Egyptian storm god Set. Thus, for the Israelite rulers of Lower Egypt, Set (not Osiris) was the rightful heir to the mantle of kingship that descended from Atum, and Set (not Osiris) was the god who died and broke the power of Death, thus safeguarding royal authority from generation to generation. This preference for Set among Lower Egypt's Israelite pharaohs might explain why the sibling rivalry stories of the book of Genesis sometimes invert the motifs of the Osiris myth. And the polemic against Ba'al that appears in the later books of the Bible only serves to confirm that Ba'al remained extremely attractive to the Israelites for many centuries. Therefore, we might consider what elements of Ba'al's cult remain a vital part of later Judaism, perhaps in a veiled form.

Consider, for example, Ba'al's mythological association with the number seven. Ba'al's house is completed on the seventh day, and Death seeks a rematch against Ba'al in the seventh year. By comparison, Jewish tradition consecrates the seventh in any series to God, including, as we have seen, the seventh of the visible planets (Saturn). Among the *sefirot*, *Malkhut* is seventh in relation to the hexad from *Chesed* through *Yesod*, and *Malkhut*—which means "kingship"—represents God's aspect as earthly sovereign, suggesting a connection to Ba'al. Moreover, the Jewish Sabbath comes on the seventh day of the week, and as part of the Sabbath liturgy, Jews praise "Ba'al of Salvations" and "Ba'al of Consolations." (See *Birkat ha-Mazon*.) The Sabbath liturgy also declares about God: "You consecrated the seventh day [(*i.e.*, the Sabbath)] *for Your name*." (See *Ma'ariv Amidah*, italics added.)

The latter expression is puzzling—it declares the holiness of the Sabbath, but it also asserts that the Sabbath is one of God's *names*. The Sabbath liturgy certainly expresses the sort of reverent devotion to the Sabbath that one would ordinarily expect to be directed toward a deity, but in what sense is the Sabbath a name of God? Recall that Ba'al is also called "Boshet" in Hebrew scripture.[59] If we rearrange the Hebrew letters of BoSHeT, we get the Hebrew word for "Sabbath" (*SHaBaT*). Thus, Ba'al/Boshet, who represents earthly sovereignty in the divine dimension, corresponds to the Sabbath day in the temporal dimension.

As discussed briefly in regard to the *Enûma Eliš*, the sanctification of the seventh day (the Sabbath) originated in ancient Mesopotamia, Abraham's homeland, and the descendants of Abraham must have brought this practice with them throughout their various migrations.[60] In Mesopotamian practice, the Sabbath (called "*sabattu*") was celebrated in conjunction with the four phases of the moon—the new moon, the waxing half-moon, the full moon, and the waning half-moon.[61] But because the lunar month is about twenty-nine and one-half days, these four lunar phases were not always exactly seven days, so an intercalary day was occasionally added. In later times these lunar Sabbaths were replaced by the strict seven-day cycle that is now recognized worldwide. Interestingly, however, every Sabbath day that occurs in the Torah falls on a new moon, a full moon, or on the

---

[59] Compare Judg 6–9 [Jeru-Ba'al] with 2 Sam 11:21 [Jeru-Boshet]; compare 2 Sam 2–21 [Ish-Boshet and Mephi-Boshet] with 1 Chron 8–9 [Ish-Ba'al and Merib-Ba'al]; see also Jer 3:24, 11:13; Hosea 9:10.

[60] Recall that, on the sixth day of receiving the manna in the wilderness, the Israelites spontaneously gathered a double portion without being commanded by Moses to do so. See Exod 16:4–22. Thus, the practice of doing so was rooted in Israelite tradition, not Moses' instruction. Moses, who was reared as an Egyptian, noticed what the Israelites were doing and acknowledged that it was what YHVH wanted. Moses then commanded the Israelites to observe the Sabbath, thus formalizing the tradition. See Exod 16:23–30; see also Deut 5:12. The foregoing interpretation of the text is, however, in tension with the rabbinic interpretation, which holds that it was at Marah that Moses commanded the Israelites to observe the Sabbath. See *BT Sanhedrin* 56b [discussing Exod 15:25].

[61] See Dalley (trans.), *Myths from Mesopotamia*, pp. 15, 255–257, 275, fn. 28.

seventh day after one or the other, suggesting that the Sabbath of the Torah was the lunar Sabbath of Mesopotamian practice.[62]

So, if Ba'al, whose "house" was completed on the seventh day (the Sabbath), is the most immanent aspect of God and the patron deity of human kings (*i.e.*, *Malkhut* among the *sefirot*), and if he corresponds to Set among the Heliopolitan gods, then who is the rightful heir to the mantle of kingship that descended from Atum? Is it troublesome Set, or is it innocent Horus? And if the Heliopolitan archetypes play out in the sibling rivalry stories of Genesis, then who is the rightful heir of Jacob? Is it Joseph, or is it Judah? And if Joseph and Judah are each the progenitor of a distinct royal house, then who is the messianic king who reveals God's immanence in the world? Is it the king of Israel, or is it the king of Judah? The Kabbalah teaches that there are actually *two* messiahs—one a descendant of Joseph and the other a descendant of Judah. But in the end, the two will be united, and every day will be the Sabbath, and all fierceness will be rendered sweet.

10. Black Fire Engraved on White Fire

Even darkness does not obscure from you,
And night appears as day.
As darkness, so light.

—Ps 139:12

---

[62] Several passages in Hebrew scripture refer, as a group, to new moons, Sabbaths, and feast days (full moons). These passages suggest that the ancient Israelites consecrated new moons, full moons, and the seventh day after each, perhaps reserving the word "Sabbath" for the half-moon phases. See Isa 1:14; Ezek 45:17, 46:1; Hosea 2:13; Amos 8:5; Ezra 3:5; Neh 10:32; 1 Chron 23:31; 2 Chron 2:3, 8:13.

We have seen that the Israelites worshiped the Canaanite god El, not YHVH, but Moses the Egyptian incorporated many Egyptian ideas into their essentially Canaanite religion, and he syncretistically associated his god, YHVH, with El. Thus, the monotheism for which Judaism is so widely admired was, in its origins, a monotheism based on cultural *syncretism*, not one based on cultural *chauvinism*. In ancient Judaism, monotheism asserted that one divine power animated all gods everywhere; it did not assert that one national god was the true god, and the others were false. But to more fully appreciate the syncretistic relationship between YHVH and El, we must also appreciate the *complementary* syncretism that characterizes the relationship between YHVH and Ba'al/Shaddai.

The Kabbalah teaches that one who wishes to understand the Torah must read the *white space* surrounding the Torah's black letters. Rabbi Levi Isaac of Berdichev (1740–1809 C.E.), among others, explained this point:

> But the truth is that also the white, the spaces in the scroll of the Torah, consist of letters, only that we are not able to read them as we read the black letters. But in the Messianic Age God will also reveal to us the white of the Torah, whose letters have become invisible to us, and that is what is meant by the statement ["a Torah will go forth from me" (Isa 51:4)].[63]

So what do we learn when we read the "white spaces" of the Torah? The illustration at the top of the next page shows the Hebrew letters *beit* (B) and *pei* (P) written according to scribal rules. Study the white space inside the *pei*. Notice the small white *beit*.

Thus, every *pei* of the Torah can be read as a *beit*, and every *beit* can be read as a *pei*. Neither letter can exist without the

---

[63] *'Imre Zaddikim*, quoted in Scholem, *On the Kabbalah and Its Symbolism*, p. 82.

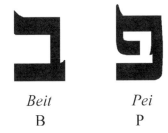

Beit   *Pei*

B   P

other, just as light cannot exist without darkness. To create a proper *pei*, one must create a *beit*, and vice versa.

In the book of Isaiah, YHVH declares: "I form light, and I create darkness; I make peace, and I create evil; I, YHVH, do all these things." (Isa 45:7.) That verse, like the negative identity between the letters *pei* and *beit*, points to a fundamental philosophical dilemma concerning the existential impossibility of light without shadow, good without evil, and, yes, God without... *anti-God*.

We have seen that YHVH permits Satan to afflict Job, and Job refers to this same afflicter by the name "Shaddai," the god of the Israelite patriarchs. We have also seen, from the Deir 'Alla inscription and Psalm 106, that Shaddai is a storm god that corresponds to the Canaanite storm god Ba'al. Shaddai's full name is sometimes abbreviated with the single Hebrew letter *shin* (SH). Take, for example, the scrolls that pious Jews attach to their doorposts. (See Deut 6:9.) On the outside of the rolled scroll, the letters *shin-dalet-yud* (spelling Shaddai) appear, but on the outside of *the box* that contains the scroll only the single letter *shin* appears (again, a reference to Shaddai). Pious Jews place similar scrolls on their foreheads while praying (Deut 6:8), and again the outside of the box has a letter *shin* embossed on the leather, signifying Shaddai. But on one side of this box, this letter *shin* is written with four "heads" instead of the usual three, as shown on the following page.

According to tradition, this four-headed *shin* depicts the way the *shin* was written on the tablets that Moses received at Sinai. Significantly, the same four-headed *shin*—again representing

Four-Headed Shin
SH

Shaddai—is also depicted in the positioning of a Jewish priest's fingers when giving the priestly blessing. About this finger positioning, YHVH tells Moses: "[The priests] will *place My name* upon the descendants of Israel, and I will bless them." (Num 6:27.) Thus, the four-headed *shin* is YHVH's *name*.

The real significance, however, of the priestly finger positioning is not the fingers themselves—which depict the four-headed *shin* of the name Shaddai—but *the blank space between the fingers*. Consider the following verse from the Song of Songs: "My Beloved. Behold, there He stands behind our wall, gazing in at the windows, *peering through the lattice*." (Song 2:9.) The ancient commentary states as follows:

> "*My Beloved…*"
> The Holy One, blessed be He…
> "*…Behold, there He stands behind our wall,…*"
> Behind the walls of the synagogues and schoolhouses…
> "*…gazing in at the windows,…*"
> From between the shoulders of the priests…
> "*…peering through the lattice.*"
> From between the fingers of the priests.[64]

This commentary directs our attention to *the blank space*

---

[64] Neusner, *A Theological Commentary to the Midrash: Volume Three*, p. 97.

between the fingers of the priests, saying that the blank space somehow depicts God (*i.e.*, "The Holy One, blessed be He"), just as the fingers themselves depict God (*i.e.*, the *shin* of the name Shaddai).

Rabbi Abraham Isaac Kook (1865–1935 C.E.) also discussed the significance of the four-headed *shin* in terms of the blank space surrounding the black letter. He wrote:

> Some commentaries connect this peculiar [four-headed] *shin* to the [traditional] description of the Torah's transmission to Israel via black fire engraved on white fire. What does this mean?... [¶] [This means that] the white parchment around the letters is an integral part of the Torah.... In fact, the white space is a higher form of Torah. It is analogous to the white fire of Sinai—a sublime, hidden Torah that cannot be read in the usual manner.[65]

Rabbi Kook is urging us not to read the letter itself, but to read the white space *surrounding* the letter.

Below is a depiction of the four-headed *shin*, shown as fire engraved on water:

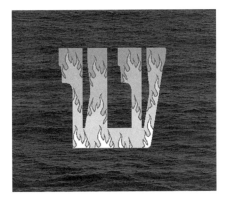

---

[65] Morrison, *Gold from the Land of Israel*, pp. 179–180 [quoting *Shemuot HaRe'iyah* IV].

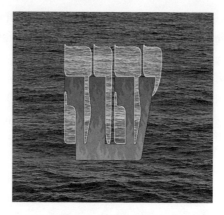

Now, focus on the water immediately surrounding the four heads of the *shin*, as shown above.

The water depicts the name YHVH.

In short, the four-headed *shin*—which signifies Shaddai, Job's afflicter—conjoins with the name YHVH to fill the two-dimensional space of the parchment on which these two names are inscribed.[66] YHVH is the negative of the letter *shin* (Shaddai), and the letter *shin* (Shaddai) is the negative of the name YHVH, a point that is hinted about in the book of Psalms: "Sitting in the hidden place of the Most High, he will lodge in the shadow of Shaddai." (Ps 91:1.)

The theological implication of this scribal trick is awesome: The part that must be removed from Infinite Presence in order to reveal a merciful God (YHVH)—that, too, is God (Shaddai). Each

---

[66] The fiery four-headed *shin* depicted in the main text was drawn to best illustrate its orthographic complementarity with the name YHVH, but the same complementarity remains valid when the letters are drawn in accordance with Jewish ritual law (Sephardic style).

member of any pair of opposites is implied in the very existence of the other member, and *duality is unreal*—two are always really one. A further example of this Jewish nondualism can be found in the Hebrew word for the "heavens" (*SHaMaYiM*), which is a contraction formed by combining the words for "fire" (*'AiSH*) and "waters" (*MaYiM*) into a single word:

The secret of the word *shamayim* ("heavens"), like the secret of the four-headed *shin*, is that perfection is realized in the alchemical unification of opposites.

A leading text of the Kabbalah, the *Bahir* (12th century C.E.), records the following mystical dialogue:

> "The letter *shin* is like the root of a Tree."
> "What is this Tree that you mentioned?"
> He said: "It represents the [two] Powers of the Blessed Holy One, one above the other."[67]

The "Tree" mentioned here is the *eitz ha-chayim*, the "Tree of Life." The "root" of this Tree is the four-headed *shin* (Shaddai), and the branches are YHVH. Together the Tree comprises "the

---

[67] *Bahir*, Nos. 118–119, translated in Kaplan, *The Bahir*, p. 45 [Kaplan's translation has been modified slightly].

[two] Powers of the Blessed Holy One, one above the other."
The *Bahir*, therefore, is describing the presence of YHVH in the
blank space of the letter *shin*, like tree branches supported by a
root. But consider also how one writes the word for "Tree" in
Hebrew:

tzadi   ayin
←←←←*direction of reading*←←←←

Now read the blank space surrounding the letters of the Hebrew
word for "Tree":

Once again, we encounter the name YHVH, this time hiding
between the branches (intentional pun) of the Hebrew letters
ayin and *tzadi*, which spell "Tree" in Hebrew.

The Song of Songs commentary teaches that YHVH is "peering through the lattice"—that is, YHVH is shining through the
blank space "between the fingers of the priests" that depict the
four-headed *shin* of God's name Shaddai. And likewise YHVH
is shining between the pointed branches of a tree, and likewise
between the crests of the mountains that rise on the distant hori-
zon, and likewise between the upraised arms of the temple's

קרוב יהוה לכל קראיו
לכל אשר יקראהו באמת

gold menorah—the menorah that shines spiritual "Light" to the world during the darkness of midwinter's moonless nights (*Chanukah*).

Ba'al Hadad, the storm god of the Canaanites, is Set, the fierce afflicter of Horus, and Ba'al is also Shaddai, the fierce afflicter of Job, but evil is implied in the very existence of good, and a fierce and punitive god (Ba'al/Set/Shaddai) is implied in the very existence of a merciful god (YHVH).

What then does it mean to believe that God is one? It means to praise God equally in suffering and in pleasure, knowing God to be the author of both. "This is the day that YHVH made; let us be glad and rejoice in it." (Ps 118:24.) God didn't just make a universe way back in the hoary past; God made *this moment right now*, whatever it may hold. If a person does not believe that God is the God of Holocausts and earthquakes, then that person does not believe in God's sovereignty in this world. Instead, that person believes there is a second force in this world that is in competition with God, a force that is the cause of suffering and that sometimes gets the upper hand. But the Torah teaches about YHVH that "he is the gods, [there is] nothing else besides him.... [I]n the heavens above and upon the earth below, [there is] nothing else." (Deut 4:35–39.) According to nondual thought, the present world, with all its ups and downs, is the world God

created, and to imagine a different world, one without evil, is to
imagine a different god that could create such a world, and thus
it is the essence of idolatry—*i.e.*, the worship of an imaginary
god of one's own making.

The Babylonian Talmud relates a story about the death of
Rabbi Akiva ben Joseph (1st and 2nd centuries C.E.) that is
directly on point. (*Berachot* 61b.) Rabbi Akiva was martyred in
a most cruel and painful way, but while he was dying, he was
repeating the *Shema* prayer ("YHVH is one") in a peaceful manner. His students asked him how he could pray calmly under
such unjust conditions. He said that usually he declared God's
unity with his heart, but in the face of an unjust death, he could
witness to the unity of God with the offering of his life. In other
words, even in the face of a cruel death, God is sovereign over
all that occurs; there is no second power, purveying evil in the
world, in competition with God.

The Ishbitzer Rebbe (Mordechai Joseph Leiner) reads the
description of Adam's sin in the Garden of Eden as a teaching
that evil must be integrated, not rejected, and then it is seen to
be good. Keep in mind that the Torah has no punctuation. The
Ishbitzer punctuates the famous Torah passage describing God's
instructions to Adam in this way: "From all the Trees of the
Garden [as a group] you may surely eat, and [also] from the
Tree of Knowledge of Good. And evil [by itself] do not eat."
(Gen 2:16–17.) In other words, all the "Trees," taken together as
an integrated whole, are nothing but good, and evil exists only
when it is isolated from its place of proper integration. Adam, in
fact, never sinned according to the Ishbitzer. He never ate "evil."
Rather, the evil was a phantasm of Adam's fragmented way of
perceiving the world.[68] What is *perceived* as evil, viewing the
world in tiny fractions of time and space, is really good when
viewed holistically. (See Job 38–39.) "And you, you intended
upon me evil," declares Jacob's son Joseph, but "God intended

---

[68] Edwards, *Living Waters*, p. 23.

it for good." (Gen 50:20.) Some people are not ready for such a radical faith that embraces the divine origin of what they perceive as evil, so they settle for dualism.

Shaddai, Job's fierce afflicter, is a variant of Baʻal, and we previously saw that Baʻal is acknowledged in the consecration of the Sabbath. The Sabbath, a day of joyous nonaction, is the appropriate way that these fierce forces within the nondual Godhead should be sanctified, for nonaction is the surrounding "blank space" of action, and the "blank space" surrounding the fierceness of Shaddai is the mercy of YHVH.

The book of Exodus says: "YHVH made the heavens and the earth in six days,… and he rested on the seventh day, therefore YHVH blessed the Sabbath day and sanctified it." (Exod 20:11.) But consider that the Hebrew verb used here for "rested" is not the verb meaning "to cease" but the verb meaning "to sit" or "to alight." Consider also that the reference to seven "days" of Creation in Genesis is an allegorical reference to seven divine powers (*sefirot*). Thus, the text is saying that YHVH sat in or *alighted* upon the "Sabbath day"—upon Baʻal/Shaddai, that is—and sanctified it. There is no merciful God without a fierce God, and there is no YHVH without the four-headed *shin* of Shaddai, but when the letters of YHVH alight down upon the four-headed *shin*, the *shin* is sanctified. (See color plate.)

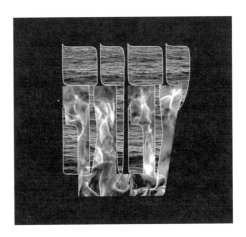

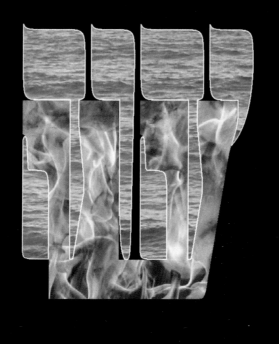

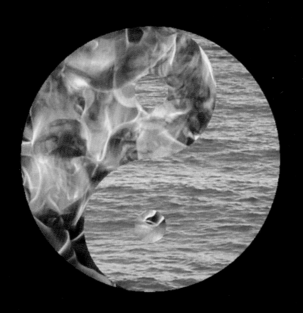

PART TWO

The Secret of the Name Yahweh
A Commentary on Exodus

"I made known to them thy name, and I will
make it known, that the love with which thou
hast loved me may be in them, and I in them."

—John 17:26 (Revised Standard Version)

1. The Fall of the Hyksos Pharaohs

Ancient Egypt was called the "Two Lands" based on the union of Upper Egypt (the upper Nile) and Lower Egypt (the Nile Delta). This union of two rival kingdoms was a critical component of ancient Egyptian myth and culture. In fact, one of the central motifs of ancient Egyptian thought, symbolized in numerous ways in the Pharaoh's royal insignia, was the motif of "opposites conjoining"—a motif that later dominates alchemical speculation (which has its roots in Egypt). But the governance of the Hyksos pharaohs (*i.e.*, the Israelite pharaohs) over the "Two Lands" did *not* comprise both lands; rather, it represented a period of *division* in ancient Egypt, and a return to a state of political rivalry between the North and the South. God made Joseph the "father to Pharaoh" (Gen 45:8), but only the father to the pharaohs *of Lower Egypt*.

According to the historical record, the authority of the Hyksos pharaohs extended up the Nile only as far as Hermopolis (modern-day El Ashmunein). A rival dynasty remained in power to the south of Hermopolis, in Thebes (modern-day Luxor), and this rival political force eventually invaded Lower Egypt, under the leadership of Pharaoh Kamose. A generation later, under Ahmose (Kamose's successor), Theban forces conquered Lower Egypt and reunited the two Egypts under Theban rule. As the Torah tells the story, "a new king arose over Egypt, who did not know Joseph." (Exod 1:8.)

The Hyksos ruling elite was the main target of this violent attack from the South. Ahmose's army took the Hyksos capital by siege, and it killed, captured, humiliated, and enslaved many of the Hyksos residents of the Nile Delta. The book of Exodus relates the story of this enslavement, and it tells of how one group of Hebrew-speaking slaves regained its freedom—or perhaps it was *two* groups…

But before we examine the surface story of the book of

Exodus, it is important to consider the subtext of that book. The first line of Exodus is "And these are the names" (*Ve'eilah shemot*), and in Hebrew, the book is called "Names" (*Shemot*). According to classical thought, the names of God are powerful incantations by which God can be invoked, and the book of Exodus reveals God's names and guards a venerable secret about the greatest of those names.

2. "A multitude of days
Israel will be without a true God"

"A multitude of days are to Israel without a true God...." (2 Chron 15:3.) Is that possible? For a long period of time, the Israelites will not know God? It seems hard to accept a literal interpretation of this prophetic verse, and in any case, the verse is surely not about present times; the rabbinic tradition asserts that its harsh implications are already a matter of bygone history.

In 1 Samuel, we read: "The lad Samuel was serving YHVH before Eli, and the word YHVH was scarce in those days.... Samuel had not yet known YHVH, and the word YHVH had not yet been revealed to him." (1 Sam 3:1–7.) In other words, Samuel was ministering to YHVH, but Samuel still did not know the secret of that obscure name.

Hebrew scripture contains thousands of names of God, all of which are said to have great spiritual power, but of all the divine names that appear in Hebrew scripture, YHVH is held to be the most sacred. It is written in Hebrew with the letters *yud, hei, vov,* and *hei* (יהוה), but it is considered to be too holy to pronounce as written, and therefore it is pronounced using the substitute Hebrew word *Adonai*, meaning "My Lord." In English translations of Hebrew scripture, the name YHVH is usually rendered as "THE LORD," and sometimes as "Jehovah" or "Yahweh." The name has no obvious meaning, although some commentators have pointed out that it is a combination of the Hebrew words for "he was" (*HaYaH*), "he is" (*HoVeH*), and "he will be" (*YiHYeH*), implying timelessness.

Of course, YHVH is not the true form of this secret name of God, for if it were, then anyone with even a beginner's knowledge of Hebrew would know this name, and it would quickly be cheapened by casual repetition. Rather, the letters Y-H-V-H (*yud-hei-vov-hei*) represent an *encoded form of the name*. The book of Exodus makes this point expressly:

> Moses said to [YHVH], "Behold, when I come to the descendants of Israel and say to them, 'The god of your forefathers has sent me to you,' and they say to me, 'What is his name?'— what shall I say to them?"
>
> And YHVH answered Moses, "*AHYeH ASHeR AHYeH*" [("I will be what I will be")]. And he said, "This shall you say to the descendants of Israel, 'AHYeH has sent me to you.'" God said further to Moses, "This shall you say to the descendants of Israel, 'YHVH, god of your forefathers, god of Abraham, god of Isaac, god of Jacob has sent me to you.' This is my name *to conceal. . . .*"[69]

The last sentence is usually translated "This is my name *forever.*" Recall, however, that the written Torah has very few vowels and that the conventional pronunciation of the letters was sometimes designed to hide the secrets of the text. To render YHVH's instruction to Moses as "This is my name to conceal," one merely vowelizes the Hebrew letters as *L'AaLaM* ("to conceal") instead of *L'AoLaM* ("forever").

Thus, the Torah is saying that the name YHVH is written in a concealed form. In other words, its letters represent a riddle. It is as if God had told Moses: "Do not tell them my name YHVH

---

[69] Exod 3:13–15.

in its revealed form for then they might profane it; instead, tell it to them in an obscured form, as YHVH, for this is my name to conceal."

According to tradition, Moses taught that God's name (*i.e.*, YHVH) would remain *incomplete* until the end of times.[70] But Abraham Abulafia, a leading 13th century Jewish mystic, urged his followers to learn the secret of the name. He claimed that the true name had tremendous power. At the end of times, Abulafia asserted, all nations would know the secret of God's name, and because of that secret, many people would come to worship the god of the Jews.[71] Scripture, too, ascribes awesome power to the secret pronunciation of the name YHVH, which it refers to as the "vocalization of YHVH" (*kol* YHVH),[72] a phrase that appears seven times in the passage below:

The <u>vocalization of YHVH</u> is upon the waters.
The glory of El thunders;
YHVH upon the great waters.
The <u>vocalization of YHVH</u> is in power.
The <u>vocalization of YHVH</u> is in majesty.
The <u>vocalization of YHVH</u> shatters the cedars.
YHVH shattered the cedars of Lebanon.
And he danced them like a calf,
Lebanon and Siryon like the son of horned beasts.
The <u>vocalization of YHVH</u> splits flames of fire.
The <u>vocalization of YHVH</u> shakes the wilderness.
YHVH shakes the wilderness of Kadeish.

[70] See, e.g., Weissman (ed.), *The Midrash Says: Sh'mos*, p. 162.

[71] See Idel, *Studies in Ecstatic Kabbalah*, pp. 47, 50.

[72] The Hebrew word *kol* means "sound" or "voice," but in the context of referring to the "sound" of an obscurely spelled name, it can be translated as "pronunciation" or "vocalization."

> The <u>vocalization of</u> YHVH brings forth the does and strips
> the forests.
> And in his temple all say, "Glory."[73]

Other psalms hint that the true form of the name YHVH is a closely
guarded secret. For example, we read: "Those who know your
name will trust in you...." (Ps 9:11; see also Ps 89:16.) And in a
different psalm, we read: "I will exalt him for he will know my
name; he will call me, and I will answer him...." (Ps 91:14–15.)
Finally, in the book of Isaiah, we find this prophetic assertion:
"Therefore, my people will know my name—therefore, *on that
day*...." (Isa 52:6.)

For you, the reader, "that day" is today.

3. The Secret Letters

The *Zohar* (13th century C.E.), one of the most respected texts of
the Jewish mystical tradition, informs us that the name YHVH—
that is, the name signified by the Hebrew letters *yud, hei, vov,*
and *hei*—includes a letter *dalet*. The *dalet* is the fourth letter
of the Hebrew alphabet, roughly equivalent to the English letter *d*. The name of the letter *DaLeT* means "door" (*DeLeT*)
and also "poor" (*DaLaH*), "poverty" (*DaLuT*), and "locks of hair"
(*DaLaT*), depending on how one chooses to vowelize the consonants. The *Zohar* speaks of the ultimate perfection of God's
name, when "ד (*dalet*) joins ה (*hei*); *hei* joins ו (*vov*); *vov* ascends
to be crowned with *hei*; *hei* is illumined by י (*yud*)...."[74] This
sequence moves in reverse order through the four letters of the
name YHVH, but the sequence inexplicably begins with a *dalet*.

---

[73] Ps 29:3–9.

[74] *Zohar* 2:219b, translated in Matt, *The Zohar: Pritzker Edition*, vol. VI,
p. 252; see also 1:51a, 1:60a–60b, vol. I, pp. 284–285, 345–346.

The idea that God's ineffable name (YHVH) includes a *dalet* fits well with the *Zohar*'s general symbolic scheme, but to understand that point, we must return to the ten *sefirot* of the Kabbalah. The *sefirot* are first identified as divine attributes in the *Bahir*, an important 12th century Jewish text, but the *Zohar* powerfully demonstrates that these ten aspects of God appear in symbolic form throughout Hebrew scripture. In Part One, we demonstrated the remarkable correspondence between the ten *sefirot* and the ten gods of the Heliopolitan pantheon, and we also described how Isaac Luria, drawing on ideas from the *Zohar*, presented the *sefirot* as components of a remarkable creation myth that parallels the Heliopolitan creation myth.

Briefly, Luria said that God opened a space within infinite divinity where Creation could occur, and then God became manifest within that space as the ten *sefirot*:

Keter ("Crown")

|

Binah ("Understanding")—*Chokhmah* ("Wisdom")

|

Gevurah ("Strength")—*Chesed* ("Kindness")

|

Tiferet ("Beauty")

|

Hod ("Splendor")—*Netzach* ("Victory")

|

Yesod ("Foundation")

|

Malkhut ("Kingship")

As noted in Part One, the entire set of ten *sefirot* is a single undifferentiated unity called "*Adam Kadmon*" ("Primordial Adam"), but within that decad there are various relationships and groupings. For example, the middle six divine powers (*Chesed,*

Gevurah, *Tiferet*, *Netzach*, *Hod*, *Yesod*) are often grouped as a single corpus, and the word *Tiferet* is sometimes used to signify the entire six-member subgroup of which it is a part. This subgroup is critically important in Kabbalah, and it has several other designations, including "Holy One, blessed be He," "Son," "Brother," and "*Zeir Anpin*" ("Small Face").

God's four-letter name (YHVH) is mapped onto the ten *sefirot* according to the following scheme: The tiny pen stroke that is the upper tip of the *yud* of God's name is *Keter* ("Crown"). The main body of the *yud* represents *Chokhmah* ("Wisdom"), and the first *hei* represents *Binah* ("Understanding"). The *vov*, which is the sixth letter of the Hebrew alphabet, and which therefore can be used to designate the number six, represents the six-member subgroup known as "*Zeir Anpin*" (the hexad from *Chesed* through *Yesod*). And, the last letter of God's name, the second *hei*, represents *Malkhut* ("Kingship").

As we have seen in Part One, the last of the *sefirot*—*Malkhut* ("Kingship")—signifies God's presence or immanence in the world, and also God's governance of the world. But according to the *Zohar*, the world was damaged as a result of Adam's sin, and therefore this divine presence or immanence (also called "*Shekhinah*") is in a state of exile. In other words, the world is in a broken condition, and we, as actors within historical time, have a role to play in repairing the world by revealing God's presence and sovereignty.

If we describe this fallen state of affairs metaphorically, we might say that the divine presence (*Shekhinah*) is "poor" (*DaLaH*) or that she is in a state of "poverty" (*DaLuT*). Here, then, we have the sense of the *Zohar*'s statement that when all is repaired and the world attains its perfection, the letter *dalet* will be joined to the *hei*, the *hei* to the *vov*, the *vov* to the *hei*, and the *hei* to the *yud*. The letter *dalet* represents the divine presence (*Shekhinah*) while in exile. When the world attains its perfection, the *DaLeT* (the *Shekhinah*) will no longer be in a state of "poverty" (*DaLuT*); she will be joined to the final *hei* of God's

Orthodox Jewish scribe [Shlomo Washadi].
Jerusalem, ca. 1935 C.E.

name YHVH, at which point she will fully manifest her aspect as
"Kingship" or "Sovereignty" (*Malkhut*).

But how can a letter *dalet* be joined to the final *hei* of the name
YHVH? To appreciate how that might be done, one must think as
a scribe, embracing the esoteric ideas of Jewish scribal hermeneutics. The *Sefer Yetzirah* is an ancient book whose authorship
is piously attributed to Abraham, the Israelite patriarch. It is full
of mystical ideas concerning the letters of the Hebrew alphabet,
and in reference to those letters, it says that Abraham "looked,
saw, probed, understood, engraved, carved, permuted, formed,
and thought, and he was successful." And what was his success?

> The Lord of all, may His name be blessed for eternity, revealed
> Himself to him, kissed him on the head, and called him,
> "Abraham My friend" (Isa 41:8). . . . He bound the twenty-two

letters on his tongue, and the Blessed Holy One revealed to him their mystery.[75]

Clearly, then, there is some great secret to be discovered in the Hebrew letters, a secret that is revealed by writing them, rearranging them, and shaping them. So let us look at some of the shapes of the Hebrew letters.

The tenth letter of the Hebrew alphabet, a *yud*, resembles a drop, very much like a seed containing the universe in potential form. The fourth letter of the Hebrew alphabet, a *dalet*, is shaped like the lintel and right post of a "door" (Hebrew: *DeLeT*)— that is, it consists of a horizontal crossbar with a vertical line descending from the right side. A *hei*, the fifth letter of the Hebrew alphabet, is formed by placing an inverted *yud* inside a *dalet*, on the lower left side.

To illustrate the latter point, a *dalet* and *yud* appear below:

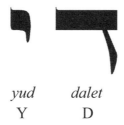

yud   *dalet*
 Y   D

The letter *hei* begins with the crossbar and right leg of the *dalet*, but then a second leg is added on the left side, in the form of an inverted *yud*. Thus, a *hei* is constructed from a *dalet* and a *yud* combined into a single letter, as shown on the top of the next page.

The *Zohar* speaks of a future time when the *dalet* (the *Shekhinah*) will be joined to the final *hei* of the name YHVH, and one

---

[75] Kaplan (trans. and ed.), *Sefer Yetzirah*, p. 281; see also *id.* at pp. 255, 267, 293.

Left leg.

hei

H

can readily see from the shapes of these letters that, when a *dalet* is "joined" to a *hei*, it can be visually *subsumed* within the *hei* (superimposed over the crossbar and right leg of the *hei*), in which case the remaining portion of the *hei* forms an inverted *yud*. In other words, the final *hei* of the name YHVH is not merely a *hei*; it conceals within itself a *dalet-yud*.

The *Zohar* highlights this scribal secret, using a sexual metaphor to describe the union of the *yud* and *dalet* to form the *hei*:

> [I]t is written: *"If there is* נערה *(na'arah), a girl, a virgin"* (Deut 22:23), spelled נער *(na'ara)*, without a ה *(hei)*. Why? Because She [(*i.e.*, the *Shekhinah*, who is the *dalet*)] has not joined a male [(*i.e.*, the seed-like *yud*)], and wherever male and female are not found, ה *(hei)* is not found but rather ascends, leaving ד *(dalet)*.[76]

Here, one should put aside any objections one might have to a gender construction that values "married and pregnant" as the feminine ideal and that associates female infertility with poverty (*DaLuT*). At an archetypal level, there is redemptive significance in the stable union of complementary opposites, and this union is effectively conveyed by the sexual metaphor of impregnation. Standing alone, the letter *DaLeT* (the *Shekhinah*)

---

[76] *Zohar* 1:51a, translated in Matt, *The Zohar: Pritzker Edition*, vol. I, p. 285; see also 1:60a, pp. 345–346 [expressing the same idea].

is barren, like Rachel (Gen 30:1), and therefore she is in a state of poverty (*DaLuT*), but when she receives the seed (the letter *yud*) from a male, she becomes pregnant, like Leah (Gen 30:22), and her poverty (*DaLuT*) vanishes; for with a letter *yud* inserted into her womb, she becomes a letter *hei*, and she is no longer a letter *dalet*.

In summary, the fourth letter of God's name YHVH is actually a *dalet* that has attained the status of a *hei* through impregnation, thereby becoming a duplicate of the second letter of the name. Recall, however, that the letters of the name correspond to the *sefirot*, with the second letter corresponding to *Binah* and the fourth letter corresponding to *Malkhut*. In the *Zohar*'s scheme, therefore, *Malkhut* (the "Daughter") attains the status of *Binah* (the "Mother") through impregnation. But by whom does she become pregnant?

The Kabbalah places great importance on the unification of *Zeir Anpin* and *Malkhut*, and many of the ritual and moral practices of Judaism are interpreted as promoting that unification. *Zeir Anpin*, we will recall, is the hexad of *sefirot* from *Chesed* through *Yesod*, a subgroup that operates as a single corpus and that is sometimes referred to as the "Son." It corresponds to the third letter of the name YHVH, which is a *vov*. Within this subgroup, each of the six *sefirot* is said to be a limb of *Zeir Anpin*'s subtle body, and *Yesod* is said to be his phallus. Thus, it is *Zeir Anpin* (the hexad from *Chesed* through *Yesod*) that impregnates *Malkhut*, and this union occurs through the mediation of *Yesod* (the phallus). The *dalet* (the "poor one") holds *Zeir Anpin*'s seed (a *yud*) in her womb and thus becomes a *hei*. *Malkhut* (the "Daughter") thus attains the status of *Binah* (the "Mother"), and the "lower world" then corresponds to the "upper world."

In terms of the letters of the name YHVH, the "unification of *Zeir Anpin* and *Malkhut*" corresponds to the unification of the *vov* (the third letter of the name) and the final *hei* (the fourth letter of the name), and the "mediation of *Yesod*" corresponds to the inverted *yud* that is an internal component of the final *hei*. That inverted *yud* is actually said to be the lower tip of the phallic-shaped *vov*, penetrating into the womb of the *dalet*, impregnating her. Thus, the last two letters of the name YHVH are metaphorically presented as a sexual coupling between a *vov* and a *dalet*, causing them to appear as a *vov* and a *hei*. (For more detail, see Appendix One.)

We now, finally, have the background information by which to decode the *Zohar*'s cryptic assertion about the ultimate perfection of God's name, when "ד (*dalet*) joins ה (*hei*); *hei* joins ו (*vov*);" etc. What appears to be the final *hei* of a name with four letters is really the final *dalet* and *yud* of a name with *five* letters.

4. Decoding the Name

(a) The Royal Name

The scribes of ancient times were experts in the use of symbols to convey meaning. In the course of their philosophical musings, they realized that *every* purposeful action produces some sort of "mark" or "sign" that conveys in some sense the intention of the actor. A mound of stones, for example, or a single elongated stone placed upright, was not, for them, just a physical monument; it was an artifact communicating some purpose. And for these scribes, even a thing of nature—a tree or a mountain—was a sign conveying an intention, for God was the master scribe, communicating God's own thoughts through the "script" of natural phenomena.

Thus, the ancient scribes learned to "read" the objective world, seeing not objects, but the intentions (the thoughts) lying behind those objects. By doing so, they turned their mundane recordkeeping profession into a spiritual practice—an *imitatio dei*. They labored to pack a superabundance of meanings into the symbols they marked on papyrus or sheepskin, or that they engraved into metal or stone, and they trusted in the power of their symbols to communicate all those meanings to the discerning reader. Thus, one must not read scripture as one might read a mere shopping list, seeking only its superficial meaning; rather, one must search for the hidden subtext of scripture, finding clues in every odd jot and tittle. We have seen a marvelous example of this approach to scriptural interpretation in the *Zohar*'s detailed explication of God's name YHVH. But what happens if we take this hermeneutical method a little further?

As mentioned, the name YHVH is usually pronounced "Adonai" ("Lord") when it is spoken out loud as part of the liturgy. The Kabbalists teach that the name *Adonai* (*alef-dalet-nun-yud*) represents "this world," whereas the name YHVH (*yud-hei-vov-hei*) represents the "world to come." Moreover, they teach that one should join this world to the world to come by thinking YHVH in one's interior thoughts while saying *Adonai* out loud. They similarly teach that one should join the two worlds by *combining the letters of these two names.*

So, recalling the *Zohar*'s assertion that the name YHVH includes a *dalet*, let us insert the *dalet* from the name *Adonai* (*alef-dalet-nun-yud*) into the name YHVH (*yud-hei-vov-hei*):

When we do, the names whisper a powerful secret: "ANiY YeH-VDaH," which means, "I am *Yehudah*."[77]

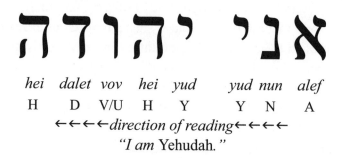

hei	dalet	vov	hei	yud	yud	nun	alef
H	D	V/U	H	Y	Y	N	A

←←←←direction of reading←←←←
"*I am* Yehudah."

In short, the name *Yehudah* is one of the secret pronunciations of the name YHVH.

In English, the name *Yehudah* is "Judah." Judah was the patriarch Jacob's fourth son, the son whom Jacob chose to be king: "A lion cub is Judah.... He bends, he lies down like a lion, and like a lion, who rouses him? The scepter [of kingship] shall not depart from Judah... until the arrival of Shiloh, and the congress of nations is his." (Gen 49:9–10.) Let us consider the explanation the Torah gives for Judah's name: "And [Leah] conceived again and bore a son and declared, 'This time let me acknowledge YHVH'; therefore, she called his name 'YeHVDaH' [(*i.e.*, *Yehudah*)]." (Gen 29:35.) Thus, Judah is expressly named for YHVH, and his name is constructed using the letters of YHVH's name but adding a *dalet* (D) before the second *hei* (H).

In Part One, we saw that the ancient Egyptians, the Canaan-ites, and the Babylonians all believed that the living king of each generation—the righteous leader who maintained civil order, showed compassion toward the weak, and upheld justice in society—was the representative of the gods on earth. We also saw traces of this concept in Judaism, particularly in the *sefirot*.

---

[77] Note that the Hebrew letter *vov* can be pronounced either like an English letter *v* or like an English letter *u*.

In present-day Judaism, this most immanent aspect of God is often called the "*Shekhinah*" (the "Presence"), a feminine term that is not usually associated with political leadership. We have seen, however, that in medieval Kabbalah, this immanent aspect was called "*Malkhut*" ("Kingship"), and according to the Torah, the patriarch Jacob expressly conferred this office of kingship on his fourth son Judah (*Yehudah*), whose name is YHVH's own name. In short, *Yehudah* is the pronunciation of the name YHVH that is associated with YHVH's immanence in the world as divine sovereign.

Not surprisingly, then, we find numerous Hebrew prayers that refer to YHVH as the "king." One notable example appears in the book of Psalms, in which we read: "God is my king from old, doing salvations in the midst of the land." (Ps 74:12; see also Jer 23:5–6; Zech 14:16–17.) And by extension, this same immanent aspect of God (*Malkhut* among the *sefirot*) is associated not just with Judah, but with the entire line of kings that descended from Judah, including King David.

A further clue, confirming that *Yehudah* is a pronunciation of the name YHVH, appears in the *Shema* prayer. The first part of the prayer is spoken out loud: "*Shema, Yisrael;* YHVH *Eloheinu;* YHVH *achod*" ("Hear, O Israel; YHVH is our God; YHVH is one and only"). (Deut 6:4.) That part of the prayer affirms that despite having diverse aspects and names, YHVH is "one" (Hebrew: *ACHoD*). The mystics urge those who recite the prayer to emphasize the *dalet* at the end of the word *ACHoD*, because the *dalet* represents the *Shekhinah*, which is in a state of "poverty" (*DaLuT*). But according to the Rabbeinu Behaye ben Asher (early 14th century C.E.), when the *Shekhinah* hears the out-loud portion of the *Shema* prayer, she feels a prick of envy. She may be earthbound, representing God's immanence in the world, but she too is perfectly united with the one indivisible divine will; she is not a separate god. Therefore, the second half of the *Shema* prayer is whispered in her honor: "*Barukh sheim kevod malkhuto le'olam va'ed*" ("Blessed is the glorious name of his kingdom forever and ever").[78] And what, at the time that this prayer was written, was the name of YHVH's earthly kingdom? That name was *Yehudah*, the Hebrew name for the Kingdom of Judah. Significantly, the same *Barukh sheim* doxology was recited when, in Temple times, the chief priest pronounced the name YHVH on Yom Kippur. (*BT Yoma* 35b, 39a, 66a.) The priest said, "*Yehudah*," and the people said, "Blessed is the glorious name of his kingdom forever and ever."

In this context, it is significant that Moses repeatedly tells the Israelites to offer sacrifices "only at the place that YHVH... will choose from among all your tribes *to place His name*." (Deut 12:5.)[79] That statement implies a location that bears the name YHVH as its own name. Significantly, from the time of King David until the destruction of the Second Temple, YHVH's cult was located in the "City of *Yehudah*" (*i.e.*, Jerusalem—see 2 Chron 25:28), again implying that *Yehudah* is a pronunciation of YHVH's name. Likewise, we read in the book of Daniel:

> My Lord, hear! My Lord, forgive! My Lord, be attentive and act! Do not delay. For your sake, my God, *because your name is called upon your city....*"[80]

In Babylon, where Daniel lived, Jerusalem was called the "City of *Yehudah*."[81] Thus, when the book of Daniel exhorts God, saying, "your name is called upon your city," it is clearly asserting that *Yehudah* is one of God's names.

---

[78] See *Commentary on the Torah*, quoted in Mopsik, "Union and Unity in the Kabbalah," pp. 232–233. On this explication of the two parts of the *Shema* prayer, see also *Zohar* 2:133b–134a, translated in Matt, *The Zohar: Pritzker Edition*, vol. V, pp. 237–245.

[79] See also Deut 12:11, 12:21, 14:23–24, 16:2, 16:6, 16:11, 26:2.

[80] Dan 9:19.

[81] See British Museum Tablet 21946, translated in Wiseman, *Chronicles of Chaldean Kings*, p. 73.

In the ancient Near East, it was not unprecedented for a place name also to be the name of the local god. Assyria, for example, was called "*Ashur*," and the Assyrians worshiped the god named Ashur. Interestingly, Hebrew scripture readily uses the name Ashur when it appears as a *national* name, but scripture obscures the name Ashur when it appears as a *divine* name. Thus, the name of the Assyrian king Esar-haddon (Akkadian: *Ashur-ahu-iddin*, "Ashur has given a brother") is obscured in the Bible as "*Eisar-Chadon*" (2 Kings 19:37). In like manner, Hebrew scripture readily uses the name *Yehudah* when it appears as a *national* name, but scripture obscures the name *Yehudah* when it appears as a *divine* name, abbreviating it as YHVH.

One final bit of evidence confirms that *Yehudah* is a pronunciation of the name YHVH. The prophet Amos (8th century B.C.E.), speaking in the name of YHVH, complains that "a man and his father go to a young woman in order to profane my holy name." (Amos 2:7.) The verse refers to a father and son sharing the same sexual partner, but why specifically does doing so profane YHVH's name? Because in Torah times, it was Judah (*Yehudah*) who did the act that the book of Amos describes (see Gen 38), and therefore it was the name *Yehudah* that was profaned by that act.

(b) The Great Name

The *Zohar* taught us that the name YHVH contains a hidden *dalet*, and by inserting a *dalet* into that name, we derived the name *Yehudah*, which is confirmed by several clues to be a pronunciation of the name YHVH (see, e.g., Gen 29:35). But were there perhaps other ways of pronouncing the same divine name?

The pronounced form of the name YHVH is sometimes called "*ha-shem ha-meforash*," which is usually translated as "the distinctive name" or "the explicit name," but the Hebrew word *meforash* derives from the root for "spread out." With that in mind, what if we simply "spread out" the letters of the name

YHVH by reading the final *hei* as the *dalet-yud* that it secretly comprises? Then the name spells YeHVDY (*Yehudi*), which is the Hebrew word for "a person from the land of Judah," or, in modern usage, a "Jew." Indeed, the name *Yehudi* all but leaps off the page once one consciously notices the *dalet* and *yud* that are subsumed within the final *hei* of YHVH. It was only a trick of the eye that saw a *hei* in place of a *dalet-yud*, as shown opposite.

If *Yehudi*, which means "Judean" or "Jew," is one of the secret pronunciations of the divine name YHVH—and it is, as we shall see—then the Jewish people wear God's name as their own name, which, for a pious Jew, must be a terrifying thought but also a source of great hope and comfort. Repeatedly, the prophets ask YHVH to save the Jewish people, not because the Jewish people have unerringly merited salvation by their actions, but for the sake of his name. In other words, YHVH should redeem the Jews because, if an individual Jew (*Yehudi*) is immersed in sin, then YHVH's own name (*Yehudi*) is immersed in sin, and if an individual Jew (*Yehudi*) is scorned for public immorality, then YHVH's own name (*Yehudi*) is scorned.

And, of course, the opposite is also true. If a Jew (*Yehudi*) is widely praised for his righteous behavior, particularly righteous behavior on behalf of all of humanity and witnessed by non-Jews, then YHVH's own name (*Yehudi*) is honored and respected throughout the world; and if a Jew is publicly martyred because he is a Jew (*Yehudi*), then YHVH's own name (*Yehudi*) is sanctified. For that reason, the idiomatic Hebrew expression used for virtuous public conduct by a Jew is "*kiddush ha-shem*" ("sanctification of the name"), and the corresponding expression used for public wrongdoing by a Jew is "*chilul ha-shem*" ("profanation of the name"). In short, what a Jew (*Yehudi*) does is done in YHVH's name, which can only mean that *Yehudi* is YHVH's name.

Consider, in this context, the third commandment received at Sinai: "You shall not take the name of YHVH, your God, in vain." (Exod 20:7; Deut 5:11.) The commandment is usually explicated as a prohibition against vain oaths. Translated literally, however,

hei   vov   hei   yud

H   V   H   Y

←←←←*direction of reading*←←←←

The Name YHVH

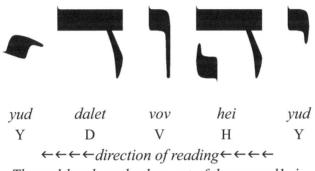

yud   dalet   vov   hei   yud

Y   D   V   H   Y

←←←←*direction of reading*←←←←

The yud *has been broken out of the second* hei, *making the* hei *into a* dalet.

yud   dalet   vov   hei   yud

Y   D   V   H   Y

←←←←←*direction of reading*←←←←←

The yud *has been repositioned at the top, to produce the name* Yehudi.

the Hebrew reads: "You shall not *bear* the name of YHVH, your God, in vain." In other words, you who bear YHVH's name as your own name should not do so in vain; rather, you have a special obligation to give glory to the name through your conduct. A 15th century kabbalist even urged Jews facing martyrdom to shout, "I am a Jew!... Jew! Jew! Jew! Jew!"—repeating, mantra-like, the word *Yehudi* ("Jew") at the moment of their death.[82] Why? Because, by doing so, they would be repeating the name of God.

For believers, the identity between YHVH's name and the name of the Jewish people (*Yehudi*) has awesome implications, explaining much about the tragedies of Jewish history. In 1981 C.E., Rabbi Yekutiel Yehudah Halberstam (the Klausenberg Rebbe) predicted that a righteous Jew (*Yehudi*) would be publicly martyred in India, and because of that martyrdom, the entire Indian subcontinent would come to know the name YHVH (*i.e.*, *Yehudi*). This prophecy came true in 2008, when Gavriel Noach Holtzberg and his wife Rivka were killed in a terrorist attack in Mumbai. Here is a translation of the Klausenberg Rebbe's 1981 prophecy:

> When you have one Jew [(*Yehudi*)] living among thousands of others, even a hundred thousand, all of them will find out that there is one God. [¶]... This way, a Jew is *mekadesh sheim shamayim berabim*, [("The one who sanctifies the name of heaven in public")].... [¶] There could be one Jew [(*Yehudi*)] living in all of India. He may be the only one there, but hundreds of people know about him. They talk about him, they discuss his situation. Is he alive? Was he killed? [¶]...Millions of people who never knew that Jews existed are now talking about Jews.... [¶]... Where there are no Jews, they wouldn't know who YHVH is.[83]

---

[82] Fishbane, *Kiss of God*, p. 55.

[83] A transcription (in Hebrew) of the Klausenberg Rebbe's talk is posted at http://www.gruntig.net/2008/12/audio-of-klausenberger-rebbe-1981-one.

In other words, Jewish martyrdom makes the name *Yehudi* known and sanctified throughout the world, which is valuable, from the Klausenberg Rebbe's perspective, because *Yehudi* is YHVH's own name and widespread knowledge and respect for that name will have a sanctifying effect on the world.

As noted, the prophets frequently plead with YHVH to have mercy on the Jews (*Yehudim*) for the sake of His name (*Yehudi*), and they assure Jews (*Yehudim*) that YHVH will not forsake His name (*Yehudi*). Consider the prophet Samuel's statement:

> Fear not. You have done all this evil—but do not turn away from following after YHVH; rather, serve YHVH with all your heart.... For YHVH will not forsake his people [(the *Yehudim*)] on account of His great name [(*i.e.*, *Yehudi*)]....[84]

Similarly, the psalms repeatedly plead with God to "save" the supplicant "for the sake of your name," or words to like effect,[85] and both Isaiah[86] and Jeremiah[87] employ this same formula. Consider also the following unambiguous statement found in the book of Isaiah:

> And now, thus says YHVH, your Creator, O Jacob, your Former, O Israel.... Fear not, for I am with you; from the east, I will bring your seed, and from the west, I will gather you. I

---

html [accessed Nov. 7, 2015]. The translation is based on a translation posted on the Internet at http://alleywaystotorah.blogspot.com/2008/12/end-is-close.html [accessed Nov. 7, 2015]. On the connection between martyrdom and the purpose of a Jew, see Lev 10:3, 22:32; see also Fishbane, *Kiss of God.*

[84] 1 Sam 12:20–22. On the name *Yehudi* being called God's "great name," see Josh 7:9; 1 Kings 8:42.

[85] See Pss 23:3, 25:11, 31:3–4, 79:9, 106:8, 109:21, 115:1, 143:11.

[86] See Isa 48:9.

[87] See Jer 14:7, 14:21.

will say to the north, "Give over," and to the south, "Do not withhold; bring my sons from afar and my daughters from the ends of the earth, [bring] *everyone who is called by my name*...."[88]

It is hard to imagine a more straightforward confirmation that the name by which the Jews are called (*Yehudi*) is YHVH's *own name*. And this confirmation is echoed in the books of Jeremiah,[89] Ezekiel,[90] Amos,[91] Daniel,[92] and Chronicles,[93] and in the Torah itself, we read: "[If you, the Jewish people, are righteous,] all the peoples of the earth will see that *the name* YHVH *is proclaimed over you*, and they will revere you." (Deut 28:10; see also Num 6:27.)

Joseph Gikatilla, a leading 13th century Kabbalist, explicitly confirmed the foregoing interpretation of scripture. He wrote: "God chose Abraham and then [God] chose [the Israelites] afterward, who are the seed of Abraham. *He then gave them His great name*...."[94] He gave them, in other words, the name *Yehudi* ("Jew"), and according to the Hebrew Bible, it is a dangerous thing to bear God's name as one's own, for God is jealous for his name (Ezek 39:25). When Jews, by their conduct, bring honor to the name *Yehudi* ("Jew"), then God blesses them, but when they fail to do so: "I [YHVH] resolved to pour my wrath upon them, to spend my anger on them,... and I acted for the sake of

---

[88] Isa 43:1–7.

[89] See Jer 14:9 ["and your name is called upon us"].

[90] See Ezek 36:21–22 ["I took pity on my holy name that the House of Israel had profaned among the nations where they came."].

[91] See Amos 9:12 [specifically asserting that the people of Judah (*Yehudah*) are those who "are called [with] my name upon them"].

[92] See Dan 9:19 ["your name is called upon... your people"].

[93] See 2 Chron 7:14 ["my people upon whom my name is called"].

[94] Weinstein (trans.), *Gates of Light*, pp. 257–258, italics added.

my name, that it be not a profanity in the eyes of the nations...."
(Ezek 20:8–9.)[95]

5. "Lest he send forth his hand and take also from the Tree of Life"

The anonymous author of *Sefer ha-Temunah* (13th or 14th century C.E.) said that in each eon of world history the Torah is read in a different way and that in the present eon *one letter of the Hebrew language is hidden*. Moreover, he added, when that one letter is revealed, the Torah will have a whole new meaning. Could he have been referring to the hidden *yud* at the end of the name YHVH—the inverted *yud* that, when elevated, transforms the name from YHVH to *Yehudi*?[96]

Numerous hints appear in Hebrew scripture about that hidden *yud*. Most of these hints are based on the fact that the Hebrew word *YaD* ("hand") is spelled without vowels, and therefore its letters can just as validly be read as *YuD*, a reference to the Hebrew letter *yud*. At first, this hermeneutical principle may seem more like homiletic invention than a legitimate method of scriptural interpretation, but the Torah itself explicitly endorses this way of decoding its text.

The Torah relates that Jacob (*Ya'aqov*, in Hebrew) was born with his "hand" (*YaD*) clasping the "heel" (*'AQeiV*) of his twin brother, and it states that therefore he was called "*Ya'AQoV.*" (Gen 25:26.) Note that in the Hebrew words written in the preceding sentence, the vowels that are shown in lowercase do not appear in the Torah's text, and therefore other vowels can be substituted. Because the physical *YaD* ("hand") of Jacob was grasping the physical *'AQeiV* ("heel") of his brother, a letter *YuD*

---

[95] See also Ezek 20:14, 20:22, 20:44. The end of the passage is more hopeful, describing how YHVH saves the Jews for the sake of his name.

[96] Cf. Scholem, *On the Kabbalah and Its Symbolism*, pp. 80–81.

(Y) became attached to the letters of the word *'AQeiV* to produce the name *Ya'AQoV*.

$$YaD + 'AQeiV =$$
$$YuD + 'AQeiV =$$
$$Y + 'AQeiV =$$
$$Ya'AQoV$$

Thus, the Torah tells us in relatively plain terms that any reference to a *YaD* ("hand") can be read as a reference to a letter *YuD*.

This bit of scribal wordplay also reveals something about the metaphysics of Jewish ritual: The significance of what one enacts ritually may have nothing to do with its external appearance in the physical world, and it may have everything to do with building meaningful letter-combinations in the spiritual world. Thus, ritual is a form of "enacted writing" in which divine powers are invoked without their names ever being uttered by a tongue or inscribed by a stylus or chisel. Only scribes could have come up with such a system, and in fact, the same metaphysics underlay the rituals that the scribes of ancient Egypt devised. Through ritual, our time-bound world became, for these scribes, a writing tablet on which one could inscribe the timeless archetypes of the divine world.

The story of how Jacob got his name informs us that any reference to *YaD* ("hand") is potentially a reference to the letter *YuD* (Y), and when we decode the stories of the Torah as "enacted writing," we find that the secret of the name YHVH is described repeatedly and explicitly—much too frequently to be mere coincidence. For present purposes, a few examples will suffice.

Consider what YHVH said after Adam ate from the Tree of Knowledge: "Behold the man became like one from us [(*i.e.*, like one particular member of the Divine Council, presumably Satan)], to know good and evil, and now lest he send forth his *YaD* [('hand')] and take also from the Tree of Life and eat and live forever." (Gen 3:22.) The phrase "his *YaD*" is better rendered "His *YuD*"—a reference to God's hidden *yud* tucked inside the final *hei* of the name YHVH. If Adam "send[s] forth [*that*] *yud*," he will see that God's name is *Yehudi*, which is the "Tree of Life."

Consider next the story from the book of Exodus of Amalek's attack on the Israelites immediately after they crossed the Red Sea: "Amalek came and battled Israel in Rephidim." (Exod 17:8.) The Babylonian Talmud (*Sanhedrin* 106a) teaches that we should not read the Torah's letters as "*BiReFYDYM*," which means "in Rephidim," but as "*BeRiF[YON] YaDaYiM*," which means "with weakness of hands." But the latter phrase can just as well be vowelized as "*BeRiF[YON] YuDaYiM*," which means "with weakness of *yuds*." In other words, Amalek was able to overcome the Israelites because of the "weakness of [the] *yuds*"—in particular, the weakness of the letter *yud* at the end of God's name, a weakness that caused it to be in a contracted position, making it appear as the left leg of a *hei*.[97]

So what did Moses do? He commissioned Joshua to fight Amalek, saying: "Tomorrow I will stand on the top of the hill with the staff of God in my hand (*YaD*)." (Exod 17:9.) The Torah next asserts: "When Moses raised his hand (*YaD*), Israel was stronger, and when he lowered his hand (*YaD*), Amalek was stronger." (Exod 17:11.) Again, the text is better understood if the phrase "his *YaD*" is read as "His *YuD*." Thus, when Moses raised the hidden *YuD*, revealing the name *Yehudi*, Israel was stronger, and when he lowered the *YuD*, concealing the name, Amalek was stronger.

At the end of the story of the battle in Rephidim, Moses says: "For a hand (*YaD*) is upon the throne of *YaH*; YHVH battles against Amalek from generation [to] generation (*MiDoR, DoR*)." (Exod

---

[97] See Weinstein (trans.), *Gates of Light*, p. 321 [teaching that Amalek attacked the *vov-hei* of the name YHVH].

17:16.) "*YaH*" is, of course, the first two letters of YHVH, and Joseph Gikatilla explains that the phrase "throne of *YaH*" refers to the last two letters of the name—the *vov-hei*.[98] Thus, if the word *YaD* ("hand") is read as *YuD*, then the verse is saying that a letter *YuD* is "upon" (*i.e.*, concealed upon) the *vov-hei* of the name YHVH.

Some readers may feel that the foregoing translations of scripture—although clever—are too contrived to be genuine interpretations of the Hebrew text. But an even clearer description of the secret of the name YHVH appears in the book of Numbers, when YHVH promises to feed meat to the pleasure-craving Israelites for an entire month. Moses pleads with YHVH, asking where he (Moses) will find so much meat. According to the conventional translation, YHVH replied: "Is the hand (*YaD*) of YHVH limited [(literally, 'foreshortened')]? Now you will see whether my word will come to pass for you or not." (Num 11:23.) According to this conventional translation, the text is saying that nothing is beyond the ability of YHVH, who needs only to speak and it is so.

But the reference to a "hand" that is "foreshortened" is a bit of an oddity, requiring the reader to assume that YHVH is using both metaphor and irony in speaking to Moses. Keeping in mind that the Torah has no question marks, the first part of the verse is better translated as a statement about the hidden letter *yud* in the name YHVH than about YHVH's metaphoric "hand." In other words, YHVH replied to Moses by explaining the secret of the name in plain terms: "The *YuD* of YHVH is foreshortened [(tucked inside a *dalet*, making the *dalet* appear as a *hei*)]. Now you will see the fulfillment for you of my word if not [(*i.e.*, if the *yud* is not foreshortened)]." Translated in that more literal way, the text makes much more sense, and it conveys to Moses that by the

---

[98] Weinstein (trans.), *Gates of Light*, pp. 321–322.

power of the name *Yehudi*, he can obtain the miraculous quantities of meat that the Israelites demand.[99]

By this hermeneutical technique, which views the episodes of Hebrew scripture as enacted writing, the text takes on a whole new significance each time some leading figure *raises* his hand (*YaD*). In the book of Leviticus, for example, we read that "Aaron raised his hand (*YaD*) to the people and blessed them." (Lev 9:22.) Likewise, we read in the book of Psalms, "Arise YHVH, God, raise your hand (*YaD*), do not forget the humble" (Ps 10:12), and the book of Psalms also urges us to "lift [our] hands (*YaDs*) in the sanctuary and bless YHVH" (Ps 134:2). The mystical significance of all these verses emerges when the word *YaD* is read as *YuD*. Thus, for example, the verse describing Aaron's blessing of the people can be translated as: "Aaron raised His *YuD* [(*i.e.*, God's hidden letter *yud*)] to the people and blessed them." (Lev 9:22.) He blessed them, in other words, using the name *Yehudi*.

Consider also the well-known scene in the wilderness when the Israelites complain about the lack of water and an angry Moses calls the congregation "rebels" and strikes a "rock" with his staff, producing abundant "water." (Num 20:2–13.) Before Moses struck the rock, he "raised his hand (*YaD*)" before the eyes of the entire assembly (Num 20:8–11), and afterward YHVH punished Moses severely, although the text is vague regarding exactly what Moses had done wrong.

This cryptic story, which has puzzled commentators for thousands of years, makes perfect sense if the statement that Moses "raised his hand (*YaD*)" (Num 20:11) is translated as "raised His *YuD*" (*i.e.*, God's hidden letter *yud*). Translated that way, the story describes an angry invocation of the name *Yehudi* before the entire assembly. Of course, God's secret name *Yehudi* should

---

[99] On the foreshortened *yud*, see also Isa 50:2 ["Is my *yud* surely too foreshortened for redemption?"].

be revealed in blessing, not in anger, and the book of Psalms tells us that Moses' sin was that "he pronounced [the name] with his lips." (Ps 106:33.)

Consider also the law of the blasphemer set forth in the book of Numbers: "The soul that acts with a raised hand (*YaD*), ... he is a blasphemer of YHVH, and that soul shall be cut off from amidst its people, for he insulted the word YHVH...." (Num 15:30–31.) What does it mean to "act with a raised hand"? Translators make sense of the passage by assuming it to be a metaphoric reference to acting arrogantly, but certainly one can be arrogant without committing blasphemy. The passage therefore makes no sense.

If, however, we translate "elevated hand (*YaD*)" as "elevated *YuD*," the passage becomes clear: A soul that elevates the hidden *yud* of the name YHVH, revealing the name *Yehudi* in a profane context, he is a blasphemer of YHVH and shall be "cut off," "for he insulted the word YHVH." (Num 15:31.)

Not surprisingly, the phrase "raising the hand (*YaD*)" is also Torah's idiomatic expression for swearing an oath in God's name. (See, e.g., Gen 14:22; Num 14:30.) If the phrase is translated as "raising the *YuD*," it becomes clear that one swears an oath using the name *Yehudi*, and the physical act of raising one's "hand" (*YaD*) is then a ritualized way of invoking *Yehudi* without ever actually uttering that name.

Yet another example of the upraised hand (*YaD*) comes from the book of Ezekiel: "Thus said Lord YHVH: 'On the day I chose Israel, I raised my hand (*YaD*) to the seed of the House of Jacob and made myself known to them in the land of Egypt, I raised my hand (*YaD*) for them, saying, "I am YHVH, your God."'" (Ezek 20:5; see also Ezek 20:15, 20:23, 20:28, 20:42.) Once again, the passage makes more sense if the word *YuD* is read in place of the word *YaD*. Read that way, it states that YHVH made himself known to the House of Jacob by raising the *YuD* hidden at the end of his name, thereby revealing the name *Yehudi*.

The scriptural puns based on the equivalence in writing between the words *YaD* and *YuD* are too numerous and meaningful to be coincidental, and many more examples are given in the footnote below.[100] Moreover, as we have seen, replacing *YaD* with *YuD* sometimes makes sensible a text that otherwise has little sense. Consider this prophecy about the ultimate redemption of Israel: "I will inform them of my hand (*YaD*)..., and they will know that my name is YHVH." (Jer 16:21.) What does informing people about God's "hand" (*i.e.*, God's power) have

---

[100] See also Exod 3:20 [YHVH says: "I will stretch forth my *yud*" and thus defeat Pharaoh], 7:3–5 ["I will multiply my letters,... and the Egyptians will know that I am YHVH when I stretch forth my *yud*"], 7:19 [Moses instructs Aaron to "stretch forth your *yud*"], 8:1–2 [same], 8:13 [same], 9:3 ["*yud* of YHVH"], 9:15 [same], 9:22 [Moses told to "stretch forth your *yud*"], 10:12 [same], 10:21–22 [same], 13:3 [redemption "with a strong *yud*"], 13:9 [same], 13:14 [same], 13:16 [same], 14:8 ["And the descendants of Israel were going out with an elevated *yud*."], 14:16 ["stretch forth your *yud*"], 14:21 ["And Moses stretched forth his *yud*"], 14:26–27 [same], 14:31 [Israel sees the hidden *yud* of YHVH], 32:11 [YHVH took the Israelites out from Egypt "with a strong *yud*"]; Num 33:3 [the Israelites escaped Egypt with a raised *yud*]; Deut 32:39–40 ["And none [who is separate] from my *yud* is a savior, for I raise my *yud* to the heavens, and I say, 'I live forever.'"]; Josh 8:19 [Joshua "stretched forth his *yud*"], 8:26 [same]; Isa 5:25 [YHVH "stretched forth his *yud*"], 9:11 ["his *yud* is stretched forth" in anger], 9:16 [same], 9:20 [same], 10:4 [same], 14:26–27 [YHVH's "*yud* is stretched forth upon all the nations" in anger], 31:3 ["YHVH will stretch forth his *yud*"], 45:11–12 [same], 49:22 ["I will raise my *yud* to the nations."], 59:1–2 ["Behold, the *yud* of YHVH is not foreshortened... but your iniquities separated between you and your God, and your sins hid the face from you...."], 66:2 ["my *yud* made all these"]; Jer 21:5 [YHVH says: "I will battle them with a stretched forth *yud* and with a strong arm"], 22:24 [YHVH says: "upon my right *yud*"]; Ezek 14:9 [YHVH says: "I will stretch forth my *yud*"], 14:13 [same], 25:7 [same], 25:13 [same], 25:16 [same], 35:3 [same]; Zeph 1:4 [same], 2:13 [YHVH will "stretch forth his *yud*"]; Pss 95:3–4 ["YHVH is El the Great and great king over all the gods, who in his *yud* has the mysteries of the earth"], 138:7 ["If I walk in the midst of distress, you vitalize me against the wrath of my enemies; you send forth your *yud*."].

to do with persuading them that God's name is YHVH? How much more comprehensible this verse is when translated as: "I will inform them of my [hidden letter] *YuD*..., and they will know that my name is *Yehudi*."

6. "Behold, the *yud* of YHVH is not foreshortened"

If we consider that the name YHVH, when written, is facing the reader, then we realize that the name's "right hand" (the reader's left) refers to hidden letter *yud* at the end of the name, in which case the Torah's hints about the secret of the name proliferate even further.

Numerous verses in Hebrew scripture refer to the elevation of YHVH's "right hand" (*yamin*) or to the extension of YHVH's "arm" (*zeroa*), and all these verses are pregnant with secondary meaning when we think of them as references to the pen strokes that a scribe uses to write the name YHVH. For example, we frequently read that YHVH redeemed the Israelites from Egypt "with a strong hand and with an outstretched arm"—that is, with the hidden *yud* at the end of the name raised up to reveal the name *Yehudi*. (See, e.g., Deut 4:34, 5:15, 7:19, 11:2, 26:8; 1 Kings 8:42; Jer 21:5, 32:21; Ezek 20:33–34; Ps 136:11–12; 2 Chron 6:32.)

Similarly, we read of how the Israelites prevailed against their enemies solely by the power of YHVH's "right hand" and "arm," not by military might. "Your right hand, YHVH, is glorified in strength; your right hand, YHVH, smashes the enemy.... You extended your right hand, [and] the earth swallowed them." (Exod 15:6–12.) "You, your *YuD*, drove out nations.... For not with their sword did they possess the land..., but [by] your right hand and your arm.... Your name we thank forever." (Ps 44:3–9.) "Why do you turn back your *YuD*, even your right hand? From the midst of your bosom remove [it]!" (Ps 74:10–11.) "Yours is the arm with power; your *YuD* is strong; your right hand is elevated.... Happy the people that knows the joyful sound of YHVH [(*i.e.*, the joyful *pronunciation* of YHVH)]; in the light of your face they walk." (Ps 89:14–16.) Many additional references to YHVH's "right hand" and "arm" are given in the footnote below.[101] There are many gods of the Torah that are powerful (Shaddai, for example), but no god other than YHVH has a "right hand" and an "arm," because these terms do not just refer metaphorically to an exercise of divine power; rather, they refer more literally and specifically to the orthographic components of YHVH's name.

In this regard, a highly respected compilation of discourses known as the *Pesikta de-Rab Kahana* (5th to 7th centuries C.E.) merits close analysis. The *Pesikta* comments on a verse from the book of Lamentations: "[YHVH] turned backward his right hand

---

[101] See Gen 48:14 [extended "right hand"]; Exod 6:6 ["outstretched arm"], 9:29 [extended "palms"], 9:33 [same], 15:16 ["in the greatness of your arm"]; Deut 9:29 ["with your outstretched arm"]; 2 Kings 17:36 ["with an outstretched arm"]; Isa 40:10 [YHVH's "arm"], 51:9 ["Awaken! Dress in strength, O arm of YHVH"], 52:10 ["YHVH has bared his holy arm to the eyes of all the nations"], 53:1 ["upon whom has the arm of YHVH been revealed?"], 62:8 [YHVH swears by "right hand" and "powerful arm"], 63:12 [YHVH's "arm"]; Jer 27:5 [YHVH says: "my outstretched arm" created the earth], 32:17 [YHVH's "stretched forth arm" created the universe]; Pss 20:7 [YHVH's "right hand"], 21:9 ["Your *yud* will find all your enemies; your right hand will find your haters."], 48:11 [YHVH's "right hand"], 60:7 [God's "right hand" saves], 71:18 ["until I tell of your arm to the generation"], 78:54 [YHVH's "right hand"], 79:11 [YHVH's "arm"], 89:10 [YHVH's "strong arm"], 89:22 [YHVH's "*yud*" and "arm"], 89:26 ["*yud*" and "right hand"], 98:1 [YHVH's "right hand" and "holy arm"], 108:7 [YHVH's "right hand"], 118:16 ["the right hand of YHVH is elevated; the right hand of YHVH does valor," prevailing against one's enemies], 138:7 ["your right hand saves me"], 139:10 [YHVH's "*yud*" and "right hand" help David]; Lam 2:3–4 [YHVH's "right hand"]; Dan 12:7 ["and he elevated his right hand and his left hand"].

(*yamin*) from the face of the enemy." (Lam 2:3.) The *Pesikta* states about the verse:

> [T]he enemies seized Israel's warriors and bound their hands behind their backs. Thereupon the Holy One declared: Scripture says of Me, "I will be with them in trouble" (Ps. 91:15), and so since My children are in deep trouble, can I remain at ease? At once,... "God bound His right hand (*yamin*) behind His back"—if one dare speak thus—"on account of the enemy" (Lam. 2:3).[102]

In other words, because of the exile of the Jews to Babylon, YHVH "turned backward his right hand from the face of the enemy"— *i.e.*, YHVH concealed his name YeHVDY (*Yehudi*), thus protecting the name from being profaned among the Babylonians.

Of course, the *Pesikta*'s commentary on God's "right hand" becoming bound can also be read as a metaphoric reference to YHVH's power being withdrawn, but it seems odd for the *Pesikta* to suggest that God chose to become powerless in order to "be with [the Israelites] in [their] trouble." What good is a God that shares one's troubles by sharing one's powerlessness? Therefore, the *Pesikta*'s statement that "God bound His right hand (*yamin*) behind His back" seems to refer to the final *yud* (Y) of the name YeHVDY (*Yehudi*) being tucked into the *dalet* (D) to produce the name YHVH, thus preserving the sanctity of the name.

The *Pesikta* next turns to a verse in the book of Daniel. When the prophet Daniel asks an angel when the redemption will come, the angel replies: "At the end of *yamin*" (Dan 12:13)— but the word *yamin* is ambiguous since it can mean both "days" (Aramaic) and "right hand" (Hebrew). The *Pesikta*, therefore, expounds the verse, imagining Daniel asking the angel for a clarification:

---

[102] This and other quotations from the *Pesikta* are taken from the translation appearing in Braude and Kapstein (trans. and eds.), *Pesikta de-Rab Kahana*, pp. 409–415.

> Again Daniel spoke up: "At the end of *yamin*, that is at the end of the world's days, or at the end of *yamin*, that is at the end of Thy right hand's being bound?" God replied: "At the end of My *yamin*—at the end of My right hand's being bound behind My back."

In other words, the redemption will come when God's "right hand" is extended once again and the name *Yehudi* is thus revealed.

The *Pesikta* then confirms that the bound condition of God's "right hand" does not refer to God's self-imposed powerlessness. In this regard, it comments on a verse from Psalms in which God's suffering devotee asserts: "My weakness is [from] the changes to the Most High's right hand." (Ps 77:11.) The *Pesikta* emphasizes that God is never powerless, and therefore "the changes to the Most High's right hand" has nothing to do with a withdrawal of God's power. Rather, the *Pesikta* asserts that "the changes to the Most High's right hand" refers to the separation between the Israelites and God. The *Pesikta* quotes this prooftext from the book of Isaiah: "Behold, the hand (*YaD*) of YHVH is not foreshortened...but your iniquities separated between you and your God, and your sins hid the face from you...." (Isa 59:1–2.) In other words, the hidden letter *YuD* at the end of the name YHVH is not "foreshortened" as it appears to be when the name is written as YHVH; rather, it is really elevated, producing the name *Yehudi*. But the errors of the Israelites hid YHVH's "face" from them, and they ceased to know the true form of YHVH's name, thus becoming separated from God.

7. "The name YHVH comes from a distant place"

Several verses of the Torah suggest that YHVH (*Yehudi*) was a widely known god of the ancient world. Why else would YHVH have been familiar to so many of the Torah's non-Israelite figures? Why, for example, would Abimelech (a pagan king) call

"in the name of YHVH, universal El"? (Gen 21:33.) Why would
he also acknowledge to Isaac that "YHVH was with you" (Gen
26:28), and why would he describe Isaac as "blessed of YHVH"
(Gen 26:29)? Similarly, why does Laban (a pagan idolater) recognize the authority of YHVH? (Gen 24:50, 30:27, 31:49.) And,
why does Potiphar—the chief priest of an important Egyptian city—likewise recognize YHVH's power? (Gen 39:3.) And
when Jethro, the priest of Midian, hears that the Israelites have
escaped Pharaoh, why does he say that "YHVH is greater than
all the gods," thus clearly distinguishing YHVH from other gods,
not just using YHVH as an alternative name for his own god?
(Exod 18:11.) And most important, why does Bala'am worship
YHVH, converse with YHVH, recognize an angel of YHVH, and call
upon YHVH, saying: "If Balak will give me his houseful of silver
and gold, I cannot transgress the mouth of YHVH, *my god*, to do
[either] small or great"? (Num 22:18.) None of these passages
makes sense unless YHVH was some widely known and respected
god of the ancient world.

Consider next the following revealing verse from the book
of Isaiah: "The name YHVH comes from a distant place." (Isa
30:27.) Read in context, this verse metaphorically describes
the ultimate vindication of the Jewish people: "The name YHVH
is coming"—*God*, in other words, is coming—"from a distant
place"—from heaven above—to make good on the Covenant, to
vanquish the forces of evil, and to establish eternal holiness. But
the phrasing of the verse seems odd. Why say that *the name* is
coming? Therefore, the verse is better read as a literal statement:
The name YHVH—the most cherished name of God in Judaism—
actually comes from a distant place; that is, it is a name of God
adopted from some foreign culture.

This literal reading of the verse from Isaiah is implied in the
following excerpt from an early Kabbalistic text. The excerpt
links knowledge of the secret pronunciation of the name YHVH
with an appearance of God in our physical world, a theophany
that the Torah calls the "Glory of YHVH":

As a consequence of our mentioning the glorious name [YHVH], He is unified with us, and is blessed in His blessing. The meaning of the name is known to the enlightened, according to the matter, "Behold, the name YHVH comes from a distant place [(Isa 30:27)]." And the meaning of the "Glory of [YHVH]" is, as it is written,... "you shall behold the Glory of [YHVH] [(Exod 16:7)],"... and many more such [verses] as these.[103]

An intriguing assertion is being made in this text: The name YHVH has a secret "meaning" known only to the "enlightened," and this secret meaning is somehow hinted at in the verse from Isaiah, "the name YHVH comes from a distant place." (Isa 30:27.)

What "distant place" in the Near Eastern world could this verse from Isaiah be referring to? What god of the ancient world bore the name that later became the name of God for both Jews and Christians? Abraham hailed from Ur Kasdim in Mesopotamia; perhaps the Jewish name for God comes from there. But YHVH specifically tells Moses: "I appeared to Abraham, to Isaac, and to Jacob as El Shaddai, and with My name YHVH, I was not known to them." (Exod 6:2–3.) This passage clearly indicates that it was only *after* the Israelites' lengthy sojourn in Egypt that they began to worship God using the name YHVH, and this passage further implies that it was specifically *Moses* who introduced the name YHVH to the Israelites. In other words, YHVH is *Moses' name for God*—the same Moses who was reared as an Egyptian prince in the pharaoh's palace.

Hence, the most likely origin of the name YHVH is Egypt. We know from the Egyptian historical record that Egyptian princes sometimes served as priests at major temples, and we know from lore recorded in Christian scripture (Acts 7:22) that Moses

---

[103] MS Oxford-Bodleian 2456 (Christ Church 198), fol. 15b, quoted in Wolfson, *Through a Speculum That Shines*, p. 263 [Wolfson's translation has been modified slightly].

was trained in all the secret wisdom of the Egyptian religion. It follows, therefore, that YHVH was an Egyptian god that Moses worshiped and that Moses later assimilated to the Israelite god.

But the verse from Exodus in which YHVH tells Moses that the Israelite patriarchs knew God as El Shaddai remains confusing. If we review the book of Genesis, we see that the patriarchs did, indeed, worship God by the names El and El Shaddai, but we also find numerous examples of the patriarchs worshiping YHVH. What then does YHVH (*Yehudi*) mean by the statement: "I appeared to [them] as El Shaddai, and with My name YHVH, I was not known to them"? (Exod 6:2–3.)

The Torah, however, must be read very closely. It tells us that YHVH appeared to Abraham, that YHVH spoke to Abraham, and that Abraham built an altar to YHVH. Nowhere, however, does it say that in these instances Abraham *knew* YHVH *to be* YHVH. But then something changes. Abraham is preparing to travel to Egypt because of a famine, and it is only *then*, when Abraham is about to enter Egypt, that the Torah tells us for the first time that Abraham "invoked [God] *with the name* YHVH." (Gen 12:8.) And also immediately after Abraham returns from Egypt, we are again told that Abraham "invoked [God] *with the name* YHVH." (Gen 13:4.) In these verses, the Torah is hinting to us that the name YHVH is, in fact, connected to Egypt.

But we need not rely on mere hints. Hebrew scripture makes the point explicitly. Through the mouth of the prophet Hosea, YHVH says: "I am YHVH, *your god from the land of Egypt....*" (Hosea 13:4; see also Hosea 12:10.) The passage is usually translated as "your god *since* the land of Egypt," thus confirming that Moses introduced the name YHVH to the Israelites, but the prefix-letter *mem*, which is usually translated in this passage as "since," means "from." The word "from" can certainly be understood temporally, but here it is better understood geographically: YHVH is the god of the Israelites "*from* the land of Egypt." In other words, YHVH—pronounced "yehudi"—is one of Egypt's gods. Which one?

Perhaps the one named Dj<u>y</u>ehudi, the author of the *Egyptian Book of the Dead*.

8. The Thrice-Great Hermes

It might be valuable at this point to consider a tradition—held by ritual magicians, occultists, and alchemists—that the Egyptian god Thoth (assimilated to Hermes in Greek mythology) was the original source of all esoteric wisdom in the world. We have already learned that Moses had a special relationship with Thoth. The Jewish historian Artapanus of Alexandria (2nd century B.C.E.) recorded that Moses was a master of the priestly sciences who was associated with Thoth and who was in fact called by Thoth's name (probably Thutmose). We have also encountered Thoth as the god of Hermopolitan Creation, the god who taught Isis and Nephthys the sacred spells by which Osiris was restored to life, and the great defender of both Osiris and Horus before the divine court.

When the ancient Greeks wrote about the Egyptian religion, they transliterated Thoth's Egyptian name into Greek, and the English name Thoth—pronounced "thoth" or "tōt"— derives from that Greek transliteration. In ancient Egypt, however, Thoth's name was pronounced "djyehudi," a name that is remarkably similar phonetically to *Yehudi*.

But is Thoth—who is depicted iconographically as an ibis and sometimes as a baboon—sufficiently consequential to be YHVH, the monotheistic God of both Judaism and Christianity?[104] Egyptian records inform us that Thoth was the god of the Egyptian scribes, and Moses was, of course, a scribe.[105] Thoth invented

---

[104] For detailed descriptions of the Egyptian god Thoth, see Boylan, *Thoth: The Hermes of Egypt*; Bleeker, *Hathor and Thoth*.

[105] In *Targum Onkelos* to Deut 33:21, Moses is called "Moses the scribe." See also Exod 17:14, 34:27.

hieroglyphs, and he acted as the scribe of the gods. Thoth "wrote *maat*," meaning that he wrote "Truth." Thoth was also the author of both ritual and civil law. A great lover of peace, Thoth was a mediator who reconciled disputants. He was the god who presided over the Egyptian calendar, and thus Thoth represented both astrological time and ritual time. Most important, Thoth was a creator god, who created through speech. And, the wonderful thing about Thoth was that, having created the heavens and the earth, he concealed himself as a mere clerical assistant to the gods—a member of the back-office staff, who records the gods' decrees.

Thoth's representation as an ibis is significant. An ibis, according to ancient legend, had the ability to discern pure from impure, and therefore Egyptian priests had their ritual baths only with water drawn from a place where an ibis had been seen to drink. Moreover, the ibis served mankind as a killer of venomous snakes. Both of these qualities conform nicely with Jewish tradition, which puts great emphasis on physical and moral purity, and which traces the origin of both evil and death to the venomous speech of a mythological serpent. Also, as we have seen, Moses used ibises to protect his army against venomous snakes during his campaign against the Nubians, and he consecrated his military camp to the ibis.

As the scribe of the gods, Thoth was the one who recorded the verdict when Osiris was tried before the divine assembly. More generally, it was Thoth who recorded the verdict when *any deceased soul* appeared before the divine assembly. As the one who recorded the verdict, Thoth had the final word regarding the outcome of trial. Thoth advocated on behalf of the deceased soul, and Thoth also knew the secret incantations that could raise a deceased soul back to life. Thoth was lauded by his devotees as the great merciful god, a friend to those who are self-restrained, modest, humble, and pious. Furthermore, Thoth was the author of the temple rites by which the other Egyptian gods were worshiped. He designed their temples, organized their cults, and composed their ritual texts.

Jews are known as the "people of the book," and as professors, philosophers, journalists, creative writers, and judges, Jews often give meaning and comprehensibility to the world we share. The idea, then, that an ancient god of scholars and scribes is the God of the Jews hardly seems surprising. But before accepting the hypothesis that YHVH is indeed the Egyptian god Thoth, we should consider a contrary hypothesis, advanced by some scholars,[106] that YHVH is actually a Midianite god that Moses first encountered after migrating from Egypt to Midian. (See Exod 2:15.)

The Midianite hypothesis is based primarily on verses from Hebrew scripture saying that YHVH comes "from the south" (Hab 3:3), "from Seir" (Deut 33:2; Judg 5:4), and "from Mount Paran" (Deut 33:2; Hab 3:3). It is further supported by the fact that Moses encounters YHVH at the "mountain of the gods" while tending the sheep of Jethro, his Midianite father-in-law. (Exod 3:1–2.) And after that encounter, during the journey of the Israelites from Egypt to Canaan, Jethro meets Moses (Exod 18) and acknowledges the supremacy of YHVH (Exod 18:11). Moses then leads the people to the "mountain of the gods," where Moses once again encounters YHVH. (Exod 19–20.) The implication of these passages is that the "mountain of the gods" (also called "Choreiv" and "Sinai") is a southern mountain on which YHVH was worshiped, somewhere in the vicinity of ancient Midian.

But these same data equally support the conclusion that YHVH is the Egyptian god Thoth. The references to YHVH being "from the south," "from Seir," and "from Mount Paran" all can refer to a location somewhere on the Sinai Peninsula, and in ancient

---

[106] See, e.g., Albertz, *The History of Israelite Religion in the Old Testament Period, Volume I*, pp. 49–52; Smith, *The Origins of Biblical Monotheism*, pp. 145–146.

times, there was an active Thoth cult at Serabit el-Khadim on the Sinai Peninsula. There, the Egyptian pharaohs maintained important mining operations, using Semitic slave labor. The temple complex at Serabit el-Khadim stood on an elevated plateau, and it included shrines to three Egyptian gods (Hathor, Ptah, and Thoth). Therefore, the phrase "mountain of the gods" would have been an apt description of that location. One should also consider in this context that in ancient times a "god" was primarily a cultic object in a temple, not an abstract omnipresence, and therefore the phrase "mountain of the gods" connotes a mountaintop *temple*. Hence, there is no location on the Sinai Peninsula that better fits the description "mountain of the gods" than Serabit el-Khadim. Furthermore, Serabit el-Khadim matches the Torah's description of a place that was a three days' journey from Egypt. (Exod 3:12, 3:18, 5:1, 5:3, 8:21–25.)

To be sure, the Torah does describe Moses migrating from Egypt to Midian, but from Midian, Moses journeys with Jethro's sheep "beyond the wilderness" to "the mountain of the gods" (Exod 3:1), where he encounters YHVH—in other words, he journeys to Serabit el-Khadim, where he encounters the shrine to Thoth. Later, during the journey of the Israelites out of Egypt, Moses meets Jethro, who acknowledges the supremacy of YHVH (Thoth), but Jethro then *returns to his land*, suggesting that Jethro was *not* in Midian when this meeting took place. (See Exod 18:27.) Then, after the meeting with Jethro, Moses leads the people to the "mountain of the gods" (Serabit el-Khadim), where Moses again encounters YHVH (Thoth). Significantly, the shrines at Serabit el-Khadim are in the form of caves, explaining why the Torah describes Moses encountering God *in* the mountain. (See Lev 25:1; see also 1 Kings 19:8–9.)

In short, the same data that are used to support the Midianite hypothesis equally support the Thoth hypothesis: YHVH is the Egyptian god Thoth, worshiped at Serabit el-Khadim. The clan of Jacob descended into Egypt, and it came back from Egypt with something quite awesome (see Gen 15:14); it came back *with an Egyptian god.*

9. Hieroglyphs and Other Alphabets— Who Wrote the Torah?

In hieroglyphs, Thoth's name was often signified by a single glyph depicting an ibis, either alone or elevated on a standard. But the name Thoth (Djyehudi) was also written with phonetic hieroglyphs as follows:

→ → → →*direction of reading*→ → → →

Our knowledge of the pronunciation of ancient Egyptian is imperfect, but scholars are able to draw a few conclusions. They find clues to ancient pronunciation by studying the ways in which ancient Egyptian words were transliterated into the alphabets of languages that are still spoken today, and they draw additional clues from present-day pronunciations of Coptic words, for Coptic is the modern language that descends from ancient Egyptian.

The first glyph of Thoth's name (ᒣ) is in the shape of a rearing cobra and was probably pronounced like the initial consonant in the French word *dieu*. It is close to an English *y* with respect to the positioning of the tongue, but it is slightly plosive rather than a mere slide. The English letters *djy* roughly capture the sound.[107]

---

[107] The pronunciations suggested here are from Collier and Manley, *Egyptian Hieroglyphs.*

The second glyph (𓏤) signifies a strongly aspirated English *h*, with a slight guttural scrape. It is probably not as guttural as the *ch* of the German word *ich*, but it is more guttural than the open-throat puff of air that we generally associate with the English *h*. It corresponds roughly to the Hebrew *hei*.

The third glyph (𓎛) was pronounced very much like the Hebrew letter *vov* when marked with the *kubootz* vowel mark. The same sound is found in the *oo* of the English word "boot" or in the *u* of the English word "rude."

The fourth glyph (𓏏) was pronounced like an English *t,* but in light of the consonantal shift in many ancient languages from *d* to *t,* this glyph might also correspond to an English *d*. In the Hebrew alphabet, it corresponds to a *dalet*.

The fifth glyph (𓏭) was a double letter that signified the long *e* sound, as in the English word "keep." It corresponds to a Hebrew *yud*, when the *yud* appears at the end of a word.

Finally, the last glyph of Thoth's name (𓅂) served no phonetic role; rather, it was a "determinative," which is the term Egyptologists use for an ideogram added at the end of a written Egyptian word to clarify (pictorially) the intended meaning of the word. The particular ideogram used here (𓅂) was generally used following the name of a god. For pronunciation purposes, it can be disregarded.

When we combine all these phonemes, we get the pronunciation "djyehudi" for Thoth's name.

But how might a Hebrew scribe, writing in ancient times, transliterate the name Djyehudi into Hebrew? Of course, the English *j* does not appear in the Hebrew alphabet, but if scholars are correct that the Egyptian cobra glyph (𓆓) was pronounced like a slightly plosive English *y,* then a Hebrew scribe might transliterate Djyehudi with a *yud* (Y) as the first letter,[108] fol-

---

[108] The Egyptian city that the Torah refers to as *Tzo'an* (Num 13:22) is identified in the Septuagint as Tanis (Egyptian: *Djanet*), a city whose Egyptian name began with the cobra glyph. Therefore, the cobra glyph

yud	dalet	vov	hei	yud
Y	D	V	H	Y

←←←←←*direction of reading*←←←←←

lowed by a *hei-vov-dalet-yud*. And that, of course, spells "*Yehudi*" (YeHVDY).

But what if this Hebrew scribe who was transliterating Djye-hudi into the Hebrew alphabet happened to be trained in all the esoteric techniques of the scribal tradition? And what if this scribe wanted to conceal the name and thereby keep it from being profaned or misused by enemies in a foreign land? What might this scribe do? One possibility would be to tuck the final *yud* into the *dalet* that precedes it, making those two letters appear to be a second *hei*. In other words, God "turned backward his right hand [(*i.e.*, his final *yud*)] from the face of the enemy" (Lam 2:3), and the result was God's four-letter name as it appears in the Torah.

Thus, Djyehudi, the god of the Egyptian scribes, became YHVH, the god of the Torah. But here an important qualification of our conclusion is necessary, requiring us to touch on the sensitive subject of who authored the Torah.

---

could sometimes be transliterated with a Hebrew letter *tzadi* (TZ). Note, however, that transliteration practices often vary considerably.

The Hebrew letters shown above derive from the *Ashuri* script. Under Jewish religious law, a Torah scroll must be inscribed in the *Ashuri* script to be ritually valid. Indeed, Jewish law is very strict in this regard because so many secrets of the Torah depend on the precise shapes of the letters. But curiously, this *Ashuri* script (also called the "Aramaic alphabet") did not come into use by the Israelites until the 5th century B.C.E., *about 800 years after Moses.*

Therefore, if—as pious tradition asserts—Moses was the great scribe who ascended the mountain, received, and wrote the Torah, and if he wrote it in the *Ashuri* script in which it appears today, then he did so using a script that did not yet exist and that no one among the Israelites of Moses' time could have deciphered. If, however, Moses wrote the Torah in a *different* script (for example, in Egyptian hieroglyphs or in the proto-Sinaitic script that Semitic people in Egypt used), then many of the most profound secrets of the Torah—secrets that derive from the *shapes* of the Torah's Hebrew letters—were not original to Moses' revelation.

In other words, Moses was *not* the scribe who wrote the Torah we have today. Rather, the Torah we have today was written by some other, equally gifted scribe (or group of scribes), writing in the mid–5th century B.C.E. or later, when use of the *Ashuri* script was widespread.

According to Hebrew scripture, Ezra was the person who, after the fall of Babylon (539 B.C.E.), brought the Torah back to Jerusalem and taught it to the Israelites. (See Ezra 7:6–10; Neh 8.) And the Babylonian Talmud adds that Ezra—who was called "Ezra the Scribe" and thus bore the same honorific as Moses—was so great that he would have merited to bring the Torah down from heaven if Moses had not done so (*Sanhedrin* 21b–22a), and the Talmud further states that the Torah was forgotten and Ezra restored it (*Succah* 20a). Do we perhaps detect here a hint that Ezra, who moved to Jerusalem in 458 B.C.E., had a much greater role in compiling our present version of the Torah than pious dogma admits?

Modern critical scholarship—focusing, among other things, on names of God, grammatical style, vocabulary, and content—has identified several interwoven textual strands within the Torah, each with its own theology and values. Meanwhile, better understanding of the ancient Near Eastern literature has confirmed that the Torah incorporates elements from Canaanite, Mesopotamian, and Egyptian traditions. This evidence all suggests a relatively late redaction of the Torah, drawing from a variety of source texts.

In addition, archaeology has discovered no evidence of a mass exodus of two million slaves from Egypt. There is simply no physical trace of such a large population meandering for forty years on the Sinai Peninsula, and Egyptian historical records make no mention of an event that certainly would have devastated the Egyptian economy. Are we to assume that a workforce two-million strong left Egypt without the Egyptians so much as mentioning the fact and that, for the next forty years, this huge group moved from camp to camp through the desert, carrying all its waste wherever it went? And are we further to assume that this group invaded Canaan, defeating thirty-one Canaanite kings and destroying Canaanite cities, but left no archaeological marks of that invasion? It doesn't seem plausible.

So what theories better fit the evidence? Was perhaps Ezra's scribal hand a late stage in an editorial enterprise that spanned centuries, weaving a variety of ancient texts, law codes, myths, legends, and songs into a single scripture that was intended to unify an ideologically fractured nation? Was perhaps the venerable out-of-Egypt story the cherished ancestral lore of only a small ruling elite within that fractured nation—lore that was taught to and eventually adopted by the native population of the land that they ruled? Did perhaps the historical exodus from Egypt involve only a few thousand people?[109] Was perhaps the name of

---

[109] See Exod 1:15 [describing only two midwives, implying at most a few thousand people]; Num 1:18–46, 3:43 [if the numbers given for male

Moses' god—Djyehudi—occulted in the form of YHVH, its fuller form more or less forgotten, even as the citizens of Judah continued to use the name *Yehudi* to identify themselves?[110] And, finally, when Ezra compiled the Torah in the *Ashuri* script, was it perhaps *he* who manipulated the letters of that script to conceal God's name?

The answer to the last question is not absolutely clear. Several inscriptions from before the time of the Babylonian exile, written in paleo-Hebrew script, use the letters *yud-hei-vov-hei* (YHVH) as the name of God, and therefore these four letters were not solely Ezra's scribal innovation based on his manipulation of the *Ashuri* script. Rather, they had some preexisting significance, probably as an abbreviated form of the name *Yehudah* (YeHVDaH). The scribes of ancient times believed that divine names had power when written, and therefore they often abbreviated divine names, just as many Jews today abbreviate "God" as "G-d." Significantly, we often see YHVH's name abbreviated in forms such as *yud-hei-vov* (*yahu*), *yud-hei* (*yah*), and *yud-vov* (*yu* or *io*). There is no reason why *yud-hei-vov-hei* (YHVH) cannot itself be one more such abbreviation, signifying *Yehudah* (YeHVDaH). But Ezra took advantage of the shapes of the *Ashuri* letters to link YHVH also to *Yehudi*, and he then dispersed throughout the Torah veiled hints about what he had done, hints that only a trained scribe would appreciate.

Thus, it appears that Ezra (or the Ezra school) put the Torah into the form we have today. By contrast, it is highly unlikely that the Torah that Moses knew contained a consistent series of wordplays—based on the word *YaD* ("hand") and the letter *YuD*—that would only become significant 800 years later, when

---

family members and eldest sons were literal, then each family would average twenty-seven sons].

[110] Many people today use terms like "Wednesday" without being aware that they are invoking the Germanic god Odin, or terms like "January" without being aware that they are invoking the Roman god Janus.

a new alphabet evolved and the Torah was rewritten using that new alphabet. Rather, someone from Ezra's time or later must have added all these wordplays to the text.

10. YHVH Sat between the *Cheruvs*

According to the philosophy of ancient Egypt, the word for an object was not merely a convenient signifier; rather, it was the spiritual essence of the object. God spoke the universe into existence, and words therefore had the power to change physical reality. Moreover, this effective power of language was not limited in ancient Egyptian thought to *spoken* words; it applied also to *written* words. Thus, sacred script—whether engraved in stone or brushed onto papyrus—had creative power; the letters brought into existence their linguistic content.

Because of the power of the written word, the Egyptians often chiseled sacred texts and the images of their gods onto "steles" (stone tablets), which they set upright. It is certainly significant, therefore, that YHVH—Torah's "god from the land of Egypt" (Hosea 13:4)—instructed Moses to hew two stone tablets (Exod 34:1), to write upon them ten words (Exod 34:27–28), and to place them in a special housing called, in English, an "ark" (Exod 25:10–16, 25:21; Deut 10:5). Significantly, the Torah never refers anywhere in its text to "Ten Commandments"; instead, it refers to "ten words"—ten powerful names that Moses inscribed onto two stone steles.

YHVH further instructed Moses that two experts in temple crafts, Bezalel and Oholiab (Exod 31:1–11), should fashion a gold cover for the ark, with a *cheruv* of "hammered gold" at either end of the cover (Exod 25:17–22). The phrase "hammered gold" (*zahav miqshah*) may refer to hammered gold plating, which was a common form of decoration in ancient times. Moses was to place the ark, with its gold cover, behind curtains (Exod 26:1), surrounded by successive zones of separation and purity, and YHVH—Thoth, that is—promised to sit, enthroned between the *cheruv*s, and from that place, speak (see Exod 25:22; Num 7:89; Ps 99:1). Of course, building a royal throne for a god that was sometimes called "king" raises at least the possibility that, at one time in the hoary past, a flesh-and-blood king sat on that throne as God's representative on earth, perhaps a flesh-and-blood king from the tribe of Judah (YeHVDaH), a name that was abbreviated as YHVH. It is significant, therefore, that Hebrew scripture uses the honorific "son [of God]" to refer to Judah's kings. (See 2 Sam 7:14; Pss 2:7, 89:27–28.) Be that as it may, the royal throne, standing by itself, functioned as a powerful symbol of the God's earthly sovereignty, a place where the invisible God "sat."

The historical record is unclear as to what exactly the *cheruv*s were. Hebrew scripture states that *cheruv*s (English: "cherubs") were winged creatures (Ezek 10), and the book of Enoch refers to *cheruv*s in close conjunction with *seraph*s, suggesting that these two mythical creatures were related to one another. A *seraph* was a fiery winged serpent. In the wilderness, when the Israelites were attacked by *seraph*s, Moses made a copper *seraph* and raised it on a pole as an apotropaic. (Num 21:4–9.) This emblem was then worshiped by the Israelites for several centuries. (2 Kings 18:4.) It is possible that, like *seraph*s, *cheruv*s were also winged serpents.

It is interesting to note in this context that the throne of Tutankhamen (14th century B.C.E.) was covered with hammered gold plating, with a winged serpent, hammered out of gold, at either side. Tutankhamen was the famous boy pharaoh who lived just a short time before Moses. It would not be unreasonable to conclude that the throne of YHVH was like that of Tutankhamen, in which case the *cheruv*s on either side of the gold ark cover were like the winged serpents on either side of Tutankhamen's throne.

Further hints about the *cheruv*s appear in the book of Ezekiel, which describes the *chayah* ("living creature") that acts as God's "vehicle" or "mount" (*merkavah*). Ezekiel's *chayah* was probably a winged sphinx with a serpent tail. A sphinx is a

Gold-plated throne of Tutankhamen.
Egyptian, 14th century B.C.E.
(Photo © Griffith Institute, University of Oxford)

composite mythical creature with the head of a person and the body of a lion. The most famous example of this biform sphinx is the Great Sphinx in Giza, Egypt. Some sphinxes, however, were composed of four animals, having the head of a person, the body of a lion, the wings of an eagle, and the tail of a serpent. This quadriform sphinx is familiar from Greek mythology as the sphinx in Thebes that posed a riddle to Oedipus.[111] In ancient times, kings and deities were often depicted sitting on quadriform sphinxes of this type.

This historical background gives context to the book of Ezekiel's description of the *chayah* that was God's "mount." Ezekiel describes God sitting on a composite mythical creature that had the "face" of a person, the "face" of a lion, the "face" of an eagle, and the "face" of a *cheruv*. (Ezek 10:14.)[112] It seems very likely that the book of Ezekiel is referring here to a standard

---

[111] Graves, *The Greek Myths*, p. 372.

[112] The book of Ezekiel describes two other composite mythical creatures, one being a man-lion-ox-eagle (Ezek 1:10), and the other being a man-lion (Ezek 41:18–19).

Deity (probably Ba'al) sitting on sphinx throne.
Phoenician, 6th–4th centuries B.C.E.
(Beazley Archive, University of Oxford)

quadriform sphinx, using the word "face" to refer to the different components of the composite creature. If that is so, then Ezekiel's use of the word *cheruv* corresponds to the quadriform sphinx's serpent tail, although the book of Ezekiel elsewhere uses the word *cheruv* to describe the sphinx in its entirety (see, e.g., Ezek 10:1–12, 10:15–21, 11:22, 41:18).

For our purposes, however, the most significant point is that, according to the Babylonian Talmud, the two *cheruv*s ("winged serpents") on either side of the ark cover were *united in sexual congress*—or, as the Talmud puts it, "genitals, this in this." (*Yoma* 54a–54b.) Of course, two winged serpents united in sexual congress suggests a caduceus—an upright staff twined by two winged serpents. Therefore, that fascinating detail from the Talmud provides yet another connection between YHVH and the Egyptian god Thoth, because the caduceus was a symbol associated in ancient Egyptian art with Thoth. The sexually united *cheruv*s atop YHVH's ark appear, then, to correspond to the twined serpents of Thoth's caduceus.

Winged sphinx with winged serpent.
Neo-Assyrian, 8th century B.C.E.
(Metropolitan Museum of Art, New York)

The latter point raises the interesting possibility that the "copper serpent" that Moses raised on a pole to protect the Israelites from *seraph*s was actually a caduceus. In the Torah, Moses' serpent-on-a-pole is called *"NeCHaSH NeCHoSHeT"* ("copper serpent"), but the same consonants can be vowelized as *NeCHaSH NeCHaSHiT*, which can be translated as "male serpent–female serpent." Read that way, the Torah would appear to be referring again to two *cheruv*s united in sexual congress.

Pious Jews wear twisted threads called "twines" (*gedilim*) or "blossoms" (*tzitzit*) at the corners of their prayer shawls (see Num 15:38; Deut 22:12), and Nahmanides (13th century C.E.) asserted that these twined threads serve to remind Jews of the cover of the ark. How so? Because the cover of the ark was decorated with two *cheruv*s ("winged serpents") twined, like the two winged serpents of Thoth's caduceus, in sexual union. About the twined threads of the prayer shawl, the Torah states, "so you may see it and remember all the commandments of YHVH" (Num 15:39), but the Babylonian Talmud (*Menachos* 43b) suggests the equally valid translation "so you may see *Him*...," indicating that one should see YHVH in these twined threads. In other words,

Caduceus

the twined serpents of the caduceus are not just Thoth's symbol; they are also YHVH's symbol, adorning the throne of God in YHVH's temple, and also the prayer shawls of pious Jews.

It merits noting that the Torah uses a singular pronoun to refer to the twined threads (plural) of the prayer shawl ("so you may see *it*"). That minor grammatical irregularity conveys a fundamental principle of the Jewish religion that we have already discussed in some detail: Two are always really one. The twined threads of the prayer shawl, like the twined serpents of the ark cover, emphasize visually the importance of harmonizing opposites and not perceiving the world dualistically. For a similar reason, the Torah treats the plural term "gods" (*elohim*) as a grammatical singular, thereby not denying the plurality and diversity of God's powers but emphasizing that they function as inseparable components of a synergistic unity, not as antagonistic rivals.

11. What's in a Name?

In his eightieth year, Moses the Egyptian prince and spiritual adept receives the call from his Egyptian god Thoth to lead the oppressed Israelite people to freedom. But the Israelites do not worship the Egyptian god Thoth; they worship the Canaanite god El Shaddai. (Exod 6:2–3.) What to do? Religious chauvinism is a strong force today, and it was a strong force in Moses' time, too, so Moses wonders how he will win the Israelites' trust. He asks Thoth about the problem:

> Behold, when I come to the descendants of Israel and say to them, "The god of your forefathers has sent me to you," and they say to me, "What is His name?"—what shall I say to them?[113]

Thoth (YHVH) understands the problem and offers a solution:

> This shall you say to the descendants of Israel, "YHVH, God of your forefathers, God of Abraham, God of Isaac, God of Jacob has sent me to you." *This is my name to conceal....*[114]

In other words, Thoth instructs Moses not to transliterate the name Djyehudi (Thoth) into the proto-Sinaitic script that the Israelites then used and certainly not to say the name Thoth out loud, for the Israelites would then recognize it to be the name of an Egyptian god, and they might doubt Moses' authority. Instead, Moses should use his skills as a scribe to encode Thoth's name in a compacted form as YHVH—for "this is my name to conceal." And, as we have seen, it was actually Ezra who did this concealing.

---

[113] Exod 3:13.

[114] Exod 3:15 [vowelizing the Hebrew word *L'AoLaM* ("forever") as *L'AaLaM* ("to conceal")].

One group, however, among Moses' followers knew the secret, for YHVH says in the book of Ezekiel (6th century B.C.E.): "On the day I chose Israel, I raised my hand [(Hebrew: *YaD*)] to the seed of the House of Jacob and made myself known to them...." (Ezek 20:5.) In other words, YHVH made himself known to the "House of Jacob" by raising his *YuD*—the *yud* that is hidden within the final *hei* of YHVH—thereby revealing his identity as YeHVDY (*Yehudi*), which is the *Ashuri* transliteration Djyehudi (Thoth).

But who constituted the "House of Jacob"? Recall that long after the time of Moses, King David's unified kingdom split into the Kingdom of Judah in the south, ruled by a royal house from the tribe of Judah, and the Kingdom of Israel in the north, ruled by a royal house from the tribe of Joseph, and a civil war raged between these two rival kingdoms for centuries. (See 1 Kings 11:26–39, 12:1–24, 14:30, 15:6, 15:16–21, 15:32; 2 Kings 9:27–28, 10:12–14, 13:12, 14:8–15, 16:5–7; Isa 7:1–9; Ezek 37:15–28; 2 Chron 28:5–8.) Recall also that the patriarch Jacob was called by two names, "Jacob" and "Israel." (Gen 32:29.) Of Jacob's two names, the name Israel obviously corresponds to the Kingdom of Israel, and thus also to the tribe of Joseph, which implies that the name Jacob corresponds to the Kingdom of Judah and to the tribe of Judah. For this reason, the later prophets and the book of Psalms often use the label "Jacob" as a poetic way of referring to the Southern Kingdom and its royal house. (See, e.g., Pss 77:16, 114:1–2.)[115] Hence, the reference in the book of Ezekiel to YHVH making himself known to the "House of Jacob"

---

[115] See also Isa 10:20, 14:1, 41:8, 41:14, 42:24, 43:1, 43:22, 44:1–5, 44:21–23, 45:4, 46:3, 48:1–2, 48:12, 49:5–6; Jer 2:4, 5:20; Hosea 12:3; Obad 1:18. In this context, consider also Exod 19:3; Num 23:7, 23:10, 23:21, 23:23, 24:5, 24:17; Deut 33:10; Amos 6:8, 9:8; Mic 3:1, 3:8–9; Pss 78:5, 78:21, 78:71, 147:19.

suggests that the tribe of Judah was specially privileged with secret knowledge of YHVH's true name.[116]

In other words, one group among the people who went up from Egypt knew Thoth—the god of Moses—to be its redeemer, while another group believed El Shaddai—the god of the Israelite patriarchs—to be its redeemer, and the descendants of the former group eventually became the ruling class of the Kingdom of Judah, while the descendants of the latter group became the ruling class of the Kingdom of Israel. But what difference does it make? Regardless of the label used, water is wet, fire is hot, and a monotheistic God is the indivisible sovereign intelligence of the universe. What's in a name?

As already discussed, the ancient Egyptians believed that the word for an object was not merely a convenient signifier; rather, it was the spiritual essence of the object, and words therefore had the power to change physical reality. Moreover, this effective power of language applied also to written words. According to this metaphysics, a deity was somehow particularly present wherever its name was properly inscribed, and Judaism fully embraces this same metaphysics, as is evidenced by the reverence Jews have for Torah scrolls and by the significance Jews give to amulets, door scrolls, and phylacteries.

According to this way of thinking, the deity named El Shaddai (*i.e.*, a variant of the Canaanite god Ba'al) is somehow present

---

[116] See also Exod 24:11 ["And to the nobles of the descendants of Israel, he did not send forth his *yud*."]. There was one instance, however, when YHVH revealed himself to *all* the people, and that was at the crossing of the Sea of Reeds. See Exod 14:8 ["And the descendants of Israel were going out with an elevated *yud*."], 14:31 ["And Israel saw the great *yud* that YHVH made in Egypt, and the people feared YHVH, and they had faith in YHVH and in Moses, his servant."]; Ps 78:40–42 ["In the wilderness... they did not remember his *yud*, the day that he redeemed them from the adversary."].

wherever the Hebrew letters *alef-lamed-shin-dalet-yud* (E-L-SHa-Da-Y) are properly inscribed, and the deity named YHVH (*i.e.*, the Egyptian god Thoth) is present wherever the Hebrew letters *yud-hei-vov-hei* (Y-H-V-H) are properly inscribed. The scribes who hold these beliefs do not necessarily deny that God is beyond name and form, but they assert that in our world of diverse names, God functions by way of diverse names, and each name draws down its own distinct attribute of divinity.

In Hebrew, El Shaddai, the fierce aspect of God that afflicted Job and that the Israelite patriarchs worshiped, is written שׁדי אל. Of course, one can rearrange those letters as ישׁד אל (which means "El Will Ravage"), and in that new configuration the deity named El Shaddai will remain associated with the letters.[117] Notice, however, the orthographic similarity between the El Shaddai anagram (ישׁד אל) and the letters that spell the name Israel in Hebrew (ישׂראל):

An anagram of "El Shaddai"

"Israel"

---

[117] Matt Davis, "Aoccdrnig to rscheearch at Cmabrigde Uinervtisy, it deosn't mttaer in waht oredr the ltteers in a wrod are…" (Cambridge Univ. 2012), posted at http://www.mrc-cbu.cam.ac.uk/people/matt.davis/cmabridge/ [Accessed January 4, 2017]; Rawlinson, *The Significance of Letter Position* [cited in Davis 2012].

From a scribal perspective, the only significant distinction between the two sets of letters is that the corner of the center letter is rounded in the word ישראל ("Israel"), making it into a *reish* (ר) (R) instead of a *dalet* (ד) (D).

The *Zohar* asserts, however, that a *reish* (ר) (R) is the same as a *dalet* (ד) (D),[118] and in fact the letters *reish* and *dalet*—whose names both mean "poor"—are interchangeable in Hebrew scripture. (See Num 1:14 [Deuel] and 2:14 [Reuel]; Gen 10:4 [Dodanim] and 1 Chron 1:7 [Rodanim].) Thus, ישד אל (an anagram of El Shaddai) and ישראל (the name Israel) are, in scribal terms, indistinguishable. More important, by this logic, the deity named El Shaddai attaches to the name Israel because Israel, when written in Hebrew, comprises the same letter shapes as El Shaddai's name. And Israel is, of course, the name of the Northern Kingdom.

A similar correspondence occurs in the case of the deity named YHVH, the merciful aspect of God that Moses the Egyptian introduced to the Israelites. In Hebrew, YHVH is written יהוה. These letters are nearly identical to the letters that spell the name Judah (YeHVDaH) in Hebrew (יהודה), the only distinction being the addition of a *dalet* (ד) (D) in the fourth position. According to scribal metaphysics, therefore, the deity named YHVH (Thoth) attaches to the name Judah (YeHVDaH) because Judah, when written in Hebrew, comprises the same letter shapes as YHVH's (Thoth's) name. And Judah is, of course, the name of the Southern Kingdom.

In other words, each of the two rival kingdoms that emerged from David's unified monarchy bears in the letter shapes of its own name the name of its predominant deity. Judah is the kingdom whose temple in Jerusalem was dedicated to YHVH, and whose people frequently used the theophoric element "*yahu*" or "*yah*" in their personal names, and the Kingdom of Judah

---

118 See *Zohar* 3:180b, translated in Matt, *The Zohar: Pritzker Edition*, vol. IX, pp. 195–196.

(YeHVDaH) bears a variant of the name YHVH as its own name. Conversely, Israel is the kingdom whose temple in Beth-El ("House of El") was dedicated to El Shaddai (a god likened to Ba'al),[119] and whose people frequently used the theophoric element "El" or "Ba'al" in their personal names, and the Kingdom of Israel bears a variant of the name El Shaddai as its own name.[120] None of this is mere coincidence.

If there is any doubt that the name Israel (ישראל) is an intentional anagram of El Shaddai (אל-שדי), consider the Torah story of how Jacob received the name Israel. (Gen 32:23–33.) A "man" (identified also as an "angel" and a "god"—see Hosea 12:3–5) wrestles Jacob at the Ford of Jabbok. When this angel cannot prevail against Jacob, he gives Jacob the name Israel. (Gen 32:29.) Jacob (now called "Israel") then says to the angel, "Tell, please, your name," and the angel answers, "You asked for my name," and blesses him. (Gen 32:30.) Jacob then calls the place "Face of El." (Gen 32:31.)

---

[119] See Gen 35:1–15 [Shaddai worshiped at Beth-El]; 2 Kings 17:16 [Ba'al worshiped at Beth-El]; Hosea 13:1–2 [Ba'al worshiped at Beth-El].

[120] Of course, we are speaking here in general terms. The element "El" or "Ba'al" sometimes appears in names from the Southern Kingdom, and the element "*yahu*" (or its Northern Kingdom variant, "*yu*") sometimes appears in names from the Northern Kingdom. There can be little doubt that by the 8th century B.C.E., YHVH worship was widespread in the Northern Kingdom (one of the priests at Beth-El was named AmatzYah, meaning "YHVH is steadfast"). Nonetheless, Yahwist names are much more common in the Southern Kingdom than in the Northern Kingdom, as is attested in both scripture and archaeological sources. A good non-scriptural source for Southern Kingdom names is the Lachish ostraca, which include several names with the Yahwist element "*yahu*." A good non-scriptural source for Northern Kingdom names is the Samaria ostraca, which likewise include Yahwist names (using the element "*yu*"), but in which Canaanite names and names using the element "El" or "Ba'al" are more prevalent.

The story is cryptic, but a different version of the origin of Jacob's new name Israel is told a few chapters later, adding more clarity. (Gen 35:9–15.) In this second version of the story, it is expressly a "god" (not a "man" or an "angel") who gives Jacob the name Israel. This god identifies himself as El Shaddai (Gen 35:10–11), and Jacob calls the place "Temple of El" (*i.e.*, Beth-El, the location of the Northern Kingdom's main temple). The added datum that it is specifically the god El Shaddai who gives Jacob the name Israel clarifies the first version of the story. In that first version, Jacob asks the angel to reveal his name (Gen 32:30), and the angel responds, "You asked for my name." The response is usually rendered into English as a dismissive rhetorical question: "You asked [to know] my name!?" But the angel's response—"You asked for my name"—can just as well be rendered as a literal assertion: "You asked for [(*i.e.*, you asked to have)] my name." In other words, the angel says, in effect, "The name I just bestowed on you (Israel, an anagram of El Shaddai), *that* is my name."

In summary, the Northern Kingdom's name, Israel, is equivalent to the name of its god El Shaddai, and the Southern Kingdom's name, Judah, is equivalent to the name of its god YHVH, and the division of the Davidic kingdom into two parts was not at its root a *political* division, but rather a *religious* and *ideological* division.[121]

Jacob blessed his son Judah (the patriarch of the Southern Kingdom's royal house), saying: "The congress of nations is his." (Gen 49:10.) That blessing implies a diverse community, comprising many ethnicities. The people of Southern Kingdom nurtured a great love for YHVH, and according to Judean lore, YHVH was the name of the god that redeemed the people from

---

[121] This idea is particularly well developed in the writings of the Ishbitzer Rebbe. The Ishbitzer draws a sharp distinction between "Judah Jews" and "Joseph Jews." See, e.g., Magid, *Hasidism on the Margin*, pp. 170, 174, 198, 206, 237.

Egypt (see, e.g., Exod 13:3, 13:9, 13:14, 13:16). In their temple in Jerusalem, the people of Judah worshiped YHVH as a speaking spirit that sat between a pair of intertwined *cheruv*s, implying the unification of opposites.

By contrast, Jacob blessed Joseph (the patriarch of the Northern Kingdom's royal house), saying: "From El, your father, and he will help you, and Shaddai, and he will bless you...." (Gen 49:25.) That blessing clearly links Joseph to El Shaddai, the god of the patriarchs. The people of the Northern Kingdom nurtured a great love for El Shaddai, and according to Israelite lore, El was the name of the god that redeemed the people from Egypt (see, e.g., Num 23:22, 24:8). In their temple in Beth-El, the Israelites worshiped El Shaddai in the form of a golden calf (see 1 Kings 12:28–29; 2 Kings 17:16; Hosea 8:4–6, 13:1–2), an image that was associated with the Canaanite Ba'al and that the Torah unambiguously condemns (see Exod 32). And the book of Hosea also makes clear that the Northern Kingdom continued the practice of child sacrifice that is linked to Shaddai by the Deir 'Alla text and Psalm 106. (See Hosea 13:1–2; see also 2 Kings 16:3, 17:16–17; Jer 3:20–25; Ezek 20:26, 20:31, 23:37–39; Mic 6:7; Ps 106:35–38.)

The book of Isaiah makes direct reference to this religious and ideological division between the two kingdoms, asserting: "This one will say, 'I belong to YHVH,'... and this one... will be surnamed with the name Israel." (Isa 44:5.) And as we have learned, this deep cultural divide eventually erupted into centuries of civil war. (See 1 Kings 11:26–39, 12:1–24, 14:30, 15:6, 15:16–21, 15:32; 2 Kings 9:27–28, 10:12–14, 13:12, 14:8–15, 16:5–7; Isa 7:1–9; Ezek 37:15–28; 2 Chron 28:5–8.) Moreover, the pain of that cultural divide continues even today.

In 1948 C.E., during the debate over the naming of the modern State of Israel, the advocates of the name Israel asserted that Israel (an anagram of the name El Shaddai) was the true name of the Jewish people, and they downplayed the significance of the names Judah (*Yehudah*) and Jew (*Yehudi*), names that are variants of the name YHVH, arguing that the latter names were provincial in origin and had become names for the Jewish people only as a result of foreign influences. One influential writer who participated in this debate argued:

> [*Yehudi*] is not our nation's primary or principal name. The name [*Yehudi*] spread to some extent after the destruction of Israel's Northern Kingdom. Judea [(*Yehudah*)] inherited Israel, but not all of it and not eternally. The name "Israel" was not forgotten and not annulled. After Judea [(*Yehudah*)] collapsed…, the name "Israel" necessarily arose again and regained primacy of place. The meaning of this is undoubtedly: The Kingdom of Judea [(*Yehudah*)] falls but the nation of Israel lives.[122]

Anyone who knows that the name Israel is an anagram of the divine name El Shaddai and that *Yehudah* and *Yehudi* are pronunciations of the divine name YHVH would recognize the reverberations of an ancient religious polemic in the foregoing quote.

But more important, it appears that Hebrew scripture relates the history of *two* nations and *two* religions, not one. In one of these two nations, God is El Shaddai, the patriarch is Israel, and his heir is Joseph. In the other, God is YHVH, the patriarch is Jacob, and his heir is Judah.

> Two names for the father of the tribes: *Jacob* and *Israel*.
> Two wives: *Leah* and *Rachel*.
> Two heirs: *Judah* and *Joseph*.
> Two groups that went forth from Egypt: *House of Jacob*
>   and *Descendants of Israel*.
> Two leaders: *Moses* and *Aaron*.
> Two gods: YHVH and El Shaddai.

---

[122] Letter by Aharon Reuveni, Israel State Archives (1965), translated in "Why not Judea? Zion? State of the Hebrews?" *Haaretz*, May 7, 2008. See http://www.haaretz.com/why-not-judea-zion-state-of-the-hebrews-1.245441 [accessed August 4, 2013].

Two kingdoms: *Judah* and *Israel.*

Two priestly houses: *Levi* and *Aaron.*

Two sets of Tablets: *The Torah of Judah* and *the Torah of Israel.*

Two Messiahs: *Messiah son of David* and *Messiah son of Joseph.*

But recall that Shaddai is the white space surrounding the letters of YHVH (see pp. 81–91, above) and that two are always really one—duality spells disaster.

Those who have closely studied the Torah delight in its circularity, observing motifs and even whole stories that repeat themselves. And, as we have noted, some passages of the Torah seem to strongly favor YHVH, while others seem to favor Elohim, El, or Shaddai. Moreover, one can discern clear stylistic and semantic distinctions within the text, as well as differences in ideological emphasis. To explain these data, modern biblical scholars have developed the documentary hypothesis, which asserts that the Torah we have today is woven together from multiple sources.

Consider, then, that in ancient times there were *two* tellings of the tale we now call Torah; one preserved in a set of texts from the Southern Kingdom that emphasized YHVH, and the other preserved in a set of texts from the Northern Kingdom that emphasized El and his pantheon. And the Bible's later prophets inform us that neither kingdom could claim to have the *true Torah.* Through the mouth of the prophet Ezekiel (*Yechezq-El*), YHVH says that, due to the intransigence of the Northern Kingdom, he "gave to them decrees that were not good and ordinances with which they could not live." (Ezek 20:25.) And through the mouth of the prophet Jeremiah (*Yirem-Yahu*), YHVH says to the inhabitants of Jerusalem: "How [can] you say, 'We are wise, and the Torah of YHVH is with us'? Indeed, behold, the pen of false scribes fashioned a lie." (Jer 8:8.) In other words, there were *two* Torahs, not one, and neither was without error.[123]

---

[123] Jewish mystics have long held that there are *two* Torahs, but this idea

But then a very wise person—or perhaps a group of people—took these two distinct scriptural records and intertwined them, like the *cheruv*s above the ark, to produce a single narrative with a single God for a single nation. By that syncretism, two localized national gods, YHVH and El, became one omnipresent universal God, and it is that syncretism that lies at the heart of Jewish monotheism.

Therefore, the documentary hypothesis appears to be valid at least in its basic premise, if not in all its specifics. There is a fundamental split that lies deep in Judaism, so deep that it goes all the way back to the man who fathered the tribes: Was he Jacob, the husband of Leah, or was he Israel, the husband of Rachel? But before we unravel all the strands of this cultural divide, let us consider that there is an important principle underlying the dogma of a monolithic Torah, for it is the very essence of Judaism to make unity out of multiplicity, to make harmony out of discord, to make synergy out of contentiousness. The Torah is the "Philosopher's Stone," fashioned from the perfect union of seemingly antagonistic elements, and the principal teaching of the Torah is the reconciliation of conflict: Do not eat from the Tree of Knowledge of Good and Evil—from the Tree, that is, of Dualistic Thought. (Gen 2:17.)

12. The Ten Words

We have now examined why the book of Exodus is called, in Hebrew, "Names" (*Shemot*), and we have explicated in detail the powerful names of God that are revealed in that book. Therefore, we are ready to return to the book's surface story.

In accordance with YHVH's instructions, Moses confronts Pharaoh, demanding the liberation of the Israelite people. (Exod

---

is generally interpreted as referring to a Torah for present times and a Torah for messianic times. See, e.g., Scholem, *The Messianic Idea in Judaism*, pp. 49–77.

7:10 to 12:36.) A battle of the wonderworkers ensues, pitting Moses and Aaron against Pharaoh's most skilled priests. Moses and Aaron, using Moses' staff, bring down ten plagues upon Egypt, each one more dramatic than the one that precedes it. The ten plagues correspond, of course, to the ten gods of the Heliopolitan pantheon. Based on type and phraseology, the plagues are neatly divisible into three sets of three, plus a tenth.[124] The tenth plague is the death of Egypt's firstborn—in other words, the death of Pharaoh's son and heir, the "Horus" of the next generation. (Exod 12:29.) That final plague is too much for Pharaoh to bear, and he acknowledges YHVH (Exod 12:31–32) and permits the Israelites to leave.

Thus, under Moses' leadership, the Israelites escape Egypt, departing in such haste that the women could not set dough aside overnight to ferment (Exod 12:34), for in those days dough was allowed to ferment naturally rather than by adding yeast. The Egyptian army pursues the fleeing Israelites, Pharaoh having reconsidered his decision to allow them to leave (Exod 14:5–18), but the Israelites—on foot and blessed by favorable weather conditions (Exod 14:21)—are able to make their way across the papyrus marshlands (the "Sea of Reeds") that separate Egypt from the Sinai Peninsula (Exod 14:22). It is possible that Moses, who had crossed the marshes several times before, knew the most favorable route. (Exod 13:17–18, 14:1–4, 14:13–16.) The

---

[124] The first three plagues establish the following pattern: forewarned, forewarned, and not forewarned. That pattern then repeats for plagues four through six, and for plagues seven through nine. Also, the first plague of each of the three triads is forewarned using the phrase "in the morning," and the instructions for the first plague of each triad includes the phrase "station yourself," while the instructions for the second plague of each triad includes the phrase "go to pharaoh." The first triad are plagues done by Aaron, the second triad are plagues done by God (with one exception), and the third triad are plagues done by Moses. On these patterns, see Hayes, *Introduction to the Bible*, p. 113.

winds then shift (Exod 14:26–28), and the rising waters make the marshes impassable for the wheels of the Egyptian chariots (Exod 14:23–30). Thus, the Israelites escape to safety.

When the Israelites finally arrive safely on the far side of the marshes, they acknowledge YHVH, Moses' god, and they sing a song of praise. (Exod 15:1–21.) The Torah hints that at that ecstatic moment the full name *Yehudi* (Thoth) was briefly revealed to all Israelites: "And Israel saw the great *YaD/YuD* that YHVH made in Egypt, and the people respected YHVH, and they had faith in YHVH and in Moses, his servant." (Exod 14:31; see Exod 14:8; Ps 78:40–42.)

Several adventures follow next, each laden with symbolic meaning. These include: the bitter waters of Marah, which Moses sweetens with a "Tree" (Exod 15:22–27); the mysterious food from heaven (manna), giving cause for instructions about Sabbath observance (Exod 16); the battle in Rephidim in which Moses raises "his hand" (*YaD/YuD*), thereby strengthening the troops (Exod 17); and the meeting with Jethro in which Jethro declares YHVH to be "greater than all the gods" (Exod 18). Finally, the Israelites arrive at Mount Sinai.

Some passages suggest that Mount Sinai—which we have identified as Serabit el-Khadim—was the original destination of Moses and the Israelites and that the idea of continuing onward to Canaan arose only later. (See Exod 3:12, 3:18, 5:1, 5:3, 7:16, 8:4, 8:21–25.) This possibility makes sense because at Serabit el-Khadim the Israelites would have encountered (and could have joined) an existing community of Hebrew-speaking mineworkers. When the Israelites arrive at Sinai, they camp at the base of the mountain, and Moses ascends the mountain to confer with YHVH—that is, with Thoth, one of the gods worshiped at the mountaintop temple in Serabit el-Khadim. Then Moses returns to the Israelite base camp, and in accord with YHVH's instructions, the Israelites purify themselves. On the third day, they witness a dramatic theophany in which the mountain seems to erupt in fire and they hear certain "words." (Exod 19; 20:1.)

As noted, the Torah never mentions "Ten Commandments"; it speaks instead of "ten words." (Deut 10:4; see Deut 4:10–13.) The Ten Commandments (*i.e.*, the list of ethical and ritual laws that appears in Exod 20) are not necessarily the same as the "ten words" that the Israelites heard God speak. It is worth noting in passing, however, that the first of the Ten Commandments ("I am YHVH, your god") uses the Egyptian word for "I" (*anokhi*), not the Hebrew word for "I" (*ani*), subtly implying that YHVH is from Egypt.

The *Bahir* (12th century C.E.) gives a much more detailed account of the mysterious "ten words" that the Israelites heard at Sinai. The ten words were actually ten *"vocalizations"* of the name YHVH—ten pronunciations of the name, that is—and seven of these vocalizations *appeared as visible entities*, one for each iteration of the phrase "vocalization of YHVH" in Psalm 29.[125] To reach this conclusion, the *Bahir* relies on a very literal reading of Exod 20:15:

> [Torah] says [in Exod 20:15], "And all the people saw the vocalizations...." These are the [seven] vocalizations [of the name YHVH] regarding which King David spoke [in Ps 29:3–9].... This teaches us that the Torah was given with seven vocalizations [of the name YHVH]. In each of them, the master of the universe revealed himself to them [(*i.e.*, to the Israelites)], *and they saw him*. It is thus written [in Exod 20:15], "And all the people saw the vocalizations...."[126]

The *Bahir* further explains that, of these seven visible vocaliza-

---

[125] The Hebrew word translated here as "vocalization" is the word *kol*, which means "sound" or "voice," but in the context of referring to the "sound" of an obscurely spelled name, it can be translated as "pronunciation" or "vocalization."

[126] *Bahir*, No. 45, translated in Kaplan, *The Bahir*, pp. 15–16 [Kaplan's translation has been modified slightly]; see also *Bahir*, Nos. 48 and 49.

tions of the name YHVH, six appeared in the sky and only one appeared on the earth. The *Bahir* says:

> One verse [(Exod 19:20)] says, "And YHVH came down on Mount Sinai…." [But another] verse [(Exod 20:22)] says, "From the heavens I spoke to you." How is this reconciled? His "Great Fire" was on earth, and this was one vocalization [of the name YHVH]. The other vocalizations [of the name YHVH] were in the heavens. It is thus written [(Deut 4:36)]: "From the heavens he let you hear his voice, that he might instruct you. And on earth he showed you his Great Fire…."[127]

Finally, the *Bahir* emphasizes God's ultimate unity, clarifying that all the "ten words" were actually heard as a *single* "vocalization" that was somehow the culmination and totality of the ten. The *Bahir* says:

> At first they saw the… vocalizations mentioned by David [in Psalm 29]. But in the end, they heard the word [(singular)] that emanated from them all.
> [Question:] But we have learned that there were ten [words]?
> [Answer:] Our sages taught that they all were said with a single utterance.[128]

What then, according to the *Bahir*'s obscure hints, were the "ten words" that YHVH spoke at Mount Sinai—that is, the ten "vocalizations" of the name YHVH? They correspond, of course, to the ten *sefirot* of the Kabbalah, the configuration of divine powers that supplanted the Heliopolitan pantheon. And if the "ten words" refer to the ten *sefirot*, what then were the six "vocalizations" that the Israelites "saw" as astrological luminaries

---

[127] *Bahir*, No. 46, translated in Kaplan, *The Bahir*, p. 16 [Kaplan's translation has been modified slightly]; see also *Bahir*, No. 49.

[128] *Bahir*, No. 48, translated in Kaplan, *The Bahir*, p. 17 [Kaplan's translation has been modified slightly].

in the "heavens"? They saw the six *sefirot* (*Chesed* through *Yesod*) that together constitute the single corpus called "*Zeir Anpin*." And what then was the one "vocalization"—the "Great Fire"—that the Israelites "saw" "on earth"? They saw the last of the *sefirot*, *Malkhut* ("kingship"), signifying God's presence in and stewardship of the world. And what was the single "word" that "emanated from them all," by which all ten words "were said with a single utterance"? Perhaps, the *Bahir* is referring to the word *Yehudi*.

In summary, the Israelites witnessed a planetary conjunction in the heavens, they saw Moses, their king, on the earth, and they heard Moses invoke the name of his Egyptian god Djyehudi. That is a radical interpretation of the theophany at Sinai, but it finds confirmation in Moses' later retelling of the event: "Moses summoned all of Israel and said to them:... '*Face in a face*, YHVH spoke with you in the mountain amidst the fire; *I stood between* YHVH *and you in that time to relate to you the word* YHVH [(*i.e.*, to reveal the name Djyehudi)], for you were afraid from before the fire, and you did not ascend in the mountain.'" (Deut 5:1–15.)

13. "Make for me a sanctuary"

Immediately after the theophany at Sinai, Moses gives the Israelites a code of civil law. (Exod 20:23–23:19.) This section of the book of Exodus is often called the "Covenant Code" (see Exod 24:3–8), and scholars have persuasively shown that it is based on the Code of Hammurabi (Babylon, 1772 B.C.E.). Moreover, scholars have found strong evidence that the Torah's revision and incorporation of this ancient law code dates to the 7th century B.C.E., more than 600 years *after* the time of Moses.[129]

---

[129] See Wright, *Inventing God's Law*, pp. 346–363.

Nonetheless, Exodus describes the Israelites at Sinai agreeing to be bound by this ancient code.

Moses then ascends the mountain to be with YHVH for forty days—that is, he ascends again to Thoth's mountaintop temple in Serabit el-Khadim. (Exod 24:1–2, 24:9–18.) There, he receives detailed instructions on the building of a mobile sanctuary. Once that sanctuary has been erected, YHVH (Thoth) will descend the mountain to live where the Israelites are camped. "They shall make for me a sanctuary," YHVH tells Moses, "and I will dwell among them." (Exod 25:8.) According to YHVH's instruction, the innermost part of the sanctuary will contain the ark and its gold cover, adorned with the twined *cheruv*s, and YHVH will sit, just like Tutankhamen, enthroned between the *cheruv*s. YHVH also provides Moses with detailed instructions about the dedication of the sanctuary and the daily offerings. (Exod 25–31.)

While Moses is up on the mountain, YHVH gives Moses "two tablets of testimony, tablets of stone, inscribed by the finger of God." (Exod 31:18.) These steles, which are to be placed within the ark, are inscribed with the same "ten words" that YHVH previously spoke to the people. (Deut 4:10–13.) The Torah further relates that "the tablets were the work of God, and the script, it was the script of God—*freedom on the tablets*." (Exod 32:16.)[130] Thus, YHVH's primary law—engraved on the first set of tablets—is the law of freedom, but perhaps the Israelites are not ready for the law of freedom.

While Moses is up on the mountain, the Israelites, waiting in the arid desert below, become impatient, and they begin to doubt Moses. (Exod 32.) They pressure Aaron, and under Aaron's leadership, they take their gold ornaments and fashion a

---

[130] This translation of Exodus 32:16 vowelizes CH-R-U-T as *CHeiRUT* ("freedom") instead of as *CHaRUT* ("engraved"). On this vowelization of the Hebrew text, see, e.g., *Zohar* 1:63b, translated in Matt, *The Zohar: Pritzker Edition*, vol. I, p. 369; 1:131b, vol. II, p. 238; 2:113b–114a, vol. V, p. 135; 2:183a, vol. VI, pp. 27–28.

golden calf (an image associated with Ba'al) to lead them on
their journey. (Exod 32:1, 32:23.) They then begin to worship
the calf in a wanton and riotous manner (Exod 32:6, 32:17–18),
saying: "These are your gods, Israel, that raised you up from the
land of Egypt" (Exod 32:4).

Meanwhile, up on the mountain, YHVH warns Moses of what
is transpiring below, and YHVH threatens to annihilate the Israelites and to make a new nation from Moses himself. (Exod
32:10.) Moses, however, pleads on their behalf, reminding YHVH
of his promise to make the descendants of the Israelite patriarchs
abundant. (Exod 32:13.) Hearing Moses' plea, YHVH eventually
relents. (Exod 32:11–14, 32:30–35.) This moving exchange
implies, of course, that Moses was not a biological descendant
of the patriarchs because, if he were, then the annihilation of the
Israelites and the making of a new nation from Moses would not
be inconsistent with YHVH's promise to make the descendants
of the patriarchs abundant. In this way, the text again hints that
Moses is an Egyptian, not an Israelite.

In the course of beseeching YHVH, Moses descends from the
mountain, witnesses the actions of the Israelites, and shatters
the tablets that God engraved. (Exod 32:19.) The tribe of Levi
then declares its loyalty to Moses. (Exod 32:26–29.) This Levite
expression of loyalty eventually becomes the basis for making
the Levites into an elite priesthood, but many centuries later, a
rivalry develops within this priestly caste, mirroring the implicit
rivalry in the Torah between Moses (the Egyptian priest) and
Aaron (the Israelite priest).

After rebuking the people for their worship of the golden calf,
Moses again ascends the mountain to speak with YHVH (Exod
32:30–31), and YHVH threatens to send his "angel"—a fierce
aspect of divinity—to lead the people, instead of YHVH doing
so directly (Exod 23:20–23, 33:1–3). It is clear at this point that
Serabit el-Khadim is no longer the destination of the Israelites;
rather, their destination is Canaan, the land of their ancestors,
but the idea that YHVH's fierce angel will lead them to Canaan

is troubling to Moses, and Moses pleads for YHVH to lead the people directly. (Exod 33, esp. 33:12–17.) Among other things, Moses reminds YHVH (Djyehudi) that YHVH has known Moses "by name," thus hinting that Moses' full name was "Djyehudi-mose" (*i.e.*, Thutmose), and Moses asks YHVH to accept the Israelites as YHVH's own.

Finally, YHVH agrees to lead the people, saying to Moses: "I will transfer all my goodness upon your face, and I will call in the name YHVH before you." (Exod 33:19.) Moses is thus commissioned to act as YHVH's earthly representative. YHVH then instructs Moses: "Carve yourself two stone tablets like the first, and I [(*i.e.*, YHVH)] will write on the tablets the [same] words that were on the first tablets that you shattered." (Exod 34:1; see also Deut 10:1–4.) The same "ten words," but not necessarily in the same configuration, for the ten *sefirot* of the Kabbalah are not in the same configuration as the Heliopolitan pantheon.

Moses hearkens to YHVH's command; he carves "two stone tablets like the first ones," and he once again ascends the mountain. (Exod 34:4.) Moses remains "there with YHVH forty days and forty nights—bread he did not eat, and water he did not drink." (Exod 34:28.) The word "forty" signifies, according to the Kabbalah, *chalav* ("milk"), because of the numeric values traditionally associated with the letters of the word *CHaLaV* (*chet*=8, *lamed*=30, *beit*=2). Although Moses did not eat bread or drink water, he did not die because he traveled, as Bedouins still do today, with a goat that could forage for food among the desert plants and provide Moses with about a liter of milk, morning and night.[131] In other words, Moses undertook a lengthy milk fast while on the mountain, and for that reason pious Jews consume

---

[131] The small Black Bedouin goat is indigenous to the desert areas of the Middle East. A female goat can travel long distances for water, returning at night to the camp to nurse her kids, and she can produce milk for up to four days without drinking. See Shkolnik et al., "Desert Conditions and Goat Milk Production," pp. 1749–1754.

milk products on Shavuot, the day in the ritual calendar that is associated with the giving of the Torah. During Moses' forty-day milk fast, YHVH writes on the tablets "the words of the covenant, the ten words." (Exod 34:28.) Moses then descends from the mountain with the two tablets, the skin of his face aglow. (Exod 34:29–35.)

The story about the golden calf and Moses pleading on behalf of the Israelites appears to be added to the Torah as a late-date religious polemic favoring the god of the Southern Kingdom (YHVH—a god worshiped on a throne between two *cheruv*s) over the god of the Northern Kingdom (El Shaddai—a god worshiped in the form of a golden calf). In any case, the Israelites follow Moses' instructions, constructing the mobile sanctuary exactly as prescribed by YHVH, and the "Glory of YHVH" then enters the sanctuary and fills it. (Exod 35–40; Num 7.) But the Hebrew term *Kevod* YHVH, which means the "Glory of YHVH," can also be translated as the "weightiness of YHVH," implying a physical form, and several statements in the Torah suggest that YHVH dwelled within the sanctuary as an anthropomorphic presence.

For example, the Torah calls Moses "the husband of God" (Deut 33:1), and it relates that "YHVH spoke to Moses face to face, as a man speaks to his friend" (Exod 33:11; see also Num 12:8). In addition, the ark in the sanctuary happens to be just large enough to fit a small person (Exod 25:10), and Aaron is instructed to wear bells on the hem of his clothing as a warning of his arrival whenever he enters the sanctuary (Exod 28:33–35). Finally, in several instances the *Kevod* YHVH is said *to appear* before Moses, Aaron, or the Israelites. (Exod 16:7, 16:10, 24:16–17; Lev 9:6, 9:23; Num 14:10, 16:19, 17:7, 20:6.)[132]

---

[132] Nahmanides (13th century c.e.), a highly regarded Jewish commentator on the Torah, asserted that YHVH can be revealed in human form. See Wolfson, "The Secret of the Garment in Nahmanides," pp. 25–49; Wolfson, *Through a Speculum That Shines*, pp. 13–51, 255–269. Moreover, as

14. Gnosis versus Praxis

With regard to the new tablets that YHVH gave Moses after Moses shattered the first set, the text does not make perfectly clear who inscribed these tablets: YHVH or Moses. Is this new law one that comes directly from YHVH, as did the law of freedom that was inscribed on the first set of tablets, or is this new law one that comes filtered through Moses? YHVH said: "Carve yourself two stone tablets like the first ones, and I [(*i.e.*, YHVH)] will write on the tablets the words [(*devorim*)] that were on the first tablets that you shattered." (Exod 34:1; see also Exod 34:28; Deut 10:1–4.) But YHVH also dictated various terms of the new covenant to Moses (Exod 34:11–26) and then said to Moses: "Write for *yourself* these words [(*devorim*)]." (Exod 34:27.) Moreover, Moses and the Israelites enter into yet another covenant when they arrive in Moab, a covenant that is expressly distinct from the covenant YHVH sealed with the people at Sinai (see Deut 28:69, 31:9, 31:24–26, 33:4), and the immediate source of *that* covenant is also unclear.

One possible solution to the puzzle lies in the specific reference to the ten "words" (*devorim*). (Deut 10:4; see also Exod 34:28; Deut 4:10–13.) According to the Torah's telling of the story, the law given directly by YHVH comprises only ten words—ten divine powers. It was these ten words that YHVH wrote on

---

Christians will point out, some Bible passages use the honorific "son [of God]" to refer to the kings of Judah. See 2 Sam 7:14; Pss 2:7, 89:27–28. Mainstream Judaism, of course, rejects the idea of divine incarnation, except to the extent that it refers to God being incarnate in all of creation or in all Jews collectively. See Exod 4:22 ["My son, my firstborn, Israel."]; Deut 4:35–39 [nothing exists besides God]; Jer 31:8 ["for I have been to Israel for a father, and Ephraim is my firstborn"], 31:19 [same]; Hosea 11:1 ["For Israel is a lad, and I love him, and since Egypt, I have called to my son."]; Ps 82:6 ["You are gods and the sons of the Most High, all of you."].

the second set of tablets. But Moses shared a critical role, for he added ritual "decrees and ordinances" that constituted the same ten words enacted in dramatic form, enabling the Israelites to unite themselves, through ritual performance, with the ten divine aspects. As Moses put it: "YHVH commanded me at that time to teach you decrees and ordinances that you shall *perform....*" (Deut 4:14.)[133] And the people agreed to do so, saying: "All the [ten] words that YHVH spoke we will *perform.*" (Exod 24:3.) Thus, through Moses' decrees and ordinances, the ten divine powers that constitute YHVH's mystical teaching became a ritualized way of living.

Consider, by way of example, the commandment related to ritual handwashing. (Exod 30:17–21.) The priest (and, by long tradition, anyone who undertakes a holy act) rinses both hands with water, raises them up, and then blesses YHVH, "who sanctifies us with his commandments and commands us concerning the elevation of the hands." In reciting this blessing, one speaks the Hebrew word *YaDaYiM* ("pair of hands"), and one elevates one's two hands, but by scribal logic, one is ritually elevating the "*YuDaYiM*" ("pair of *yud*s") of the name YHVH, including the hidden *yud* at the end of that name, thereby ritually revealing the name *Yehudi*.

In that way, one expresses the secret name by way of enacted writing rather than ordinary speech, and enacted writing is, according to ritual thought, much more powerful than ordinary speech because it requires more intentionality and because it is not easily done with a profane intent. A similar metaphysics underlies the sacrificial ritual at the temple. The sacrificer "supports his hand" (*samakh YaDO*) upon the head of the sacrificial animal (see, e.g., Lev 1:4, 3:2), and by doing so, the sacrificer subtly "supports His *yud*" (*samakh YuDO*)—that is, he supports

---

133 See also Exod 35:1; Lev 8:5, 8:36, 9:6; Deut 1:14, 1:18, 24:18, 24:22, 28:58, 29:8, 29:28, 31:12, 32:46.

the hidden *yud* at the end of YHVH's name. The Torah includes many more examples of rituals that can be explained as a form of enacted writing based on the shapes and components of Hebrew letters and the alternative meanings of their names.

In summary, Moses took the "ten words" that are the essence of Heliopolitan Creation, and he transliterated them into the alphabet of sacred deed, making them something a person could *do*, not merely *know*. We are physical creatures living in a world of action, not disembodied spirits living in a world of the imagination. Therefore, according to ritual thought, it is not enough for a spiritual seeker to sit in a cave and contemplate high ideals; rather, a seeker must act out those ideals, making them real. Moses' decrees and ordinances represent an opportunity not just to know the highest truth intellectually, but also to be it with one's limbs and with one's vital energies, for action is perhaps the most profound form of knowing.

But there is another reason why one might want to observe the rituals of the Torah. One might want to do so in order to be called "*Yehudi*" ("Jew"), for to be called "*Yehudi*" is to be called by God's own name. Moses explained: "It shall be that if you listen carefully to the vocalization of YHVH, your god, to observe [and] to perform all his commandments that I command you this day, then... all the peoples of the earth will see that the name YHVH [(*i.e.*, *Yehudi*)] is proclaimed over you, and they will revere you." (Deut 28:10.)

15. Names

In this commentary on the book of Exodus—a book called "Names" (*Shemot*) in Hebrew—we have learned a few of the names of God that are encoded in Hebrew scripture, but there are many others that we might also have discussed. There is the name Emet ("Truth"), which is similar to the Egyptian word *maat* (also meaning "Truth"). Maat was an Egyptian god, and as we will recall, Djyehudi was the one who "wrote *maat*." There is also the name Amein ("Amen") that Jews, Christians, and Muslims repeat after a blessing (see e.g., Num 5:22; Deut 27:15–26; Jer 28:6), thus invoking the Egyptian god Amun. The book of Isaiah makes the connection to Amun explicit, asserting: "The one who blesses in the land, he will bless by the god of AMuN, and the one who swears in the land, he will swear by the god of AMuN." (Isa 65:16). In addition, there are the personal gods of the Israelite patriarchs, the "Magein of Abraham" (Gen 15:1), the "Pachad of Isaac" (Gen 31:42, 31:53), and the "Avir of Jacob" (Gen 49:24; Isa 60:16), each being an invocation of a particular divine potency. There is the god called "Makom Acheir," invoked in the book of Esther (Esther 4:14), and also Elyon and Tzur, names of God invoked in the song of Moses (Deut 32:8). And there are the names of the twelve stones on the breastplate of the chief priest (Exod 28:17–20), names that some people consider to be divine potencies. In addition, there is the seventy-two-letter name by which Moses split the Sea of Reeds. (Exod 14:19–21.) Likewise, there is the forty-two-letter name (the initial letters of the *Ana B'Koach* prayer), a divine name that derives from the letters of the first two verses of the Torah. There is YHVH's statement of the thirteen attributes of mercy, which together constitute a single powerful name of God. (Exod 34:6–7.) And there is also the name Achod ("One") from the *Shema* prayer: "Hear, O Israel; YHVH is our God; YHVH is *Achod*." (Deut 6:4; see also Zech 14:9.) Some mystics even assert that the Hebrew word for "Love" (*Ahavah*) is a particularly potent name of God, and of course for the faithful, the entire Torah is nothing but divine names, from beginning to end.

Two names, however, are particularly important. A people went forth from Egypt, worshiping El the Magnificent, the foremost deity of the Canaanite pantheon. Another people walked beside them, worshiping Djyehudi, the Egyptian god of scribes and scholars. Rivalries, especially religious rivalries, often run deep, but the book of Psalms boldly asserts that "Djyehudi is El the Magnificent." (Ps 95:3.) The two gods are really one.

If God is called "Gesu" in Rome and "Shiva" in Benares and "Yehudi" in Jerusalem and "Allah" in Mecca, but God is nevertheless one, then does God have a true name? If water is called "*acqua*" in Italian and "*paani*" in Hindi and "*mayim*" in Hebrew and "*maa*" in Arabic, and water is nevertheless one, then does water have a true name? Is *mayim* water's true name, being the name from the oldest language? But what name did the ancient Egyptians use for "water"? What name was used in the Vedas? The further back in history we go, the more the names resonate with primordial power. But stand at the bank of a river, reach out, and cup the water in one's palms. Watch the sun glisten and sparkle on the surface. Feel the drops pour through one's fingers. Hear it splash back to the river below. Taste it on one's lips. Inhale its pure fragrance. That's the true name of "water." The other names are just invocations.

PART THREE

The Enacted Metaphor
A Commentary on Leviticus

With the sacrifice the gods sacrificed to the Sacrifice.

—*Rg Veda* 10.90.16

1. Fractal Geometry—
The Whole in Each of the Parts

In a psalm of praise to YHVH, King David sings: "For I see your heavens, the works of your fingers, the moon and the stars that you set. What is man that you remember him?" (Ps 8:4.)

"What *isn't* man?" YHVH might have responded. "Man—male and female—is the most marvelous, most complete, creature of the universe, replicating the union of heaven and earth by combining in a single integrated being a refined soul and a material body."

But, we may ask, isn't man merely a complex self-replicating series of chemical processes whose so-called "consciousness" is an illusion explained by functionalism? Isn't man merely an accident of trillions of incremental and random mutations? Isn't man an infinitesimally small and insignificant animal, walking the crusty ridges of a watery planet somewhere on a rather unimportant edge of a vast, swirling galaxy in an unimpressive corner of an even vaster expanding universe? Isn't man merely a highly evolved primate, having developed both language and analytical reasoning, endowed with inventiveness and ingenuity, seeking ever-greater security, pleasure, and amusement, producing offspring, and then dying a permanent death? Isn't *that* man?

Or, is Man—male and female—nothing less than the conscious universe itself, the whole reiterated in the part, a reference point within a fractal that is the same on every scale of perception? The notion that man is the most highly evolved animal ever to roam our planet's surface represents a very noble self-vision. But the notion that Man—male and female—is nothing less than the universe itself elevates humanity to the level of the sacred.

Most readers are familiar with the Mandelbrot image of fractal geometry. Each part, when enlarged, replicates the whole, and this self-replication continues infinitely, on every scale of perception (see next page). But how, then, can we distinguish

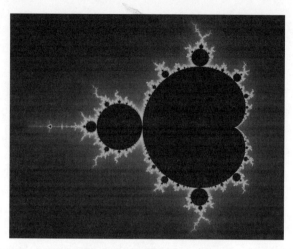

The Mandelbrot set.

one scale of perception from another? Can we even speak of different scales of perception if every scale is a replica of the scale "above" and the scale "below"? It is like attempting to identify the center of a line that extends infinitely in both directions; every point is the center. Thus, in reference to the Mandelbrot image, we cannot speak of different scales of perception; instead, there is only infinite replication of a single pattern wherever one casts one's attention. What then is man, this most intelligent of animals roaming the surface of the planet Earth? According to fractal geometry, Man—male and female—is one scale of perception at which the entire universe replicates itself, not distinguishable in any way from the whole.

Imagine, for the sake of a thought experiment, that a person has somehow been born without normal human senses and that this person can only perceive through a tiny camera and microphone located somewhere inside his or her own physical body. That person would certainly believe that all the diverse organs of the body were *outside*, not inside—just as we think the vast world that we perceive around us is *outside*, not inside. Ideas like "outside" and "inside," then, are just illusions created by the mechanics of our sensory perception. What if the world is really *inside* each of us, not outside? What if the world only *appears* to be outside because our perception is temporarily confined to the senses of a human body made of flesh? What if we are witnessing no less than the efficient functioning of our own cosmic form when we look around ourselves at the "outside" world?

It requires a great leap of the imagination to think of the universe in that way. How, for example, would that self-perception impact one's beliefs and actions? If the consciousness in each of us is actually the undivided consciousness of the entire universe, and if the human body is, in some subtle sense, a replica of the whole, then what individual can be devalued without devaluing everyone? And if each of us replicates the whole, then who among us is a moral island, and how can we say that a person's private thoughts and actions are his or hers alone, having no effect on others or on the world as a whole?

Where the rationalist sees metaphor, the mystic sees equivalence. Where the rationalist finds in the natural world many useful analogies for describing inner emotional experiences, the mystic denies the outer world an independent existence, interpreting it instead as a hall of mirrors that merely reflects back multiforms of the viewer wherever the viewer happens to cast his or her attention. The rationalist believes the human being to be small and the universe to be immense, but the mystic asserts that one just keeps seeing one's own self, over and over, in each part and on every scale. And if the mystic's understanding is correct, then by doing an action in the outer world, one can effect a change in one's soul, for the two are really one.

This mystical way of interpreting human experience may strike some people as fanciful; for others, it may feel intuitively correct. One must come to recognize that consciousness is the common ground of all objective phenomena—whether large or small, near or far, external events all happen on the screen of consciousness, and therefore whatever event one may observe, one is always only observing one's own self. Indeed, an external object can be known only because of the existence, in the observer's own thoughts, of an archetype (a Platonic "Idea") associated with that object. Thus, *subject*, not object—*consciousness*, not matter—is the foundation of being. But more important, in our *knowing* of the objective world, likenesses are not mere likenesses; rather, they are equivalences. There are not a thousand trees covering a forested hillside; there is only the one archetypal Tree in the consciousness of the observer by which each tree on the hillside is recognized to be a tree, and it is always that one archetypal Tree that one is seeing, over and over, whenever and wherever one happens to see a tree.

It is in the foregoing sense that we can begin to understand temple-based worship. Today, many people associate temple-based worship with primitive religion. A temple implies a localized conception of divinity—a particular god serving a particular community, not a universal God belonging to all—and thus temple-based worship seems to foster religious rivalry. In addition, a temple implies a priestly professional class mediating between God and the devotee, thus offending modern notions of self-reliance and social equality. Finally, a temple implies sacrifices and other offerings that, to a modern understanding, are quite unlikely to please a self-sufficient, all-powerful God that has no need for food or clothing. Nonetheless, there is a power in temple-based worship that we can come to appreciate when we learn to think about "self" and "other" in a new way.

Today, India is one of the few places where temple-based worship—and fire sacrifices, in particular—remain a vital part of the religious culture. Not surprisingly, then, Hindu tradition preserves, like a time capsule, many ideas from the ancient world concerning temple practice, and when we examine these ideas, we find that many of them have parallels in descriptions of the Jewish temple service.

At the end of the book of Exodus, the Israelites have completed the construction of a sanctuary dedicated to YHVH, but they do not yet know how to operate it—YHVH must provide them with a user's manual. The English name for that user's manual (*i.e.*, the third book of the Torah) is "Leviticus," from the Greek word *Leuitikos*, which means "that which concerns the Levites [(*i.e.*, the priests)]." Leviticus relates the specifics of the Jewish temple service, and a brief study of the Hindu tradition helps to unlock many of Leviticus's secrets, as we shall see.

2. Fire Sacrifice in Image and Intuition

When the river Ganges reaches Benares in the middle of India's Great Plain, it turns sharply to the left and drifts for a while northward—vast and silent, garlands of marigolds and cups of burning camphor floating serenely upon its surface. At about the midpoint of its slow journey past this "Jerusalem" of India, the river reaches Manikarnika Ghat. There, in the darkness sloughed off by a sun that has just marked its daily retreat to the underworld, half a dozen cremation fires glow and sparkle. The fires are a beautiful, irresistible sight as they gaily light up the night—flames dancing right and left, sparks streaming weightlessly upward, like rivers of golden stars.

Human corpses lie on the pavement, pointed this way and that, like grain tossed on the ground, seed kernels wrapped in golden husks of fine cloth. Each looks so small, so benign, and yet powerful on account of the immediacy of death that each silently conveys. The funerary workers have just placed one body atop a square stack of logs. The deceased's eldest son—dressed in white and head shaved—awkwardly, dutifully, performs the ancient rituals, while trained experts casually instruct him in his uncomfortable task. The family gathers near to watch. The fire is lit, using an ember from the eternal fire that burns there at the ghat. The smoke rises, forming a long black curl that grasps the sky. The golden cloth surrounding the corpse begins to burn, and then the flesh begins to cook. Atop another fire, a body is nearly consumed, and above the smoldering coals of a third, funerary workers chat casually, warming themselves against the cool, evening air.

The Brahmin priests teach that Manikarnika Ghat is both the womb of the city and the navel of the new emergent universe.[134] Thus, the cremation of a person's body does not just have implications for the soul of the individual who has died; it also has implications for the entire world. The sacrificial oblation of a single corpse into the funeral pyre is the oblation of the entire cosmos, and it regenerates the cosmos as nothing else can do,[135] but to perfect this cosmic regeneration, the offering must be a worthy one, and the soul's renunciation of life in the earthly body must be total.[136]

A thousand miles southwest of Manikarnika Ghat, the diamond-shaped continent of India is adorned, along its western coast, by a maze of estuaries that wind like cobras through a landscape of rice paddies and palm forests. The banks of these meandering waterways are dotted by tent-like fishing nets, each with a small light attached at its peak to attract fish into the net. At night, these lights look very much like the camphor fires that float on the surface of the Ganges so far to the north.

On the veranda of a small temple nestled beneath the coconut palms at the bank of one of these coastal estuaries, in the pure hours just before dawn, a Brahmin priest performs the daily fire sacrifice. The fire rises toward the sky, its smoke streaming through small openings in the veranda's roof, and outside, the monsoon rains pour down, easing the South Indian summer heat. The shadow of the priest's lean, erect body flickers

---

[134] Parry, *Death in Banaras*, pp. 13, 179. Jewish literature characterizes Jerusalem in the same terms.

[135] Parry, *Death in Banaras*, pp. 30–32, 178–184, 189; Parry, "Sacrificial Death and the Necrophagous Ascetic," pp. 82–83; Vesci, *Heat and Sacrifice in the Vedas*, pp. 275–276.

[136] Parry, *Death in Banaras*, p. 158.

on the smoke-stained wall behind the low platform on which he sits. He wears only a waistcloth and has the three lines of Shiva drawn in ash across his limbs and forehead. His complex hand gestures tell a ritual story that, like a pantomimed poem, only reveals itself indistinctly, in fragmented suggestions of meaning. The vibrations of carefully articulated mantras resonate in the air, making palpable the mystical teaching that God created this world through sound.

A few people have emerged from the shadows of pre-dawn darkness to bathe in the light of the fire sacrifice. They gaze down at the shining brass implements, the golden butter dripping from the priest's ladle into the fire, the flames licking upward toward the smoke-blackened beams overhead. The priest feeds the sacred fire with bits of coconut, fragrant wood, grass, flower petals, incense, curd, jaggery, herbs, seeds, and grains. Then, the priest stands and pours the remaining butter into the fire, all at once. The flames suddenly rise up as tall as a man, and the people who are watching bow their heads to the floor in unison. For a second, perhaps, they glimpsed the deity of the fire, like a picture projected among the dancing flames.

Butter is the refined essence of cream, which is the refined essence of milk, which is the refined essence of the cow. The cow's milk is truly her own precious vitality, which she pours out lovingly as food for her newborn calf, and butter is the vigor of that milk. Thus, it is the cow, not butter, that is being placed on the fire—it is her life that pours out from the ladle in the form of melted fat.

Long strings of butter fall gracefully into flames that leap upward to meet their lord. The rain falls down in streams that fertilize a chaste soil that is heaven's bride. Is this small temple in South India somehow the same as Manikarnika Ghat? Is it somehow the same as the ancient temple in Jerusalem? Is it the same as Calvary Hill? Is it the same as Auschwitz? What ties these disparate images together? Sacrifice, of course. The fire sacrifice is a beautiful, versatile metaphor, but for the faithful, it is so much more; it is an enactment of *one's own being*. On the veranda of that small temple in South India, one is able to witness one's own innermost self, dramatized before one's eyes. One's own self is the butter being poured out. One's own self is the flame rising up to receive it. One's own self is the firepit. One's own thoughts are the fragrant wisps of smoke rising toward the sky. One is the sacrificer, the sacrifice, the fire, and its victim.

As noted, the book of Leviticus was the handbook the priests followed in their service at the Jerusalem temple, including the details of the fire sacrifice that they conducted at that temple. Scholars assert that Leviticus was probably added to the Torah at a relatively late date, perhaps as a result of a priestly redaction of the Torah's text long after the construction of the Jerusalem temple. The conceptual content of Leviticus, however, is very ancient. Fire sacrifice as a method of worship probably originates with the domestication of fire, and the methods and principles that the priests in the Jerusalem temple followed were those that had been passed down to them through countless generations.

As we know, however, Roman soldiers destroyed the Jerusalem temple nearly two thousand years ago. Since that is so, are not the details of the temple service a matter of mere academic interest? What practical need have we today to study these things? The answer to that question lies in fractal geometry. If the temple is a multiform of the human being, and the latter is a multiform of the universe, then the book of Leviticus—the manual of the priests—is really *about us* and our relationship to the world around us. In that case, Leviticus is arguably the most relevant, not the least relevant, book of the Torah.

3. The Broken Universe

In Vedic times, God was not merely a philosophical abstraction called "Brahman"; God was also a story figure named Prajapati ("Lord of Creatures").[137] For the Vedic seers, stories and parables did not trivialize or demean God; rather, they were symbol-rich ways of teaching the most subtle and sophisticated ideas about God, for a metaphor can speak in a thousand ways at once.

Prajapati—God—"sacrificed himself into existence,"[138] pouring out his own substance to give rise to this world—to give rise, that is, to a revealed form of himself, for this world is in the form of that divine Man. Thus, Prajapati made himself many; he created multiplicity from his own unified being.

In Prajapati's self-revelation as the universe, the correspondences overlap without contradicting. His mind became the cool white moon that sheds its nectar upon the earth. His eyes became the sun and the moon, from which his inner light still flows, and through which he, as the soul of the universe, still sees. His hungry mouth became fire. His vital forces, too, became fire. His life breath became the wind. His ear became the directions. The crown of his head became the heavenly vault. His chest became the atmosphere. His feet became the earth. His mouth, full of holy utterances, became the prophets and the priests. His arms

---

[137] On Vedic thought in general, see Mahoney, *The Artful Universe*; Panikkar (trans. and ed.), *The Vedic Experience*; O'Flaherty (trans. and ed.), *The Rig Veda*; O'Flaherty, *Hindu Myths*; Eliade, *A History of Religious Ideas, Volume 1*; Kaelber, *Tapta Marga*. On Vedic ideas about ritual fire sacrifice, personal sacrifice, and death, see also Heesterman, *The Broken World of Sacrifice*; Kramrisch, *The Hindu Temple*; Vesci, *Heat and Sacrifice*; Bodewitz, *Jaiminiya Brahmana I*; Bodewitz, *The Daily Evening and Morning Offering*; Tachikawa et al., *Indian Fire Ritual*; Parry, *Death in Banaras*; Parry, "Sacrificial Death and the Necrophagous Ascetic"; Coomaraswamy, "Atmayajna: Self-Sacrifice."

[138] Kramrisch, *The Hindu Temple*, p. 68.

became the rulers who maintain civil order. His thighs became the merchants and the artisans; his feet, the laborers. He became the spoken word; he became the flowing waters and the firm ground; he became the gods and the demons. From his dismemberment arose all creatures. And he also became human beings (male and female)—replicas of himself on a smaller scale.

But after Prajapati poured himself out, he felt weak, dissipated, and disconnected. Prajapati was spent, like a man enervated by sexual emission, like a woman who has emptied her breast for the love of her child. A myth from the *Aitareya Brahmana* makes the sexual metaphor explicit, describing a sexual union between the "Father" and his "Daughter."[139] Incest is a frequent motif in creation stories and should not distract us here; one could say that the Creator (the "Father") seeks to reunite with the Creation (the "Daughter"). But at the critical moment of this intended union, the "Father" suddenly withdraws, pierced unexpectedly by a hunter's arrow. The Father's seed—his soul, that is—spills on the earth. Like a raging bull, the Father runs; like one rejected, the Daughter flees. The universe is broken, and to heal the breach and protect the cosmic order, the gods compose a poem. Then, the sound of the Father's progeny arises from the surface of the earth.

The Father in this story is Prajapati, the "Lord of Creatures." The pitter-patter of the Father's earthly progeny is mankind—a product of the accidental impregnation of earthly matter with divine soul. According to this myth, the universe was broken in the making, and mankind is both the product of that brokenness and, through the recitation of Vedic hymns, the means of repair.

Does the story sound familiar? The description of Prajapati's sacrifice recalls Atum of the Heliopolitan creation myth, and it recalls Adam of Isaac Luria's creation myth. As Luria described it, "Light" poured forth from Adam's nose, mouth, ears, and

---

[139] See O'Flaherty, *Hindu Myths*, pp. 25–35, 116–118, esp. pp. 25–26, 29–31; Kramrisch, *The Presence of Śiva*, pp. 3–26, esp. pp. 3–4, 6.

eyes, and it arranged itself into ten divine potencies. But the cosmic "vessels" were too weak to contain the divine Light. They shattered and the Light fell, trapped among the fragments of the broken vessels—again, a universe broken in the making.

And a broken universe yearns, of course, to be reintegrated, reordered, and rebuilt. Prajapati created the universe by an act of sacrifice, and by sacrifice, Prajapati's disjointed body is reconnected, the universe is repaired, and the soul-sparks that fell to earth are reunited to the sky.

Vedic mythology asserts that Prajapati is the year—he is, in other words, the cycle of time. But when the universe broke, time also broke.[140] How can we understand this assertion that time is broken? Consider that we inhabit a giant astrological clock, but the planetary gears of that astrological clock are slightly miscalibrated, and the orbits of the planets do not quite align. When the minute hand (the lunar month) has completed its twelve revolutions, the hour hand (the solar year) has not quite completed its full revolution. The astrological clock is not keeping the correct time, and as occurs when the gears of any ordinary mechanical clock are miscalibrated, each turn of the cycle of time manifests a new permutation of the cosmic misalignment. The result is that astrological time, which is circular, becomes linear; it begins to progress, that is, along a linear dimension. Thus, according to astrological thought, linear history represents time's brokenness, its leakiness, the failure of its cycles to restore us, in every particular, to the place where we began. Because of time's brokenness, the cycles of time fail to sustain us; instead, they slowly dissipate us. In short, broken time means that we inhabit a universe that is subject to decay and ultimately death.

Broken time consumes all forms, but according to Vedic

---

[140] See *Brihad-Aranyaka Upanishad* 1.5.14, translated in Hume, *The Thirteen Principal Upanishads*, pp. 88–89; see also Bodewitz, *The Daily Evening and Morning Offering*, pp. 71, 128; Kramrisch, *The Presence of Śiva*, pp. 265–278, 281–287.

speculation, the universe "outlasts death" through sacrifice. In other words, sacrifice liberates living creatures from the mortality of broken time. The *Satapatha Brahmana* explains: "Man, so soon as he is born, is to be regarded, his whole person, as a debt owed to death. When he performs sacrifice he is purchasing himself back from death."[141]

In Vedic cosmogony, therefore, creation and sacrifice are inextricably linked. Nothing that is decaying and old can become new again without sacrifice. In other words, sacrifice is gain, not loss; it is the source of life, not its end. By the sacrifice of one living organism into the digestive fires of another, life is sustained. By the sacrifice of seed into the womb, life is sustained. By the sacrifice of a coin into the hand of a helpless beggar, life is sustained. By many small acts of self-sacrifice done throughout one's life, one builds for oneself a heavenly home and a heavenly body, and by the final sacrifice of one's earthly body into a cremation fire, one attains that heavenly home and body—or, according to an alternative model, one ensures one's reincarnation among one's earthly descendants.

Likewise, the natural world remains ever new through sacrifice. Each year, summer sacrifices itself into the fiery colors of autumnal death only to be born again as spring. Each month, the moon makes an oblation of itself into the fire of the sun only to return, a fortnight later, to wholeness. Each evening, the sun offers itself into the inky dark waters of the western sea only to arise, the next day, on a newborn world. These are, of course, the images of poetry, not of science, but for the Vedic seers, they convey an important principle: Forms arise, forms decay, and new forms arise. Those who cling to old forms live amidst decay, and they clothe themselves in mortality. Those who identify instead with constant change gain immortality. Hindu mythology asserts that the serpent attained its immortality by molting its skin, and

---

[141] Panikkar (trans. and ed.), *The Vedic Experience*, p. 393, quoting source text.

by the same principle, the natural world heals the cosmic breach through sacrifice.

Thus, according to the Vedic model, sacrifice is the very soul of the universe, and by internalizing the sacrifice, we reintegrate ourselves, recognizing our essential unity with all that is. Then, we are not the performers of the sacrifice, nor are we its victim, nor is God the performer, nor is God its victim, nor is God the one for whom the sacrifice is performed. Rather, the Sacrifice itself is the deity. There are no longer any actors in the drama, nor are there objects acted upon; only the Sacrifice remains. The Vedas teach that "[w]ith the sacrifice the gods sacrificed to the Sacrifice,"[142] gods who themselves were instantiations of the Sacrifice.[143]

In later Vedic literature, the word *brahman* became a label for the Absolute—the one, uncreated, infinite, and transcendent God. But in earlier texts, the *brahman* was the mysterious power that made the sacrifice effective, and the *brahman* was also the point of intersection between all the disparate elements of the sacrificial ritual.[144]

> The *brahman* is the invocating priest;
> the *brahman* is the sacrificial offering;
> by the *brahman* are the sacrificial posts set in place.
> The officiating priest is born of the *brahman*;

---

[142] *Rg Veda* 10.90.16, translated in O'Flaherty, *The Rig Veda*, p. 31.

[143] Panikkar (trans. and ed.), *The Vedic Experience*, p. 396, referencing the *Satapatha Brahmana*.

[144] Mahoney, *The Artful Universe*, pp. 114–116. In early literature, the word *brahman* was closely related to the idea of *rta*, the organizing force in the universe. The *rta* was the invisible force that made the sacrifice a wellspring of fertility and renewal. *Id.* at pp. 46–52. As the literature developed, the word *brahman* sometimes took the place of the word *rta*, with only shades of difference in meaning. *Id.* at pp. 114–119; see also Panikkar (trans. and ed.), *The Vedic Experience*, pp. 350–351.

into the *brahman* is put the offering.

The *brahman* is the ladle dripping with clarified oil;
by the *brahman* is the fire altar established.

The *brahman* is the true essence of the sacrifice.[145]

Similarly, Krishna declares in the *Bhagavad Gita*: "I am the ritual, I am the sacrifice, the oblation, and the herb. I am the Prayer and the melted butter, the fire and its offering."[146] According to these texts, the sacrificial drama is God's own form, and God is also the regenerating power of that drama.

Prajapati's soul spilled upon the earth, giving rise to mankind. The divine "Light" streamed from the face of Adam, but the "vessels" were too weak to contain the Light; they shattered and the Light fell, trapped among the fragments of the broken vessels. Thus, the universe was born, but a broken universe, and in this broken universe, bits of divine soul are trapped amidst the retrograde forces of decay, submerged in the brokenness of time, constantly needing to chase life just to live.

The motif of trapped spirit needing to be rescued from earthly matter recurs throughout world literature. We find it, for example, in the many Indo-European myths describing the hero's quest for the nectar of immortality, a precious ambrosia held captive by tellurian forces. The *Rg Veda* relates that the demons have trapped milk-producing cows deep in a cave, and Brhaspati must descend to free them; he must descend, in other words, to free the forces of life from the grip of earthly darkness. Likewise, Indra must free the flowing waters—again signifying the forces of life—from the grip of the serpent Vrtra,

---

[145] *Atharvaveda* 19.42, quoted in Mahoney, *The Artful Universe*, p. 116; see also *Bhagavad Gita* IV, 24.

[146] *Bhagavad Gita* IX, 16, translated in Panikkar, *The Vedic Experience*, p. 430.

who holds them stagnant in the belly of a mountain.[147] And in Gnostic mythology, this same motif assumes the form of a harsh duality in which matter is evil, and spirit is good. But in Vedic and Jewish thought, it is not the union of matter and spirit that is the source of evil; rather, it is *the way* spirit has conjoined matter—their imperfect union—that is the problem.

"Humpty Dumpty sat on a wall. Humpty Dumpty had a great fall." We live in a universe that was broken in the making. "All the king's horses and all the king's men couldn't put Humpty together again"—all the wealth and political power that one might accumulate cannot renew life in a universe that is subject to death. But sacrifice outstrips death. From Prajapati's act of sacrifice, the universe was born, and from the repetition of that act in circular time, the universe is ever new.

4. The Jewish Temple Service

A close study of the first seven chapters of the book of Leviticus offers the reader a fascinating journey to a ritual world that is unfamiliar to many people today. On any day of the year, the air above the Jerusalem temple was not scented with the diesel fumes and car exhaust that characterize modern urban life but with a potpourri of sweet fragrances. The golden incense altar poured lazy plumes of pungent smoke toward the sky, and that smoke mingled with the distinctively pleasing aroma of burning wood and roasting meat and oiled wheat cakes toasting over hot flames. During a festival like Passover, the smoke of

---

[147] See O'Flaherty (trans. and ed.), *The Rig Veda*, pp. 148–151 [slaying of Vrtra], 151–156 [Brhaspati and the cows]; O'Flaherty, *Hindu Myths*, pp. 74–90 [slaying of Vrtra]; Dimmitt and van Buitenen, *Classical Hindu Mythology*, pp. 303–306 [slaying of Vrtra]; Mahoney, *The Artful Universe*, pp. 126–128 [discussing both myths]; Eliade, *History of Religious Ideas, Volume 1*, pp. 205–208 [slaying of Vrtra].

thousands of sacrifices filled an atmosphere that was charged with the potent rhythms of Levites chanting psalms and *kohanim* ("priests") intoning sacred benedictions.[148] And on such a day, a vast crowd of devotees stretched in all directions, filling the temple compound and overflowing into the city's bustling streets and alleys, talking together, arguing, laughing, waiting. There were pious supplicants mumbling their pleas and praises beneath fringed prayer shawls; there were bearded preachers shouting heartfelt sermons to all who might stop to listen; and there were limbless beggars soliciting meager alms. Animals bleated and brayed under the warm sun, and temple business-men noisily plied their age-old trade.

And, in the center of that awesome din was the relative silence of the altar, where no one uttered a word,[149] where there was only the crackling roar of the sacred fire to speak the devotions and aspirations of a nation that hoped to reconnect earth to heaven and thus to redeem mankind. When Solomon dedicated the first Jerusalem temple, the Levites chanted, the *kohanim* blew trumpets, and twenty-two thousand oxen and a hundred and twenty thousand sheep were sacrificed (1 Kings 8:63; 2 Chron 7:4–6), their blood soaking the altar stones and streaming through the temple gutters, their fats melting and flaming brightly toward the bright blue sky, their sacred vitality electrifying an atmosphere that was so palpably affected that it seized the attention of even the most callous observer.

Prior to the destruction of Jerusalem's second temple, the fire sacrifice was the central devotional event of the Jewish religion. The sacrifice took several forms, and each had its distinct purposes and meanings, but the common metaphysics of all these forms was the flow of vitality into the altar's life-generating heat. For the faithful, the temple was not a mere building made

---

[148] On singing and recitations in the Jerusalem temple, see Lev 9:23; 2 Chron 7:6; see also Milgrom, *Leviticus 1–16*, pp. 19, 60–61, 219.

[149] Milgrom, *Leviticus 1–16*, pp. 19, 60–61.

of wood and stone; it was a conscious living being. The altar was the digestive fire of that living being, and the sacrifices were the holy food that sustained its life.

The sacrifices of the Jerusalem temple can be divided into five main types—(1) the whole offering (*olah*), (2) the well-being offering (freewill or fulfillment of a vow) (*zevach shelamim*), (3) the thanksgiving offering (*zevach todah*), (4) the purification offering (*chatat*), and (5) the reparation offering (*asham*)—and the psalms the Levites sang in the temple can be divided into corresponding categories. An individual devotee might present a whole offering, known in Hebrew as an "*olah*" (literally, "that which ascends"), to expiate sin, to entreat God, or to elevate himself and his family spiritually. In addition, an institutional *olah* was offered at appointed times as a matter of temple routine. (Num 28–29.) In each case, the sacrificial animal had to be unblemished (Lev 22:17–25), and the priest had to meet similar qualifications (Lev 21:16–24; see also Deut 23:2).

As the English name "whole offering" implies, the *olah* entailed a complete incineration of the animal on the altar, causing it to rise entirely to the sky as smoke. Other sacrifices required only a partial burning of the animal, with the distribution of the remainder to the offeror and the priests as food for a feast. Such a sacrifice was called a "*zevach*" in Hebrew. The portion of a *zevach* that was burned on the altar included certain specified fats—in particular, the omentum, which is the layer of fat covering the stomach, kidneys, liver, and loins.

The omentum was also the critical offering of the Vedic fire sacrifice. In Vedic thought, the fat of the omentum constituted the spiritual essence of the entire animal, and therefore when the priest offered the omentum, the sacrifice was complete and fully effective, even if other parts of the animal remained to be offered.[150] The Vedic seers also identified the omentum with *soma*, the semi-mythical plant sap that was the Vedic fire offering *par*

---

[150] Vesci, *Heat and Sacrifice*, pp. 119, 131–133.

excellence. When the omentum was placed on the fire, it quickly melted and burned brightly, producing a pleasant fragrance. Its elevation skyward as light and fragrance was, in Vedic thought, an effective means of repairing the cosmic breach. It restored the spilled sap to Prajapati's fragmented being, and derivatively, it restored the sacrificer's own lost wholeness. Thus, the rising smoke of the omentum was like a ladder by which the Vedic seers hoped to regain their place in the heavens above.

In Jewish ritual, the offeror of an *olah* supported "his hand" (Hebrew: *YaDO*) upon the head of the animal. (Lev 1:4.) In other words, he supported "His *yud*" (Hebrew: *YuDO*), the hidden letter *yud* at the end of YHVH's name, thus ritually revealing the name *Yehudi*.[151] The offeror then slaughtered the animal, and the *kohein* ("priest") poured the animal's blood on the base of the altar. (Lev 1:5.) The blood was not burned. Blood exudes a foul odor when burned, just as it fouls the mind when heated internally by passion,[152] and the whole point of the burned offerings was to produce a pleasing fragrance. After pouring the blood on the base of the altar, the priest placed the rest of the animal on the fire, causing its fats and flesh to ascend skyward as smoke, a "satisfying aroma for YHVH" (*rei'ach nicho'ach ladonai*). (Lev 1:8–9.)

In Jewish and Vedic metaphysics, we encounter the idea that the quality of one's thoughts is linked to the vapors and breaths that pervade one's body, with pleasant fragrances corresponding to noble thoughts, and foul smells corresponding to base thoughts. Jewish metaphysics even correlates the most refined part of the human soul—the *neshamah*—to a "breath" (*neshimah*) that YHVH-God blew into Adam's brow, implying the unity of vital breath, consciousness, and God. (Gen 2:7.) In this

---

[151] Cf. Milgrom, *Leviticus 1–16*, pp. 151–153. Milgrom argues that the purpose of pressing the hands was to establish ownership.

[152] Vesci, *Heat and Sacrifice*, pp. 116–117, 132 [expressly linking the cooking of blood with base desires].

sense, the sweet fragrances of the temple sacrifices corresponded to the noble thoughts of the living temple.

The *olah* was accompanied by a wheat offering, known in Hebrew as a *minchah*, and by a libation of wine (*yayin*). (Num 15:1–12, 28–29.)[153] Recall in this context that, in our knowing of the objective world—in our comprehension of it, that is—likenesses are not mere likenesses; they are really equivalences, because they invoke the same archetypes and thus are one in the world of Ideas. Wheat is the central source of nourishment for an agrarian people, representing the triumph of civilization over hunter-gatherer subsistence. But much more important, wheat is the fat of the land, and the wheat offering was often mixed with oil, which is liquid fat. The wheat offering (*minchah*) was therefore a multiform of the fats of the sacrificial victim.

Wine, on the other hand, is dark red and produced from vines, suggesting the blood that courses through the body's veins. Vines (like veins) do not support themselves, clinging instead to an external support, and vines (like veins) meander from one place to the next, branching, twisting, and flowing with vital juice. Moreover, wine (like blood) invigorates the body, and wine (like blood) also intoxicates the mind with passion. Wine (*yayin*) was therefore a multiform of the blood of the sacrificial victim. Thus, the wheat offering (*minchah*) and the libation of wine (*yayin*) did not merely *symbolize* the fat and blood of the sacrificial animal; they actually *were* the fat and blood of the sacrificial animal by reason of the archetypes they invoked in the consciousness of the offeror.[154]

Vedic fire sacrifices likewise included cereal offerings. According to Vedic sacrificial theory, the spiritual essence of the animal was likely to flee on account of its resistance to being

---

[153] See Milgrom, *Leviticus 1–16*, pp. 195–202 [discussing the wheat offering].

[154] On the identification of fat with wheat, and blood with wine, see Deut 32:14.

194

TORAH AND NONDUALISM

slaughtered. For this reason, only a *willing* victim could guarantee that the sacrifice would be effective, and the cereal offering served as that "willing" victim. The commentaries on the Veda explain that the spiritual essence that flees the animal at the moment of slaughter enters the earth, and from the earth, it enters plants. Thus, the cereal offering served to restore the lost essence of the animal to the sacrifice, perfecting the sacrifice.[155]

The book of Numbers specifies the precise quantities of wheat and wine that accompanied certain obligatory whole offerings. (Num 15:1–12, 28–29.) The wheat had to be unleavened (Lev 2:11, 6:9–10), the best quality available, thoroughly winnowed, finely ground, and mixed with specified amounts of oil. A wheat offering was also made in connection with a *zevach*—that is, a sacrifice that provided consecrated food for a feast. (Num 15:1–12.)

In some cases, wheat and wine could also be offered alone, as a *substitute* for the fats and blood of a sacrificial animal. (Lev 2, 6:7–11.) Like the animal offering, an offering of wheat alone was a "satisfying aroma for YHVH" (*rei'ach nicho'ach ladonai*). (Lev 2:2, 2:9.) Thus, in appropriate situations, its status was equal to that of the animal offering. One could offer the wheat uncooked, placing a lump of frankincense on top, or one could bake or fry the wheat, using either a shallow or a deep pan. (Lev 2:1–11.) The offeror generally mixed the wheat flour with olive oil, but in the case of a purification offering (*chatat*), the wheat was presented without oil or frankincense (Lev 5:11), reflecting an attitude of humility. In every case, the wheat offering was salted. (Lev 2:13.) Salt represents the absence of decay, but more important, it represents the presence of soul, for just as soul invisibly pervades the body, giving sentience to all its limbs, so salt invisibly pervades food, intensifying all its flavors.

The priest broke the wheat cake into small pieces. He then scooped up a memorial portion (*azkarah*) with his three middle

---

[155] Vesci, *Heat and Sacrifice*, pp. 137–138; Kaelber, *Tapta Marga*, p. 26.

fingers and burned that portion, along with any frankincense, producing a "satisfying aroma for YHVH" (*rei'ach nicho'ach ladonai*). (Lev 2:2, 2:9, 6:8.) The unburned portion of the wheat offering was consumed by the priests as consecrated food, to be eaten only in a holy place by one in a state of ritual purity. (Lev 2:3, 2:10, 6:9–11.)

The eating of the remnant of the sacrifice by the priest was a critical part of the ritual. (See Lev 5:13, 6:9–11, 6:19, 6:22, 7:6–7.) The priest's body was a microcosm of the entire temple. His digestive fire corresponded to the altar, and his noble thoughts corresponded to the fragrant smoke rising heavenward. In the case of a purification offering (*chatat*), the atonement came in part from the priest's consumption of the remnant; the priest actually digested a portion of the sin.[156]

We encounter this same principle in the Vedic tradition. For example, in the case of Vedic funerary rites, it is said that the cremation fire cannot complete the work of atonement, and therefore the Brahmin priest must symbolically eat and digest a portion of the deceased's sin.[157] The Brahmins add that, unless the priest is exceedingly holy and righteous, the sin *digests him*, and this potentially dangerous effect of the sacrificer's sin on the health of the priest is also recognized in the Jewish tradition.[158]

The three-finger scoop of wheat that the priest burned on the altar, the *azkarah*, was referred to above as the "memorial portion." The Hebrew word *azkarah* comes from the root *zkr*, connoting "memory," "remembering," and "holding in thought," but in scriptural usage, a "memory" also suggests the enduring

---

[156] *Pesachim* 59b; see also Luzzatto, *Mesillat Yesharim*, p. 329, quoting *Pesachim* 59b ["If one sanctifies himself with the Holiness of his Creator, even his physical actions come to partake of Holiness.... 'The priests eat and the owners [of the offered food] are atoned for.'"].

[157] Parry, *Death in Banaras*, pp. 76–77.

[158] Reznick, *The Holy Temple Revisited*, p. 74.

mark a person or event leaves in the world.[159] Thus, the *azkarah* portion of the sacrifice was the enduring ritual legacy of some past event, bringing that event into the present.

The Torah uses the same word, *azkarah*, when describing the weekly service related to the showbread (*lechem ha-panim*; literally, "face bread"). (See Lev 24:5–9; see also Exod 25:23–30.) These twelve loaves were on display in the temple at all times, placed in two stacks on a specially designed rack, with incense atop each stack. Each Sabbath, the priests replaced the loaves, and they burned the incense as an *azkarah* ("memorial portion"). The week-old loaves were then distributed among the priests as consecrated food.

As noted, the *azkarah* ("memorial portion") was the enduring mark of a past event that brought that event into the present. Thus, it served as a physical and spiritual link between the ongoing temple service and every significant sacrificial event of history, including Isaac's archetypal offering of himself at the request of his father, Abraham (Gen 22:1–19). It was that total self-dedication to God—typified by Isaac—that was the real purpose of the temple service, a point that is emphasized in numerous biblical texts: "Is YHVH's delight in whole offerings and sacrifices comparable to [YHVH's delight in] hearkening to the voice of YHVH? Hearkening is better than sacrifice; heeding is better than the fat of rams." (1 Sam 15:22.) "For if you raise up to me whole offerings and your wheat cakes, I will not desire [them], and peace [offerings] from your stall-fed animals I will not regard.... Let judgment be revealed like water, and righteousness like a continuous stream." (Amos 5:22–24.) "For you[, O God,] do not delight in sacrifice, or I would give; whole offering you do not desire. The sacrifices of God are a shattered spirit, a shattered heart...." (Ps 51:18–19.) These passages and

---

[159] Examples from scripture include Exod 17:14, 30:16; Deut 25:19, 32:26; 2 Sam 18:18; Isa 26:14, 56:5; Jer 11:19; Mal 3:16; Pss 9:6, 34:16, 45:17, 109:15; Job 18:17; Eccles 1:11, 9:5; Ws 4:1.

many others like them[160] reiterate a single essential point of Jewish thought: One who aspires to true service of God must transform all his or her actions and thoughts into a "satisfying aroma for YHVH" (*rei'ach nicho'ach ladonai*).

5. The Morality of the Fire Sacrifice

But does the ritualized slaughter and immolation of innocent animals really constitute the height of moral perfection to which a devotee of God should aspire? To many modern observers, animal sacrifice seems senseless and barbaric. The irony in this attitude is that in ancient times most animal sacrifices were for the purpose of eating a consecrated holiday meal with family and friends, whereas modern society unceremoniously slaughters millions of animals every day, often for meals that are consumed with much less noble intention. The parts of the animal that in ancient times were burned on the altar are, generally speaking, discarded today. Thus, from the perspective of religious devotion, modern meat-eaters are the barbaric ones, not those of ancient times who performed animal sacrifices, for the latter consecrated the life of the animals they ate, whereas the former just kill and eat, sometimes without even reciting a blessing.[161]

But what about the *olah* (the whole offering), which was burned entirely on the altar? Even if the ritual sacrifice of feast animals can be justified as an act of religious piety, how can one

---

[160] See Isa 1:10–17, 66:3; Jer 6:20, 7:21–23; Hosea 6:6; Mic 6:6–8; Mal 1:7–14, 2:13; Pss 40:7, 50:12–13, 69:31–32.

[161] On the strict ethical rules that applied to meat-eating in ancient Jewish and Vedic culture, see Lev 17:1–9; Deut 12:15–16, 20–25; Milgrom, *Leviticus 1–16*, pp. 221, 704–713; Weissman (ed.), *The Midrash Says: Vayikra*, p. 203; *The Laws of Manu* 5.26–56, translated in Doniger and Smith, *The Laws of Manu*, pp. 102–104.

morally defend the vain incineration of an entire animal on an altar? Obviously, for the worshipers of ancient times, the *olah* was not a vain act; for them, it had a meaning and a spiritual significance that the modern observer fails to intuit.

As already noted, the Jerusalem temple was not merely a place where pious people gathered to worship, analogous to a modern church or synagogue. For the worshipers of ancient times, the temple made of wood and stone constituted the physical body of a living person, and that "person," like any other, was animated by the metabolism of food. To understand that principle more deeply, we need to recall the theory that the universe we inhabit is a fractal very much like the Mandelbrot image. Thus, every scale on which the universe is observed is, in some subtle sense, identical to every other scale. According to that model, the human person (the microcosm), the temple (the mesocosm), and the universe (the macrocosm) are iterations of the same thing. The person *is* the temple *is* the universe. Diversity is really unity.

We encounter this idea in both Vedic and Jewish tradition. Vedic thought asserts that the person, the temple, and the universe are all in the form of the divine *Purusha* ("Cosmic Person," a/k/a Prajapati).[162] In other words, by laying out the temple complex according to scriptural precepts, the temple's architects reproduce, in wood and stone, the form of a person. Of course, a Hindu temple does not *look* like a person, but according to the Vedic understanding, the Hindu temple comprises proportions

---

[162] See Kramrisch, *The Hindu Temple*, pp. 67–97, 161–176 [person = temple = universe]; Fuller, *The Camphor Flame*, p. 209 [person = temple = universe]; Parry, *Death in Banaras*, pp. 170–171 [person = temple = universe]; see also Bodewitz, *The Daily Evening and Morning Offering*, pp. 42, 113, 160–161, 171 [human "breaths" = "breaths" of ritual fire = cosmic "breaths"]; Bodewitz, *Jaiminiya Brahmana I*, pp. 220–229, 240, 259–264, 267, 276–283, 318–322 [human "breaths" = "breaths" of ritual fire = cosmic "breaths"].

and symmetries that function, spiritually speaking, like a person: "In the net of this [temple design] the figure of [the *Purusha*] is caught."[163] And by a similar logic, the temple patron who subsidizes the construction of a Hindu temple builds up, stone by stone, both the universe and himself, and likewise the sacrificer who subsidizes the construction of a fire altar does the same thing.[164]

Similarly, Jewish tradition asserts that the Jerusalem temple corresponded in a subtle sense to both a person and the universe.[165] The anthropomorphic correspondences were quite specific. The ark, which contained the tablets of the law, corresponded to a person's higher soul (*neshamah*), the aspect of the soul that makes a person capable of knowing God. The anteroom corresponded to a person's face, complete with eyes (the

---

[163] Kramrisch, *The Hindu Temple*, p. 71.

[164] Kramrisch, *The Hindu Temple*, pp. 68–71; Vesci, *Heat and Sacrifice*, pp. 37–45, 74, 93–94; Parry, *Death in Banaras*, p. 133; Mahoney, *The Artful Universe*, pp. 134–140, 207, 219; Eliade, *History of Religious Ideas, Volume 1*, pp. 220–223, 229–232.

[165] See, e.g., *Zohar* 2:140b [person = temple = universe], 2:149a [temple = universe], 2:162b [person = temple = universe], 2:220b–221a [temple = universe], 2:231b [temple = universe]. These *Zohar* passages are translated in Matt, *The Zohar: Pritzker Edition*, vol. V, pp. 293 [2:140b], 366 [2:149a], 438–439 [2:162b]; vol. VI, pp. 260–264 [2:220b–221a], 332 [2:231b]. See also Reznick, *The Holy Temple Revisited*, pp. xiv–xvi [person = temple]; Scholem, *On the Kabbalah and Its Symbolism*, pp. 166–167 [temple = universe]; Hallamish, *An Introduction to the Kabbalah*, pp. 232, 248 [person = universe]; Weissman (ed.), *The Midrash Says: Sh'mos*, pp. 243–244 [person = temple = universe]; Dresner, *The Zaddik*, pp. 122–132 [person = temple]; Green (trans.), *Menahem Nahum of Chernobyl*, pp. 71–79, esp. pp. 73, 75, 78 [person = temple]; Nachman of Breslov, *The Aleph-Bet Book*, "A Righteous Man," pars. A35, A46 [person = temple]; Gottlieb, *The Lamp of God*, p. 147 [temple = universe]; Starrett, *The Inner Temple*, pp. i, v–vii, x, 37, 55, *passim* [person = temple]; Kramer, *Anatomy of the Soul*, pp. 32–33 [person = temple = universe].

menorah and the showbread), nose (the incense altar), and mouth (the door through which the priests spoke blessings to the congregation). The pure and holy fire of the temple's main altar was the temple's metabolic engine, and the altar's fragrant smoke was the temple's holy and virtuous thoughts. According to this logic, the daily burning of pure food on the temple's altar renewed the vitality of the living temple, stemming the forces of death and decay at all levels of the cosmic fractal.[166]

Thus, the temple was not merely a place where the pious gathered for worship; rather, it was a living being capable of transforming ordinary people by providing them a direct encounter with an ideal that existed in both them and the universe. And if we accept the premise that the temple was a living being, then the moral dilemma associated with the temple sacrifices expands to become the moral dilemma of eating in general, and the crux of that dilemma is the jarring observation that *life lives by consuming life*. Life simply cannot be sustained without killing— neither the life of the human body, nor the life of the temple.[167]

Under the influence of Buddhist values, which put great emphasis on *ahimsa* (non-injury), the Brahmins of South Asia became increasingly sensitive to this moral dilemma, and post-Vedic Brahmin culture embraced vegetarianism, offering butter, grains, seeds, flowers, and similar ingredients to the temple's

---

[166] It might be argued that this explanation of the temple sacrifices is not sufficiently detailed in its assignment of meaning to the complex specifics of sacrificial ritual law. Such specifics are, however, simply a matter of observing proper culinary etiquette in feeding the metabolic fires of the living temple. In every culture, it is important to serve certain categories of food in certain sequences and combinations. These cultural rules are often both complex and contextual, and to an outside observer, they may even seem overwrought and arbitrary, but they are nonetheless meaningful in all their details, and their meaning is to honor those who consume the meal. See Weissman (ed.), *The Midrash Says: Vayikra*, pp. 289–290 [priests must be pure because they are cooks for a very noble king].

[167] Cohen, *Everyman's Talmud*, p. 77.

altar fire, and corresponding vegetarian sustenance to the internal fires of human digestion.[168]

The Torah also favors vegetarianism. For example, God did not designate any animal products for Adam to eat. (Gen 1:29.) Rather, only in the instructions given to Noah ten generations later did God permit the consumption of meat, subject to the rule of blood avoidance. (Gen 9:3–4.) But even then, meat continued to be a disfavored food. When the Israelites craved meat in the wilderness (despite having food from heaven), YHVH expressed anger over their lack of refinement and decided to feed them meat until they vomited. Then, while the meat was still in their teeth, YHVH struck them with a plague. (Num 11:4–23, 11:31–34.) It is hard to interpret that story as a strong endorsement of a meat diet; rather, meat-eating is presented as a concession to human weakness and associated with a lower level of spiritual insight. The latter point is confirmed by the description of Moses' austere diet while residing with YHVH on Mount Sinai. (Exod 34:28; Deut 9:9, 9:18.) And the book of Daniel also endorses a vegetarian diet. (Dan 1:8–16.) Interestingly, Rabbi Abraham Isaac Kook (1865–1935 C.E.) asserted that when the Jerusalem temple is rebuilt, the sacrifices will be vegetarian sacrifices.

A vegetarian diet and temple sacrifices consisting of butter, grains, seeds, and flowers are not, however, a complete solution to the moral dilemma presented by the need of all living creatures to sustain themselves through eating. For example, draining a cow's milk to make butter taxes her vitality just as surely (though by small increments) as a knife across the throat, and scything grass to harvest grain is, to the sensitive observer, just as much an act of violence as the slaying of a calf or a lamb. Even for a vegetarian, the paradox remains: *life lives by consuming life*. Eating is not possible without killing, and if the eating stops—that is, if vitality stops flowing from one life form to another—then there is only universal death, not more life.

---

[168] Doniger and Smith (trans.), *The Laws of Manu*, pp. xxx–xl.

In other words, life is sustained by sacrifice, and the moral dilemma is resolved so long as sacrifice is dedicated to that which is good. Thus, death can be seen as the antithesis of sacrifice; when we cling to old forms, unable to let things go, we dwell in death. In ancient times, the altar fire of the temple, like the metabolic fire of the body, was understood to be a fire of regeneration, not a fire of destruction. Hence, the life of a sacrificial animal was not poured out in vain; rather, the animal attained its ultimate apotheosis in the fire of the altar, becoming the sustaining food of a living temple that mediated between God and mankind.[169]

6. Holy Fire

But the philosophers of ancient times did not just view the temple as a person made of wood and stone; they also viewed each person as a temple made of flesh, blood, bone, and marrow, and to understand more clearly how each of us is like a temple, we must consider what fire is in its broadest sense.

In ancient times, people knew fire much more intimately than we know it today. For them fire was a visible and gaily dancing wood-flame in a family hearth, not a hidden and precisely regulated gas-flame confined within a machine. People cooked with fire. They warmed themselves by it. They ate their food and talked and laughed in its company. For many hours, late at night, they gazed into fire. They meditated on it. They knew what a life-generating fire was. It crackled cheerfully in a firepit, producing a bright light, a pleasant aroma, and a benevolent, warm heat that maintained the spirit and joy of the home. They also knew what a destructive fire was. It hissed, sputtered, and popped, producing thick clouds of smoke and exuding the

---

[169] See, e.g., Krassen (trans.), *The Generations of Adam*, p. 224; Jacobs, *Hasidic Prayer*, p. 109; Cohen (trans.), *The Holy Letter*, pp. 120–124.

putrid odors of rotting unburned residue, or it flared wildly out of control, leaping angrily and unpredictably from structure to structure.

One can think of fire as the energy of dynamic change, capable of regenerating life but just as capable of destroying it.[170] The warmth of the womb gestates the embryo to maturity, and the warmth of the digestive fire restores vitality to the body. But the fierce and volatile heat of a forest fire destroys everything that comes in its way. The holy fire produced on an altar by the combustion of animal fats and wood resins was, according to classical thought, a life-generating fire, recognizable by its shiny light and sweet fragrance. By contrast, the unholy "fire" produced by slow decay at the center of a garbage heap was a destructive fire, recognizable by its darkness and its foul smell. The philosophers of ancient times studied the types of fire that they encountered around them, and from that study, they derived lessons about themselves.

All the diverse metabolic processes of the body—processes that break down organic matter and then distribute and build up new organic matter—can be characterized as a kind of "fire," and the energy that animates the body's limbs and warms its blood is likewise a kind of "fire." Moreover, just as fire in the outside world can have different qualities (life-generating and destructive), so the metabolic processes that burn within a person's body can have different qualities (life-generating and destructive). And with that insight, the sacrificial rite of the temple became a ritual enactment of the observer's own self and a meditation on self-perfection.

Vedic mythology relates the cosmic battle of the gods against the demons, a battle for immortality in which priests are the

---

[170] See Vesci, *Heat and Sacrifice*, pp. 37–45, 74, 93–94, 181; Doniger and Smith (trans.), *The Laws of Manu*, p. 103; Parry, *Death in Banaras*, pp. 171, 213–214.

warriors and sacrifices are the weapons.[171] At the beginning, both
the gods and the demons are mortal. Agni, however, is immortal.
Agni is Fire. The gods said: "Come, let us establish this immortality in our inmost self!... The Fire is with both [us and our
demon rivals]; let us then speak openly with the [demons]...."
But the demons responded: "[W]e shall set [Fire] in place, saying: eat grass here, eat wood here, cook rice here, cook meat
here." The demons, in other words, domesticated fire, turning
it into a valuable household tool, but the gods did something
much greater: They "established that Fire in their inmost self
and, having established that immortality in their inmost self and
become immortal and unconquerable, they defeated their mortal
and conquerable enemies."[172] The gods were not satisfied with
fire as a mere domestic tool capable of serving creaturely needs.
They recognized that the same life-generating fire that eternally
builds and maintains the entire universe exists also inside each
person as the life-generating energy of the body, and by establishing that life-generating fire within themselves, they became
immortal beings.[173]

The mythological battle between the gods and the demons
takes place, of course, within the human psyche, and the sacrifices that are the weapons in that battle occur in the human body's
metabolic fires. Thus, the myth teaches that it is a person's task
to achieve internally the same victory the gods achieved. When a
person succumbs to mundane or selfish thoughts, the demons are
offering sacrifices in that person's inner metabolic fires. When
virtuous thoughts arise, the gods are offering those sacrifices.
The vitality that animates the human body is nothing but a series

---

[171] The myth related here, from the *Satapatha Brahmana* (I.5.2.6), is
translated in Panikkar, *The Vedic Experience*, pp. 382–383.

[172] Panikkar (trans. and ed.), *The Vedic Experience*, p. 383.

[173] See Bodewitz, *The Daily Evening and Morning Offering*, pp. 42, 113,
137–138, 160–161, 171, *passim*; Bodewitz, *Jaiminiya Brahmana I*, pp.
220–229, 254–264, 318–338, *passim*.

of fire sacrifices, and by internalizing the noble fire sacrifices of the temple, a person transcends what is time-bound and attains what is immortal. "The [fire] sacrifice is man," asserts the *Satapatha Brahmana*. "[I]n being spread out, it assumes exactly the same stature as man. For this reason, the sacrifice is man."[174]

Classical South Asian medicine identifies several types of "fire" that animate the body of a living person, the most familiar of these being the digestive "fire" (*jatharagni*). Other important "fires" operate in the muscles, burning carbohydrates to power the movement of the limbs, and in the synapses of the neural network, using electricity to communicate information. Ultimately, all the subtle "breaths" that constitute the lifeforce of the body are, in Vedic thought, animated by fire,[175] and when all these "fires" are functioning efficiently, they produce the sweet incense of noble thoughts and actions.[176]

In the Jewish tradition, we encounter the same constellation of ideas. For example, Rabbi Mordechai Twersky of Chernobyl (1770–1837 C.E.), a leading Hasidic master, identified the body's internal metabolic functioning with the fire sacrifice of the

---

[174] *Satapatha Brahmana* I.3.2.1, translated in Panikkar, *The Vedic Experience*, p. 393; see also pp. 390–391, 410–411, 412–413.

[175] See *Pranagnihotra Upanishad, passim*, translated by A.G. Krishna Warrier, posted at *http://www.astrojyoti.com/pranagnihotraupanishad. htm* [accessed Feb. 4, 2019]; *Chandogya Upanishad* 3.16, 5.19–24, translated in Hume, *The Thirteen Principal Upanishads*, pp. 211–212 [3.16], 238–240 [5.19–24]; *Maitri Upanishad* 6.9, translated in Hume, at pp. 429–430; *Mahabharata*, Book 14, §§ 20–25, translated by Kisari Mohan Ganguli, posted at *http://www.sacred-texts.com/hin/m14/* [accessed Feb. 4, 2019]; see also Bodewitz, *The Daily Evening and Morning Offering*, pp. 42, 113, 137–138, 160–161, 171, *passim*; Bodewitz, *Jaiminiya Brahmana I*, pp. 220–229, 254–264, 318–338, *passim*; Eliade, *History of Religious Ideas, Volume 1*, p. 234; Heesterman, *The Broken World*, pp. 213–215.

[176] Svoboda, *Ayurveda*, pp. 51–52.

temple, doing so in the context of a moralistic sermon about natural bodily functions, faithlessness, and illicit sex:

> When a man gets up in the morning... he should first evacu-
> ate his bowels in order to push the waste away so as to give
> the "wicked man" his portion so that he [(the "wicked man")]
> should not be envious and seek to enjoy the holy. It is also to
> avoid the vapours ascending from the dung to the mind since
> when this happens the mind can become contaminated with
> strange thoughts of unbelief and fornication and these invali-
> date the sacrifices of the brain, the Temple of the soul. He will
> then find it easy to purify the brain and to turn away from all
> [inappropriate] thoughts....[177]

Likewise, the Talmud records the following prayer, which again assimilates the body's internal metabolic fire to the fire on the temple's altar:

> Lord of the Universe! it is revealed before Thee that when
> the Sanctuary was in existence, a man sinned and brought an
> offering, of which they sacrificed only the fat and the blood,
> and atonement was made for him. But now, I observe a fast,
> and my fat and blood are diminished. May it be Thy will,
> that my fat and blood which have been diminished may be
> accounted as though I had offered them before Thee upon the
> altar....[178]

According to Jewish ritual law, a Jew must fast on Yom Kippur (the Day of Atonement), but at the inauguration of Solomon's temple, which coincided with Yom Kippur, the people ate.

---

[177] Jacobs, *Hasidic Prayer*, p. 51, quoting source text.

[178] Cohen, *Everyman's Talmud*, pp. 107–108; see also *Zohar* 2:20a–20b
[*Midrash ha-Ne'lam*], translated in Sperling et al., *The Zohar, Vol. III*, pp.
66–67 [fasting is a sacrifice into the body's metabolic fires].

According to tradition, the reason their eating was not accounted as sin was that they were in such a state of spiritual elevation on that particular day that their consumption of food was not eating but rather the offering of sacrifices.[179] Similarly, Rabbi Moshe Chayim Luzzatto (1707–1746 c.e.) uses images from the temple service to describe the temple-like body of a person who has achieved perfect purity of heart:

> One who is Holy... and clings constantly to his God, his soul traveling in channels of truth... — such a person... is himself considered a tabernacle, a sanctuary, an altar.... The Divine Presence dwells with the Holy as it dwelt in the Temple. It follows, then, that the food which they eat is as a sacrifice offered upon the fire.... As our Sages of blessed memory have said..., "If one brings a gift to a Scholar, it is as if he offers up first fruit" and..., "In the place of libation, let him fill the throat of the Scholars with wine." The meaning here is not that Scholars should lust, glutton-like, to fill their throats..., but rather... that Scholars, who are Holy in their ways and in all their deeds, are literally comparable to the sanctuary and the altar, for the Divine Presence dwells in them just as it dwelled in the sanctuary.... [A]nything at all which is made use of by them in some way is elevated and enhanced through having been employed by a righteous individual, by one who communes with the Holiness of the Blessed One.[180]

A similar teaching is recorded in the Jewish classic, *Pirkei Avot*:

---

[179] Weissman (ed.), *The Midrash Says: Vayikra*, p. 202.

[180] Luzzatto, *The Path of the Just*, pp. 329–331; see also *Zohar* 2:168a–169a, translated in Matt, *The Zohar: Pritzker Edition*, vol. V, pp. 476–483 [holy eating took the place of temple sacrifices]; *Zohar* 3:7a–7b, translated in Simon and Levertoff, *The Zohar, Vol. IV*, p. 339 [same]; Weissman (ed.), *The Midrash Says: Vayikra*, p. 202 [same].

Three who have eaten at one table and have not said over it words of Torah are as if they had eaten of the sacrifices of the dead, as it is said, "For all tables are full of vomit *and* filthiness without God" [(Isa 28:8)]. But three who have eaten at one table and have said over it words of Torah are as if they had eaten from the table of God, as it is said, "And he said to me This is the table which is before THE LORD" [(Ezek 41:22)].[181]

Thus, in the Jewish tradition, as in the Vedic tradition, one attains perfection and immortality by establishing the altar fire in one's inmost self. According to Jewish legend, the angel of Esau wrestled with Jacob, trying to frighten him with fire, but Jacob said: "What! thou thinkest thus to afright me, who am made wholly of fire."[182] Like the gods of the Vedic myth, Jacob recognized that human beings are essentially made of fire, and when one has purified the inner altar, as Jacob did, the fire that burns as one's own internal metabolism, like the altar fire, draws down the divine Fire that is the source of eternal life. Hence, the Torah tells us about Jacob: "And God went up from upon him." (Gen 35:13.) This verse does not mean—as is usually thought—that God left Jacob to return to the heavens above; rather, it means that Jacob became the resting place of God below.

---

[181] *Pirkei Avot* III, 4, translated in Herford, *Pirke Aboth*, p. 67; see also Karo, *Maggid Mesharim*, translated in Jacobs, *The Schocken Book of Jewish Mystical Testimonies*, p. 140 [same]; Green (trans.), *Menahem Nahum of Chernobyl*, p. 99 [same]; Nachman of Breslov, *Likutey Moharan* I, 17 [blemished eating is like sacrifices offered on a blemished altar].

[182] Ginzberg, *The Legends of the Jews, Volume 1*, p. 384.

7. The Relevance of Leviticus

The correspondence between the temple and the human body made the sacrificial rite of the Jerusalem temple into an effective pedagogical tool that could catalyze inner transformation. The external ritual laid down tracks in the mind of the observer, slowly constructing in him or her a new self-understanding. In that way, the sacrifice was the external performance of a liberating gnosis, communicating that gnosis not by speech but by presenting it in enacted form.[183]

In other words, the temple ritual gave people an external model of the interior environment they hoped to create. Their goal was to sanctify their own bodies, cell by cell, tending daily to their own inner fires, cultivating the life-generating fire, and avoiding the fires of destruction, until ultimately their consciousness merged into divine consciousness. By meditating on the external temple and its rituals, one erected an inner temple, becoming that ideal. In the book of Exodus, YHVH told Moses that the Israelites should build a temple sanctuary "and I [(YHVH)] will dwell *betokham*." (Exod 25:8.) The Hebrew word *betokham* is usually translated as "among them" or "in the midst of them," but it can just as correctly be translated as "within them" (*i.e.*, "within each of them"). In other words, YHVH intended the Israelites to build an *inner* temple so that YHVH could dwell in their hearts.

The destruction of the Jerusalem temple in 70 C.E. was certainly a great tragedy of history, but in one important sense nothing changed. The temple of wood and stone lay in ruins, but according to the fractal metaphysics of sacrificial ritual, the devotee's own body remained as the ultimate place of atonement.[184]

---

[183] See, e.g., Coomaraswamy, "Atmayajna," pp. 381–382.

[184] See Green (trans.), *Menahem Nahum of Chernobyl*, pp. 71–79, esp. pp. 73, 75, 78.

Thus, a psalm entreats YHVH: "[Let] my prayer stand [like] incense before You; the lifting of my palms, [like] an afternoon wheat offering." (Ps 141:2.)[185] And many mystics of the Vedic tradition likewise recognize that, in the modern age, prayer is an appropriate equivalent to the fire sacrifice.[186] By the recitation of holy texts, by small acts of kindness, and by a life dedicated to pious observances, the satisfying aroma (*rei'ach nicho'ach*) of one's inner metabolic fires rises up to God, and in that form, the daily offerings of the temple service continue, even while the temple of wood and stone lies in ruins.

Thus, the Jerusalem temple—as mesocosm—mediated the cosmic and human levels of a marvelous fractal geometry,[187] but even when the temple was standing, the cosmos and the human body were always God's true temples. The continuing relevance of the book of Leviticus lies, then, in the insight that Ezekiel's vision of a future Jerusalem temple (Ezek 40–48) refers to each of us.

8. Ritual Purity

The book of Leviticus is the manual of the priests, and among classical priestly values, ritual purity ranked high. Hence, we are not surprised to find that Leviticus includes detailed rules of ritual purity. But ritual purity is a concept that is particularly

---

[185] Additional examples of this idea in scripture include Pss 40:7–11, 69:31–32, 119:108; Hosea 14:3. See also *Zohar* 1:244a, translated in Matt, *The Zohar: Pritzker Edition*, vol. III, pp. 492–494 [prayer replaced temple sacrifices]; Cohen, *Everyman's Talmud*, pp. 157–158 [prayer, righteousness, and kindness replaced temple sacrifices]; Weissman (ed.), *The Midrash Says: Vayikra*, p. 9 [prayer replaced temple sacrifices].

[186] See, e.g., Panikkar (trans. and ed.), *The Vedic Experience*, pp. 392, 394.

[187] Cf. Vesci, *Heat and Sacrifice*, pp. 188–191.

obscure and offensive to the modern mind, and therefore it calls for close analysis.

"Do not eat this food." "Do not touch that object." "Do not take from that person." These laws give rise to an intense consciousness of the physical self and its interactions. But to what end? If the rules of ritual purity are simply a matter of hygiene, then the modern mind has no disagreement with them in principle, but in that case, soap and hot water have rendered them more or less obsolete. When, however, emphasis is placed on a lingering spiritual contamination resulting from seminal emissions or menstruation, the modern mind sees only a hodgepodge of baseless fears and superstitions that work, in practice, to justify unacceptable forms of bigotry.

Nearly every classical culture accepted the metaphysics of spiritual pollution. This concern of our ancestors is evident in the Greek concept of miasma,[188] in the painstaking purity protections that Zoroastrian priests applied not only to the body but also to the natural elements,[189] in the Brahmin purity injunctions detailed in the *Laws of Manu*,[190] in the Jewish restrictions found in the Torah,[191] in Islam's purity observances set forth in *Shari'a* law,[192] and even in Lady MacBeth's concern about the indelible stain of murder.

Are these traditional beliefs rightly rejected? Has modern

---

[188] See Parker, *Miasma*.

[189] See Choksy, *Purity and Pollution in Zoroastrianism*.

[190] See Doniger and Smith (trans.), *The Laws of Manu*; Carman and Marglin (eds.), *Purity and Auspiciousness in Indian Society*; Dumont and Pocock, "Pure and Impure," in Dumont and Pocock (eds.), *Contributions to Indian Sociology*, pp. 9–39.

[191] See Neusner, *The Idea of Purity in Ancient Judaism*; Klawans, *Impurity and Sin in Ancient Judaism*; Milgrom, *Leviticus 1–16*; Milgrom, *Leviticus 17–22*; cf. Jon 4:11 [people of Nineveh don't know right from left (*i.e.*, pure from impure)].

[192] See Katz, *Body of Text*; Reinhart, "Impurity/ No Danger," pp. 1–24.

religion progressed beyond ancient religion at least insofar as it
no longer concerns itself with ritual purity? In modern society,
after all, we routinely touch one another. We shake hands, we
exchange from hand to hand, we embrace, and it matters not
whether the person we embrace is a man who recently had a
seminal emission, a woman who is menstruating, a stylist who
cuts hair for a living, a domestic helper who washes bed sheets
and undergarments, or an undertaker who handles corpses. No
one has "cooties" in modern society; we have no pariahs. Rather,
we are all equals in one great human family. That, at least, is our
ideal, and even when we fall far short of that ideal, we recognize it and reconfirm it in the breach. One could even say that
the ideal of human equality characterizes modern society just
as strongly as the ideals of tribe, caste, and purity characterized
ancient society. To validate purity laws, then, is to undermine
much of the progress the world has made in the last two thousand years. But before dismissing purity laws as superstitions
that rationalize bigotry, we should try to understand the conceptual basis of these laws.

The specific laws differed from culture to culture, but they
all derived from the basic principle that death—particularly
human death—is somehow contaminating:

> See—I have given before you today the life and the good, and
> the death and the evil.... The life and the death I have given
> before you, the blessing and the curse, and you shall choose
> life, so that you will live, you and your offspring....[193]

This text from the Torah links life conceptually to virtue and
blessing, and it links death to evil and curse, and it urges the
reader to shun death and cling to life. According to purity values,
anything that implies death, even by mere association, is contaminating, and this includes not only human corpses but also

[193] Deut 30:15–19.

any portion of the human body that decays or dies.[194] Hair clippings and fingernail parings are minor forms of such "life leaks," decaying skin and household molds are somewhat more significant, and infertile sexual emissions are particularly dangerous on account of the concentrated loss of vitality they represent. Consistent with these principles, the book of Leviticus closely regulates exposure to human corpses (see Lev 21:1–4, 21:11, 22:4–7; see also Num 6:6–7, 19:11–20), and it distinguishes animals as clean or unclean based in part on their association with decay and death (see Lev 11; see also Deut 14:3–21). Leviticus also regulates exposure to skin ailments and fungal infestations (Lev 13–14), and it categorizes sexual emissions according to graduated degrees of impurity (Lev 12, 15). Most modern people are not willing to accept that death is somehow contagious by contact or proximity, or that a mere fingernail clipping can somehow expose a person to this death contagion, so they dismiss these rules as ill-informed precautions against bacterial infection.

To understand these rules, however, we have to consider that ritual impurity refers to *spiritual* infection, not *physical* infection—it is the contamination of the *psyche*, not that of the *body*, that is so offensive to priestly values. In other words, it is not death but the *knowing* of death that is the cause of spiritual pollution. According to the logic of the purity laws, spiritual germs (bad memes) damage one's mind just as much as physical germs (bad bacteria) damage one's body. When a person has close contact with a dead thing or with something associated with death,

---

[194] See, e.g., Biale, *Eros and the Jews*, pp. 28–31 [Jewish purity observances]; Fuller, *The Camphor Flame*, pp. 15–16 [Hindu purity observances]; Alter, *The Wrestler's Body*, p. 240 [same]; Obeyesekere, "The Impact of Ayurvedic Ideas on the Culture and the Individual in Sri Lanka," in Leslie (ed.), *Asian Medical Systems*, p. 215 [same]; Katz, *Body of Text*, pp. 4 [Zoroastrian purity observances], 4–5 [Christian purity observances], 135–140 [Islamic purity observances].

he or she has close contact, spiritually speaking, with the Idea of Death—the death archetype. Thus, physical proximity to death has the power to distort the archetypal Ideas by which a person interprets sensory data, causing one to see the world as dead matter rather than as conscious soul.[195]

Jewish prophecy asserts that, in messianic times, ritual impurity will no longer exist. In the book of Zechariah, we read: "It will be on that day—the word of YHVH of hosts—…I will pass [away] the spirit of impurity from the land." (Zech 13:2.) Moreover, it is possible, according to Jewish thought, to live in that state of messianic freedom before its time.[196] A close examination of Hebrew scripture reveals two distinct principles by which God orders affairs in the world—one is the rule of strict retributive justice, and the other is the rule of mercy. According to retributive justice, what a person does comes back to the person, measure for measure. If one steals; one will be stolen from. If one kills; one will be killed. By contrast, the rule of mercy, which is generally associated in the Torah with the name YHVH (see Exod 34:5–7; Num 14:18–20; Deut 5:9–10), shields one from the rule of retributive justice.

We encounter the retributive principle in the well-known passage from the book of Leviticus that speaks of "an eye for an eye" and "a tooth for a tooth." (Lev 24:20.) This passage should not be read as setting forth a governing principle for civil justice systems, for such systems are created for the protection of society, not for the judgment of souls. Rather, the passage sets forth

---

[195] Regarding spiritual germs that damage one's mind just as much as physical germs damage one's body, Jacob Milgrom gives the example of finding one's half-filled teacup in the bathroom and then not wanting to drink from it. Milgrom, *Leviticus 1–16*, p. 720. On death contamination as the basis of Torah's purity laws, see *id.* at pp. 766–768, 1000–1004.

[196] See, e.g., *Zohar* 2:183a–183b, translated in Matt, *The Zohar: Pritzker Edition*, vol. VI, pp. 27–29.

a principle of nature that is familiar to anyone who has studied Eastern philosophy, where it is referred to as the "law of karma." It simply describes a morally charged version of Newton's third law of physics. Consider, for example, the covenant that God—Elohim, not YHVH—made with Noah: "The one who spills the blood of man, by man his blood will be spilled." (Gen 9:6.)

Significantly, however, a distinctive feature characterizes the verses from the Torah that set forth this rule of retributive justice: They employ a chiastic structure, meaning that as one reads in either direction away from the central pivot of the verses, the provisions repeat one another, like reflections in a mirror. Consider, for example, the complete text of the "eye for an eye" passage from Leviticus (Lev 24:15–23):

[A] Any man who will denigrate his god, he will bear his sin. . . .
    [B] Stranger and native alike. . . .
        [C] And a man who smites any human soul will surely die.
            [D] And the smiter of an animal soul will pay, soul for soul.
                [E] And a man who gives a wound in his people—as he did, so will be done to him.
                    [F] Break for break,
                        [G] Eye for eye,
                    [F] Tooth for tooth.
                [E] As he gave a wound to man, so will be given to him.
            [D] And the smiter of an animal shall pay.
        [C] And the smiter of a man shall die. . . .
    [B] Stranger and native alike. . . .
[A] And they took the one who cursed to the outside of the camp, and they stoned him. . . .

Likewise, consider the covenant against murder that God (Elohim, not YHVH) made with Noah (Gen 9:6):

[A] The one who spills
  [B] the blood
   [C] of man,
   [C] by man
  [B] his blood
[A] will be spilled.

Finally, consider the commandment to atone for sin on Yom Kippur through acts of self-affliction (Lev 16:29–31):

[A] And this shall be for you for an eternal decree....
  [B] You shall afflict your souls,
   [C] and you shall not do any work....
    [D] For on this day he will atone for you to purify you;
    [D] from all your sin before YHVH you will be purified
   [C] It is a Sabbath of ceasing for you,
  [B] And you shall afflict your souls.
[A] An eternal decree.

What we learn from these passages and many others like them is that when the Torah is invoking the divine principle of retributive justice (the law of karma), the text employs a chiastic structure that imitates its unforgiving quid-pro-quo content.

Significantly, many of the purity laws of the book of Leviticus are set forth in this same chiastic verse structure. For example, the laws governing sexual emissions can be categorized as follows (Lev 15:2–30):

[A] Abnormal male genital emissions (vv. 2–15).
  [B] Normal male genital emissions (vv. 16–17).
   [C] Procreative sexual relations (v. 18).
  [B] Normal female genital emissions (vv. 19–24).
[A] Abnormal female genital emissions (vv. 25–30).

The reader can also consult chapter 14 of Leviticus, which

describes the sacrificial rituals necessary in the case of impure skin diseases (Lev 14:11–20, 14:21–32); again, the text employs a chiastic structure. What these verses communicate through the subtlety of their structure is that purity laws relate only to the rule of retributive justice; they do not govern a person who, through humility and selflessness, has come under the rule of mercy.

Consider, in this context, the story of Gehazi the servant of Elisha. (2 Kings 5.) An Aramean general named Na'aman suffered from a ritually impure skin affliction (*tzara'at*), and he came to the prophet Elisha with a large sum of money, hoping Elisha would heal him. Expecting Elisha to perform an elaborate ritual, Na'aman was disappointed when Elisha merely sent him to immerse seven times in the Jordan River. Na'aman scoffed: "Are not... the rivers of Damascus better than all the waters of Israel?" Nonetheless, he went to the Jordan and immersed in accordance with Elisha's instruction, and his skin was healed, becoming "like the skin of a small child." Na'aman then humbled himself before Elisha and sought to compensate Elisha generously, but Elisha took no interest in Na'aman's gift, and Na'aman went on his way.

Elisha's servant Gehazi, however, ran after the general, coveting the general's wealth. He told Na'aman, untruthfully, that Elisha had sent him to collect the payment, and the general gave a large amount of money to Gehazi, who put the money away and returned to Elisha. Gehazi then lied to Elisha about where he had been, but Elisha knew and predicted that Na'aman's state of ritual impurity would be transferred to Gehazi, which is exactly what happened.

What this Bible story suggests is that ritual impurity only affects a person who is arrogant and self-seeking in his or her interactions with others. Thus, it is the *thoughts* a person has, not the *things* he or she touches, that make a person pure or impure. A well-known Buddhist story illustrates the same point. Two mendicant monks were journeying together, and they arrived at the bank of a shallow river. There they encountered an attractive young woman who asked them to help her cross. The older monk lifted the woman and waded across the river, putting her down on the opposite bank. Then the two monks continued their journey, but after some time, the younger monk expressed a doubt that had been troubling him. He complained that the older monk had compromised his monastic purity by touching a young woman. The older monk answered the complaint, saying: "I put her down after crossing the river, but you're still carrying her." In other words, the younger monk had allowed his *thoughts* to be affected by the beauty of the woman. The only impurity that he experienced was the impurity of his own mind.

9. The Enacted Metaphor

We have discussed in some detail the correspondence, in both Vedic and Jewish thought, between eating and temple sacrifices. But Rabbi Isaac of Acre (13th and 14th centuries C.E.) instead employs a sexual metaphor to describe the temple service, relating a story that equates the sacrifices in the Jerusalem temple with procreation:

> A certain sage asked his colleague about the subject of the [temple] sacrifices, and said: How is it possible that a matter as disgusting as the burning of fat and the sprinkling of blood, with the smell of the skin and hair of the [whole offering], should be a matter by which the world is sustained, that it be a cause for unification above and for blessing and for the sustaining of all that exists? He answered: I will tell you a parable, as to what this resembles. A child is born and is left alone when he is little, and he sustains himself by herbs and water, and he grows up and it happens that he comes within the habitation of human beings, and one day he saw a man coupling

with his wife. He began to mock them and say: what is this foolish person doing? They said to him: you see this act; it is that which sustains the world.... He said to them: how is it possible that from such filth and dirt there should be the cause for this good and beautiful and praiseworthy world? And it is nevertheless true....[197]

Not surprisingly, the same sexual metaphor appears in Hindu texts.[198] The kindling of the altar fire is closely related to the mechanics of conception. The sticks—one phallic and the other bowl-shaped—are said to be male and female. The male stick is churned within the female stick until a spark emerges.[199] The spark entering the firepit corresponds to semen entering the womb, and the result in both cases is the regeneration of life.[200] Likewise, the strands of butter that the priest pours into the sacrificial fire are like emissions of semen into a womb.[201]

So what is the correct metaphor—eating or sex—that best conveys the power and meaning of the sacrificial rite? Perhaps the sacrificial rite will not be constrained by any metaphor, because the sacrifice is not a *representation* of a thing; rather, it

---

[197] Isaac of Acre, *Me'irat 'Enayim*, quoted in Idel, *The Mystical Experience in Abraham Abulafia*, p. 203; see also *Zohar* 1:244a, translated in Matt, *The Zohar: Pritzker Edition*, vol. III, pp. 492–494 [sacrifices = sexual union].

[198] See, e.g., Bodewitz, *The Daily Evening and Morning Offering*, pp. 26–27, 34–35, 38–39, 41–46, 51–53, 61–63, 80–84, 92–95, 97, 145–153, 158–159, 170–171; O'Flaherty, *Women, Androgynes, and Other Mythical Beasts*, pp. 20–21, 26–28, 48–53; O'Flaherty, *Śiva: The Erotic Ascetic*, pp. 90–110, 273–282.

[199] *Ṛg Veda* 3.29.1–3; O'Flaherty, *The Origins of Evil*, p. 333.

[200] Vesci, *Heat and Sacrifice*, pp. 204–206.

[201] O'Flaherty, *Women, Androgynes, and Other Mythical Beasts*, p. 49.

is the thing. Perhaps the life-generating activities of the natural world, including both eating and sex, are representations of *the sacrifice*, not the other way around. By this way of thought, even the sacrificial rite of the temple is a representation—an enacted metaphor—signifying the true Sacrifice. The true Sacrifice, in other words, is an archetype, an Idea, that preexists any of its instantiations, including its ritual instantiations. "With the sacrifice the gods sacrificed to the Sacrifice."[202]

According to Plato's theory of Ideas, wood cannot be known unless one has in one's mind an Idea of Wood by which to interpret the sensory data associated with wood, and even if one has the Idea of Wood in one's mind, a musical instrument, for example a lyre, is just a random arrangement of wooden pieces, not a lyre, unless one has in one's mind the Idea of Lyre.[203] Thus, Ideas—also called "forms" or "supernal images"—enable us to measure and evaluate the incoming flow of data and construct from it a world. Moreover, in our *knowing* of the world, those archetypal Ideas—which exist in our own minds—are the immediate objects of our perception, and without those Ideas, external objects are only unintelligible data, for all knowing is really interpretation.

So according to the theory of Ideas, what is the sacrificial rite? Is it an external drama that takes place in a temple in Jerusalem or on the coast of South India? It is not. Rather, the sacrificial rite is an Idea in the world of Ideas, and without the Idea of Sacrifice, the external drama would be unknowable. Moreover, the world of Ideas is, according to both Platonic and Jewish thought, the true world, and the physical objects of the external world are merely shadows on the wall of Plato's allegorical

---

[202] *Rg Veda* 10.90.16, translated in O'Flaherty, *The Rig Veda*, p. 31.

[203] See Plato, *Cratylus* 389–390; see also *id.* 439–440.

cave,[204] or, according to the Jewish model, projections of the Hebrew language into dense matter.[205]

Consider, however, that if eating, sex, and ritual sacrifice all invoke a common archetype of Sacrifice, then any of these activities has the power to affect the others. In other words, if any of them is demeaned, the Idea that they all invoke is demeaned, causing all of them to be demeaned, and if any of them is honored, that same Idea is honored, causing all of them to be honored. Therefore, whether we are eating, having sex, or performing the temple service, the same archetypal Idea—the Sacrifice—is bearing the moral burden of our conduct and our intentions.

This theory has powerful implications. Because very different external activities are linked by the common archetypes they invoke, the repair and restoration of those archetypes is the master key to spiritual and psychological health. According to this theory, the root problem in our experience of the world is not the state of the world but the state of our Ideas. When we degrade the Ideas by which we know the world, we see ugliness where we should see beauty, and then we act based on that ugliness, spreading more ugliness. Thus, for example, because eating and sex are metaphors for sacrifice, we degrade the Idea of Sacrifice through profane eating and profane sex, and by sanctifying the sacrificial rite in the temple, we repair and restore the Idea of Sacrifice. Physically speaking, the sacrificial rite affects only the temple's altar made of metal and wood, but our *consciousness* of the rite affects our Ideas, and thus it has the power to heal our perception of the world.

---

[204] For Plato's famous cave allegory, see Plato, *The Republic*, Book VII, 514a–520a.

[205] See, e.g., Scholem, *Major Trends*, p. 17; Scholem, *On the Kabbalah*, pp. 74–77; Krassen (trans.), *The Generations of Adam*, pp. 30–31, 164–165.

The first part of Leviticus (Lev 1–16) describes the temple service and the ways in which the priests carefully guarded the purity of the temple, and the second part of Leviticus (Lev 17–27)—often called the "Holiness Code"—focuses on the "land" and the ways in which moral transgressions defile the land (see Lev 18:24–30). Moreover, the book of Leviticus asserts that moral transgressions taking place far from the Jerusalem temple somehow also defiled *the temple*, which then had to be purified by ritual sacrifices. (Lev 16:16–19.)[206] But how is the temple defiled by moral transgressions taking place far away? The answer is apparent when we focus on our *knowing* of the world, for regardless of how distant two things are externally, they are known by an observer on the same screen of consciousness and thus are one.

According to the logic of Leviticus, the "land" (like the temple) is holy, a place where people are expected to share wealth and to help one another, and where real estate and labor contracts are temporary and revocable (see Lev 25). Thus, if a person, through moral transgression, degrades the "land," he or she degrades the Idea of Holiness, and by degrading that Idea, the temple is also degraded. In other words, distant things affect one another through the common Ideas by which they are known, and by sanctifying the temple's altar made of metal and wood, the Idea of Holiness is repaired, and the holiness of the "land" is restored.

We have seen that the metaphor of sacrifice links many superficially distinct events. The Brahmin priest sacrifices *soma* (plant sap) into the hungry mouth of *agni* (fire) and thus restores the lost sap to Prajapati's enervated body. The dying man sacrifices his body to the hungry flames of the cremation pyre and thus reemerges whole. The spiritual aspirant sacrifices pure food into the digestive fire of his or her stomach and thus generates

---

[206] See Milgrom, *Leviticus 1–16*, pp. 48–49, 254–261, 1033–1040; cf. *id.* at pp. 718–736.

pure thoughts. The husband sacrifices his semen into the life-generating warmth of his wife's womb and thus conceives a child. The wealthy man sacrifices a few coins into the palm of a beggar and thus restores hope to a world that has lost hope. And, every kind act, every recited prayer, every repetition of a divine name is an oblation of one's vital energies.

The sacrifice is a versatile metaphor, and therefore in the knowing of so many diverse actions, we know the one Idea of Sacrifice. In that sense, diversity is really unity. But our actions have degraded the Idea of Sacrifice, thus damaging our perception of the world, and the sacrificial rite can be a way of beginning the important work of restoration. No ritual, however, matches the power of loving-kindness to restore the Idea of Sacrifice. "For if you raise up to me whole offerings and your wheat cakes," YHVH says, "I will not desire [them], and peace [offerings] from your stall-fed animals I will not regard.... Let judgment be revealed like water, and righteousness like a continuous stream." (Amos 5:22–24.)

A story from the *Mahabharata* conveys this principle quite beautifully.[207] Yudhishthira, the king of Hastinapur, organizes the greatest horse sacrifice ever held, thus attaining the heavenly realm. As part of this unsurpassed ritual, the sacrificial horse is let loose to roam the entire world, and Yudhishthira's brother Arjuna follows it, conquering the world and inviting the world's kings to attend Yudhishthira's great sacrifice. Yudhishthira then gives away generous gifts of rich food, spices, garments, horses, elephants, jewels, and billions of gold coins. He gives three times the required fee-gift for the rite. Yudhishthira even gives away the world itself, which his brother has conquered for him, and he then departs to the forest to live as an ascetic.

When the horse sacrifice is finally complete, an unusual mongoose is seen rolling in the dust where the sacrifice has just been conducted. Half the body of this mongoose is gold; the

---

[207] *Mahabharata*, Book 14, §§ 70–96.

other half is normal. The mongoose then complains that Yud-hishthira's awesome sacrifice—the most elaborate ritual sacri-fice ever conducted—is not equal to the sacrifice of a pound of barley meal by a single poor man. The mongoose relates the following story.

There was a poor pious man who lived a life of simplicity and austerity, surviving from gleanings and eating only once per day. A famine came to the land where that poor man lived with his wife, son, and daughter-in-law. For many days, the family went without food. Then, at last, the poor man was able to glean a pound of barley (animal fodder). His wife ground the barley and prepared four small loaves. The family was about to eat, when an unknown mendicant arrived.

Aware that a home is sanctified by serving a guest, the poor man invited the mendicant inside and offered the guest his own barley loaf. The guest ate but was not satisfied. The poor man's wife then offered the barley loaf that had been prepared for her. Again, the guest ate but was not satisfied. Then the son and next the daughter-in-law offered their loaves. Finally, when the last barley loaf was offered to the guest, the guest revealed that he was a celestial being and that the family would be rewarded with immortality for their willingness to sacrifice their own lives for the sake of another.

The mongoose relates this story and then reports that, hav-ing observed all these events, he went to the place where a few barley crumbs had spilled on the floor of the poor man's house. He rolled among those crumbs, and wherever the barley crumbs touched his body, his body was transformed into incorruptible gold. It was for this reason that half the mongoose's body was gold, and the mongoose had come to Yudhishthira's sacrifice, hoping to turn the other half of his body to gold, but without success.

The message of the story is, of course, that even the great-est ritual sacrifice ever conducted is not as powerful a means of repairing the Idea of Sacrifice as one poor family's sacrifice of their own humble meal. True righteousness consists of renunciation, generosity, and compassion, not rote ritual.

There is a great sacredness in sacrifice. Consider the palpable holiness of places like Arlington National Cemetery, the beaches of Normandy, the concentration camps of the Holocaust. Consider also the awesome power of Abraham Lincoln's timeless words, spoken on the battlefield in Gettysburg, where perhaps as many as fifty thousand Americans saturated the ground with their lifeblood:

> [W]e cannot dedicate—we cannot consecrate—we cannot hallow—this ground. The brave men, living and dead, who struggled here have consecrated it, far above our poor power to add or detract.... It is... for us to be here dedicated to the great task remaining before us—that from these honored dead we take increased devotion to that cause for which they gave the last full measure of devotion—that we here highly resolve that these dead shall not have died in vain—that this nation, under God, shall have a new birth of freedom....[208]

In that moment, Lincoln was the chief priest, the fifty thousand were the bulls and lambs, and a "new birth of freedom" for a multiethnic nation was the holy benediction—a cause for which Lincoln would soon pour out his own lifeblood, on Good Friday no less, the Christian day of sacrifice.

---

[208] President Abraham Lincoln's Gettysburg Address, Nov. 19, 1863.

PART FOUR

Moses' Sin at the Rock
A Commentary on Numbers

An ignorant man is a rock from which no water flows.

—Ali ibn Abi Talib (601–661 C.E.)

1. "In a little while they will stone me!"

In Parts One and Two, we developed the thesis that the Torah has its roots in *two* religious cultures (Egyptian and Canaanite), that it expresses devotion to *two* deities (Thoth and El), that this division within the Torah reflects the history of *two* rival kingdoms (Judah and Israel), and that the ultimate purpose of the Torah was (and is) to interweave the sacred texts of these traditions, making *two* into *one*. "In that day," the prophet asserts, "YHVH will be one, and his name [will be] one." (Zech 14:9.) That powerful quote from the book of Zechariah simultaneously affirms unity and concedes that unity remains elusive.

In Judaism as in the world, the centrifugal forces of separation too often operate beneath the surface of oft-repeated assertions of unity, and although many people piously invoke the dogma of a unified Torah, scholars who closely study the Torah quickly see that it is a tapestry of competing ideas, values, and perspectives, drawing from multiple literary sources. And at the root of that complexity is the historical fact of two rival kingdoms with two distinct religious cultures.

That is a provocative idea, and therefore it is intentionally obscured beneath the Torah's surface story. But here, in Parts Four and Five, we encounter a thesis that is even more provocative. Parts Four and Five argue that, as the Israelites set out from Mount Sinai toward Canaan, a deadly confrontation broke out among the leaders of the people, and a band of rebels seized power. Moses and Aaron were arrested, charged with capital offenses, tried, convicted, and executed. A close reader of the Torah will recall that shortly after leaving Egypt, Moses—a prophet, whose every word is true—declares: "In a little while they will stone me!" (Exod 17:4.) The provocative thesis of Parts Four and Five is that in a little while they *do* stone him and that both Moses and Aaron die as martyrs.

Some readers will summarily dismiss this thesis as mere fantasy, but as we shall see, it is the rivalry between the Kingdom of Judah and the Kingdom of Israel—not a scholar's overactive imagination—that best explains this hidden drama of the Torah. Indeed, the puzzle of the Torah is half solved when the pro-Judah bias of Hebrew scripture is taken into account. (Examples of this bias are set forth in Appendix Two.) The goal of Parts Four and Five is not to make up fantasies about the figures described in the Bible; rather, it is to unlock the secrets of the Torah using the techniques of biblical hermeneutics that are recorded in the ancient commentaries and in the Torah itself. If there is a different explanation of the textual evidence, one that is more plausible than the one presented here, then the present author looks forward to learning about it. But before we reject the thesis of Parts Four and Five, we should fairly consider the evidence mustered here in its support.

The book of Numbers relates a series of seemingly disjointed episodes, and the reader is left to wander aimlessly through its plotless narrative like the Israelites wandering through the desert. But according to the Babylonian Talmud, the sequence of Torah's verses is scrambled to obscure Torah's true story (see, e.g., *Pesachim* 6b; *Sanhedrin* 65b), and every odd phrase, every misspelled word, every stray letter is intentional—a signal designed to connect disparate parts of the story to one another. Therefore, it is not enough just to read the Torah as one might do a newspaper. One must read it as a master scribe would read it; one must read it like a detective searching for the clues that solve a crime. And when one learns how to read Numbers and Deuteronomy, those books are transformed. They then relate a gripping tale of rebellion culminating in the execution of Moses and Aaron on capital charges.

It takes a certain amount of courage to proceed down the path that Parts Four and Five set before the reader. Courage to search out the Torah's hidden narrative. Courage—for those who read their own national story in the Torah—to think about that story in a new way. Courage to embrace a deeper understanding of the myths that shape Western culture.

2. The Blasphemer

The first important clue regarding the martyrdom of Moses and Aaron is not in the book of Numbers; it is the story of the blasphemer in the book of Leviticus. Chapter 24 of Leviticus describes a mysterious episode in which "the son of an Israelite woman expressed the name [YHVH] and cursed" (Lev 24:11), and the law of the blasphemer is then announced. The episode is unconnected to the surrounding sections of the Torah, and it appears to be intended simply to provide a basis for promulgating the rule regarding blasphemy. But as with all things in the Torah, the story is more than what appears on the surface. On closer analysis, the blasphemer story from Leviticus turns out to be remarkably similar to a story from Numbers that tells of a confrontation between Korach and Moses, culminating in Moses angrily expressing the name YHVH and cursing Korach to die an unnatural death. (See Num 16.) In other words, Moses does exactly what the blasphemer did: "he expressed the name and cursed." (Lev 24:11.)

Looking first at the blasphemer story, we learn from the chiastic structure of the text (the significance of which we have already discussed) that the blasphemer's capital offense was not simple blasphemy; it was invoking the name YHVH in a curse that resulted in death. The relevant verses (Lev 24:15–23) are set forth at the top of the next page.

We begin with the first line. To better illustrate the chiasmus, the text of the first line shown on the next page is abbreviated. The complete line actually announces two contradictory rules: "[1] Any man that will denigrate his god, he will bear his sin, and [2] [he who] expresses the name YHVH will surely die; the entire Assembly will surely stone him." (Lev 24:15–16.)

[A] Any man who will denigrate his god, he will bear his sin....

  [B] Stranger and native alike....

    [C] And a man who smites any human soul will surely die.

      [D] And the smiter of an animal soul will pay, soul for soul.

        [E] And a man who gives a wound in his people—as he did, so will be done to him.

          [F] Break for break,

            [G] Eye for eye,

          [F] Tooth for tooth.

        [E] As he gave a wound to man, so will be given to him.

      [D] And the smiter of an animal shall pay.

    [C] And the smiter of a man shall die....

  [B] Stranger and native alike....

[A] And they took the one who cursed to the outside of the camp, and they stoned him....

Rule [1] of the complete text of the first line asserts that a blasphemer "will bear his sin"—that is, the evil that follows from his inappropriate invocation of God's name will be revisited upon him. But rule [2] asserts instead that anyone who "expresses the name YHVH" (*i.e.*, reveals the secret pronunciation of the name)[209] will be stoned to death regardless of how he used or misused the name. The apparent contradiction is

---

[209] The Hebrew word translated as "expresses" is *noqeiv*, which means "to specify" or "to express in a direct way" (*i.e.*, not by mere allusion). In the verse under discussion, the word is sometimes translated as "blasphemes," but it certainly does not mean that. For example, in Num 1:17, the same word is used to describe the specification by name of the leaders of the tribes, and the context there does not imply any sort of condemnation or reproach. The word does, however, imply a formal invocation, using the full and true name of a person or thing, not a pseudonym.

resolved, however, if we recognize that the first part of the statement announces the operative rule of the blasphemer ("he will bear his sin"), and the second part announces what became of a *particular person*, the person in the blasphemer story who expressed the name YHVH ("he will surely die"). In other words, the second part of the statement is descriptive, not prescriptive.

Many provisions of the Torah that appear on their face to state laws of general application are actually descriptive, not prescriptive, stating only what happened to a particular person who acted in a particular way. We can deduce this point from, among other things, the list of forbidden sexual unions listed in chapters 18 and 20 of Leviticus. The list is incomplete, prohibiting some slightly irregular sexual unions (such as sex with two women who are sisters, or sex with a menstruating woman), while remaining silent about other sexual unions that, by most standards, are much more irregular (such as father-daughter incest). The oddity is explained when we see that some of the prohibited sexual unions listed in Leviticus are unions that actually take place somewhere in the Bible's narrative. Thus, the list in Leviticus is not necessarily intended to be complete; rather, it is intended, in part, to be descriptive of the lives of specific biblical figures.

Regarding the statement in Leviticus relating the punishment of the blasphemer, the first half of the statement states the law of strict retributive justice or karma ("he will bear his sin"). In the Jewish legal tradition, "blasphemy" is an act that diminishes the dignity of God's most revered name, YHVH, and it includes expressing that name in a context, such as public anger, that brings the name into disrepute. The name YHVH is associated with divine mercy (see Exod 34:5–7; Num 14:18–20; Deut 5:9–10), but by abusing that name in public, the blasphemer alienates himself from God's mercy and brings himself under the law of retributive justice ("he will bear his sin"). And the blasphemer story relates in detail the harsh, measure-for-measure reality of that retributive justice.

234

TORAH AND NONDUALISM

The chiastic structure of the text naturally focuses the reader on the pivot: "Eye for eye" (Hebrew: *ayin tachat ayin*). The symmetry of this "pivot" is the key that unlocks the entire passage. The central point is the letter *chet* (CH) of the word *TaCHaT*, a letter whose name means "sin" (Hebrew: *cheit'a*). As one moves in either direction away from the letter *chet* ("sin"), the letters, and then the words, and then the ideas repeat one another almost verbatim, as if the *chet* ("sin") were a mirror. According to this chiastic principle, the punishment line of the blasphemer story (the last line) must match substantively the line describing the blasphemer's crime (the first line), and thus the punishment line reveals *an undisclosed detail* about the blasphemer's crime. The punishment line states: "They took the one who cursed to the outside of the camp, *and they stoned him.*" (Italics added.) They killed him, in other words, and therefore, according to the story's rule of retributive justice, and also according to its chiastic structure, the blasphemer of the first line must have invoked the name YHVH in a curse that resulted in death.

Next, let us consider the story from Numbers of Korach's confrontation with Moses. In the story, Moses angrily invokes the name YHVH and curses Korach to die an unnatural death, a death that then transpires. In other words, Moses does precisely what the blasphemer from the Leviticus story did, although the Korach story makes no mention of blasphemy.

Korach is the son of Izhar, Moses' uncle (see Exod 6:16–27), and he is one of the leaders of the Assembly of Israel (*Adat Yisrael*)—also called the "Sanhedrin"—which is a governing council consisting of representatives from all the Israelite tribes. (See, e.g., Num 11:16–17, 11:24–26; Deut 1:9–18; cf. Exod 18:13–26.)[210] Over time, a group within the Assembly has grown frustrated with the leadership of Moses and Aaron, and it eventually chooses Korach—who aspires to be chief priest in

---

[210] See also Rashi on Lev 4:13, translated in Yitzchaki, *Rashi: Commentary on the Torah*, vol. 3, p. 38.

place of Aaron—to lead the people back to Egypt, thus invoking Moses' wrath. (See Num 14:4; 16:1–34; Neh 9:17.)

As mentioned, some passages of the Torah suggest that the Israelites left Egypt only temporarily, intending to worship at Mount Sinai and then return to Egypt. (See Exod 3:12, 3:18, 5:1, 5:3, 7:16, 8:4, 8:21–25.) Other passages, however, invoke YHVH's promise to give the land of Canaan as a homeland for Abraham's descendants (see Gen 12:7, 13:14–18, 15:7–21, 26:3–5), and these passages suggest that the Israelites intended to leave Egypt permanently, relocating to Canaan (see Exod 3:8, 3:17, 13:5, 32:13, 33:1–3; Num 11:12, 14:23, 32:11; Deut 1:6–8). It may be that these conflicting passages reflect conflicting expectations among the people whom Moses and Aaron were leading. Thus, when the Israelites leave Mount Sinai, heading toward Canaan (Num 10:11; Deut 1:6–8, 1:19), a large group begins to rebel against Moses' leadership, frustrated by the austere conditions of the desert, fearing the uncertainties of migrating to Canaan, and seeking instead to return to Egypt, where, even in servitude, they enjoyed a relatively comfortable way of life (see Num 11:4–6). Indeed, at this critical point in the story, even Aaron and his sister Miriam begin to doubt Moses, criticizing him concerning his Nubian wife. (Num 12.)[211]

Faced with this growing resistance and hoping to reassure

---

[211] The leading commentary (Rashi, 11th century C.E.) explains that under the influence of this Nubian wife, Moses was practicing sexual abstinence in order to cleave to God without interruption and that this practice was the basis of Miriam and Aaron's criticism. Interestingly, the Torah relates that, as a punishment, YHVH made Miriam's skin white "like snow." Num 12:10. The form of Miriam's punishment seems symbolic, drawing an intentional contrast to the dark skin of the Nubian wife. That fact could be read as an indication that Miriam's criticism had a racial element that was offensive to YHVH. Significantly, the Bible includes several assertions that YHVH "dwell[s] in thick darkness" (1 Kings 8:12; 2 Chron 6:1; see also Exod 20:18), and the Hebrew word for "thick darkness" (*'arafel*) contains the root letters of "skin" and "dark."

the people, Moses reluctantly (see Deut 1:21–23) allows the Israelites to send scouts to Canaan to examine the situation there and report back (Num 13). The scouts return with a positive report about the quality of the land but with grave doubts about whether the Israelites will be able to settle there in the face of opposition from powerful local kings. Only Caleb the son of Jephunneh and Joshua the son of Nun offer encouraging reports, but their minority view is not heeded. (Num 13:30, 14:6–9.)

God had previously warned that the Israelites would return to Egypt if they feared war (Exod 13:17), and this warning now proves true; the discouraging report about Canaan fuels the rising flame of rebellion, and the Israelites resolve to appoint a leader who will return them to Egypt. (Num 14:1–5.) The Torah clearly denounces these rebels. Once again, YHVH threatens to annihilate the Israelites on account of their lack of faith (Num 14:11–12), and Moses again pleads on their behalf (Num 14:18–19). YHVH then declares that the entire generation will wander like Bedouins in the desert for forty years and that only their children will cross the Jordan into Canaan—although YHVH makes an exception for Caleb and Joshua. (Num 14:20–39.)

With the news that Moses has no immediate intent to relieve the people from the austerity of desert life, the crisis only worsens. A defiant group now rejects the idea of returning to Egypt and embraces the opposite extreme, deciding to ascend the hill country of Canaan immediately, without YHVH in their midst— that is, they decide to seize the land of Canaan by military force without awaiting the providence of God to deliver the land to them in peace (see Neh 9:24–25). Moses warns that the group will "fall by the sword," but they nonetheless "ascend to the head of the mountain," and they are struck down, as Moses predicted. (Num 14:40–45; Deut 1:41–45.)

It is at that point that Korach, taking advantage of the discontent of the people and, in particular, their frustration with the austere desert conditions, initiates his rebellion, aligning himself with three members of the tribe of Reuben. Korach hopes to be named chief priest in place of Aaron, and the Reubenites seek to depose Moses as leader. (Num 16:1–14; Neh 9:16–18.) YHVH instructs Moses to "speak to the Assembly" and to urge its members to distance themselves from the sanctuary of Korach and his supporters (Num 16:24), but Moses does something more. He expresses the name YHVH and, in great anger (Num 16:15; Ps 106:32–33), curses Korach and his supporters to die an unnatural death, and the ground then opens its "mouth" and swallows Korach and his closest supporters alive (Num 16:26–33). The text uses the Hebrew term for descent to the netherworld (*vayeirdu… sh'eolah*), implying that this earth-swallowing event is a figurative way of relating the fact that the rebel leaders died.

As noted, blasphemy includes pronouncing God's name in a context, such as public anger, that brings dishonor to the name. Certainly, Moses did that in the case of Korach; "he expressed the name and cursed" (Lev 24:11). Thus, the story from Numbers of Korach's confrontation with Moses and the story from Leviticus of the blasphemer are remarkably similar.

The Leviticus story tells us: "[1] any man who will denigrate his god, he will bear his sin, and [2] [he who] expresses the name YHVH will surely die; the entire Assembly will surely stone him." (Lev 24:15–16.) As discussed, the second part of this statement is descriptive, not prescriptive. In other words, it does not *prescribe* what ought to be done to someone who expresses the name YHVH; rather, it *describes* what was actually done to a particular figure in the Torah who expressed the name YHVH. Perhaps, in other words, it describes what happened to Moses, who expressed the name YHVH and angrily cursed Korach to die an unnatural death.

In this context, it is worth considering in greater detail the exasperated statement Moses made about the Israelite people shortly after he and the Israelites left Egypt: "Moses cried out to YHVH, saying, 'What will I do for this people? *In a little while they will stone me!'*" (Exod 17:4; see also Num 14:10.) According to the rule set forth in the Torah, words have power and every utterance of a true prophet becomes manifest as an actual event. (See Deut 18:22; see also Isa 55:10–11.) For example, Jacob's rashly uttered words to Laban—"with whom you find your idols, [that person] will not live" (Gen 31:32)—foretold the death of Rachel, for Rachel was the one who had taken Laban's idols (Gen 35:18–20), and by the same rule, Moses' rashly uttered words to YHVH—"In a little while they will stone me!" (Exod 17:4)—foretold the death of Moses. It is also worth noting that when Moses makes this exasperated prediction that the Israelites will soon stone him, YHVH does not contradict him. We can deduce, then, according to the logic of the Torah, that in a little while, the Israelites *do* stone him.

But the thesis that Moses was executed is still only very weakly supported, dependent on a tenuous link between two stories that appear in different books of the Torah and that are not obviously connected. Moreover, the foregoing discussion of the blasphemer story omitted details of that story that strongly undermine the claim that Moses was the blasphemer in question. In particular, it omitted details about the blasphemer's identity, and it omitted the fact that Moses appears in the blasphemer story as judge, not as offender.

The story opens with this description of the blasphemer's offense: "The son of an Israelite woman—and he was the son of an Egyptian man—went out amidst the descendants of Israel; and the son of the Israelite [woman] and an Israelite man fought in the camp, and the son of the Israelite woman expressed the name [YHVH], and he cursed, and they brought it [(the legal matter)] to Moses, and the name of his mother was Shelomit daughter of Divri of the tribe of Dan." (Lev 24:10–11.) A quick scan of the text seems to make clear that Moses was *not* the blasphemer, for the story says that (1) the blasphemer "was the son of an Egyptian man," (2) "the name of his mother was Shelomit daughter of Divri of the tribe of Dan," and (3) they brought the legal matter of the blasphemer's offense "to Moses."

We will discuss the reference to "an Egyptian man" (*ish mitzri*) (Lev 24:10) in more detail below. For now, it will suffice to note that Moses was called "an Egyptian man" (*ish mitzri*) by Jethro's daughters (Exod 2:19), and thus "Egyptian man" can be a discreet way of alluding to Moses himself. But what about the story's statement that "his mother" was Shelomit?

Here, we encounter one of those marvelous ambiguities that make the Torah so rich from a literary perspective. The Torah is not specific concerning the antecedent of "his" in the phrase "his mother was Shelomit." The phrase's placement leads the reader to think that the blasphemer is the antecedent of "his"—that is, that Shelomit is the *blasphemer's* mother—and the Torah's premier commentator, Rashi (11th century C.E.), adopts that reading.[212] But the text can also be read to say that the Israelite man who fought with the blasphemer is the antecedent of "his"—that is, that Shelomit was the mother of the blasphemer's *antagonist*. Significantly, the name Shelomit was an alternative name for Korach. (See 1 Chron 23:18.) Thus, by saying that "the name of his mother was Shelomit," the text might be hinting in a discreet way that Korach was the "Israelite man" who fought the blasphemer.

But there remains the statement that "they brought" the legal matter of the blasphemer's offense "to Moses." If the

---

[212] Rashi asserts that Shelomit was married to the Hebrew slave whom Moses defended when, as a young prince, Moses encountered an Egyptian overseer striking a Hebrew slave (see Exod 2:11–12). Rashi further implies that this woman (the wife of the rescued Hebrew slave) had been raped by the Egyptian overseer and that the offspring of that rape was "the son of an Egyptian man" who later blasphemed.

blasphemer is Moses, then how can the legal matter of the blasphemer's offense be "brought... to Moses"?

The expression "and they brought it to Moses" (*vayaviu oto
el Moshe*) is not meant to be literal; rather, it is a formulaic way
of saying that the legal matter was one that had to be decided at
the highest level of the judiciary. We derive this reading from
chapter 18 of Exodus, where we learn that the judges whom
Moses selected "judged the people in all times, but the difficult
matter they brought to Moses" (*y'viun el Moshe*) (Exod 18:26;
see also Deut 1:17). In other words, in the context of a legal dis-
pute, the phrase "brought to Moses" (*y'viun el Moshe*) signifies
a "difficult matter" that had to be decided at the highest level of
the judiciary.

The Babylonian Talmud confirms this reading and develops
the point further. (See *Sanhedrin* 16a and 18a–18b.) The rule
that a "difficult matter" had to be "brought to Moses" derives
from the advice of Moses' father-in-law Jethro, who counseled
Moses to select subordinate judges who "will judge the people
in all times, and it will be, *every great matter* they will bring to
you" (Exod 18:22). But here the Torah uses idiomatic phrasing that must be smoothed in translation. Its literal word-for-
word translation is not "every great matter" but "all the matter
the great" (*kol ha-davar ha-gadol*). The Talmud states that *kol
ha-davar ha-gadol* should be read as "every matter [involving]
the great [one]," which the Talmud specifies as being a matter
involving the chief priest. Moreover, the Talmud asserts that the
reason the word "matter" is singular with a definite article ("the
matter") is that the text does not refer to just any matter involving the chief priest; rather, it refers only to the single most seri-
ous matter that might involve the chief priest, which the Talmud
implies is *an accusation of intentional murder*. It is *that* matter
that should be "brought to Moses" (*i.e.*, brought to the highest
level of the judiciary).

The Talmud notes that after Moses' appointment of the Sanhedrin (see Num 11:16–17, 11:24–26), the phrase "brought to Moses" meant "brought to the Sanhedrin," and the Talmud thus concludes that any capital charge against any chief priest, whenever it might occur, must be "brought to Moses" (*i.e.*, brought to the Sanhedrin).[213] Be that as it may, when the rule was first adopted shortly after the Israelites left Egypt (see Exod 18:24), it necessarily applied to a capital charge against the chief priest *of that time*, who was Moses himself, for Aaron had not yet been anointed as chief priest (see Lev 8:12).

Thus, the Talmud makes clear that not only is it *possible* for a legal matter involving Moses to be "brought to Moses" (*i.e.*, brought to the highest level of the judiciary) but that, at the time the rule was first adopted, there was only one legal matter that was especially reserved for adjudication at that level, and that was a capital charge against Moses himself. Later, when Aaron was anointed as chief priest, a capital charge against Aaron would need to be "brought to Moses," but even then Moses retained his priestly rank (Ps 99:6). Therefore, the statement in the blasphemer story that "they brought it [(the legal matter)] to Moses" signifies that the offender was either Moses or Aaron and that the charge was intentional murder or some other capital offense.

In conclusion, despite the presence of superficial details that seem to distinguish the blasphemer story from the Korach story, the two stories might be two tellings of the same event,

---

[213] The Talmud's instruction is cast as a theoretical discussion about what should happen if the chief priest is accused of intentional murder, concluding that the Torah provides for that situation and referencing the phrase "the matter [involving] the great [one]." Exod 18:22. Of course, the very existence of this purportedly theoretical discussion, focusing as it does on such an unlikely event—the holiest man in the community standing trial for capital murder—suggests that the event must have actually occurred and that the Talmud's discussion is intended to gloss secrets of the Torah.

and the blasphemer might be Moses, who was sometimes called "an Egyptian man" (Exod 2:19). But the evidence is weak and contrary to tradition. So let us dig deeper. Might there be a *third* telling in the Torah of the same blasphemous confrontation?

3. The Rock in Kadeish

Commentators on the Torah have long wondered about the undisclosed sin at the rock in Kadeish (Num 20:1–13) that caused YHVH to decree the death penalty for both Aaron (Num 20:23–24) and Moses (Num 27:12–14; Deut 32:48–51). The Israelites arrive at Kadeish, where Miriam—the sister of Moses and Aaron—dies, and there is no water for the people to drink. The people complain to Moses, and YHVH tells Moses that he and Aaron should "speak to the rock" to obtain "its waters." But instead, Moses angrily calls the congregation "rebels," and then he "raise[s] his hand and str[ikes] the rock with his staff twice," bringing forth "abundant waters." (Num 20:1–13.) The place is then called "Waters of Contention" (Num 20:13), and because Moses did not obey YHVH's instruction—that is, because he *struck* the rock instead of *speaking* to the rock—YHVH condemns Moses and Aaron to die. (Num 20:23–24, 27:12–14; Deut 32:48–51.)

Obviously, there is more to the story than appears on its face. Certainly, Moses and Aaron were disobedient, but their disobedience hardly seems to merit a decree of death. Commentators have suggested many creative explanations for why Moses' minor act of disobedience called forth such a harsh decree: (1) Moses was such an advanced soul that he was held to a higher moral standard than an ordinary person; (2) Moses' error was not his act of disobedience, but rather the anger he exhibited when he called the Israelites "rebels"; and (3) Moses missed an opportunity to perform a miracle by mere word of mouth (speaking to the rock), rather than by a physical act (striking the rock), and the former would have so awed the Israelites that they would have followed Moses faithfully. All of these explanations have merit, but none wholly satisfies; the secret of the episode remains elusive. But we begin to unlock that secret when we recognize that the story of Moses' sin at the rock in Kadeish and the earlier story of Korach's confrontation with Moses, which also took place in Kadeish (Num 13:26), constitute two tellings of the same event, an event that is likewise described in the blasphemer story from the book of Leviticus.

Regarding the sin at the rock in Kadeish, the Torah relates: "Moses *raised his hand*, and he struck the rock with his staff twice." (Num 20:11.) We have seen in Part Two, that the phrase "raised his hand [(*YaD*)]" should be read as "raised His *YuD*," indicating the raising of the hidden letter *yud* at the end of the divine name YHVH, revealing the name *Yehudi*. Thus, the statement that "Moses raised his hand" indicates that Moses expressed the name *Yehudi* in its unabbreviated form, and because Moses was clearly angry at the time (see Ps 106:32–33), calling the congregation "rebels" (Num 20:10), this public revelation of the secret name was not one likely to win the Israelite's admiration and devotion. Rather, it brought the name into disrepute. In short, Moses committed blasphemy.

This interpretation of Moses' sin at the rock may seem doubtful, but the Torah confirms it expressly. Just a few chapters earlier, the Torah states: "The soul that acts with a raised hand, … he is a blasphemer of YHVH." (Num 15:30.) Most readers assume that this verse sets forth a normative rule and that "act[ing] with a raised hand" connotes violence or arrogance (high-handedness). But why then is a simple act of violence or arrogance equated with blasphemy? Many figures in the Bible are violent or arrogant, but they are not charged with blasphemy. The answer lies in the now-familiar explanation that this so-called "law" of the Torah is descriptive, not prescriptive. It does not prescribe norms of behavior; rather, it tells us the code the

Torah will use to identify a specific person as a blasphemer. The accusation of blasphemy against a prophet is no small thing, and the text will only make such an accusation discreetly, by way of an encoded signal. It tells us, in effect: "Hey, reader. Psst. Read the next few chapters carefully. The soul that acts with a raised hand,... he is a blasphemer of YHVH." (Num 15:30.) And then, just a few chapters later, Moses "raise[s] his hand and str[ikes] the rock." The text could not be clearer: Moses is a blasphemer of YHVH.

So there we have it in the plainest terms. Moses' sin at the rock, the sin that scholars have puzzled over for centuries, was blasphemy. And this point is confirmed when Moses' sin at the rock is retold in the book of Psalms: "They provoked at the Waters of Contention, and it was bad for Moses because of them, for they defied his spirit, and he pronounced [the secret name] with his lips." (Ps 106:32–33.) In other words, Moses uttered the secret unabbreviated form of the name YHVH in a moment of public anger, thus blaspheming the name.

With this confirmation that Moses was guilty of blasphemy, the previously described connection between the blasphemer story from Leviticus and the story of Korach's confrontation with Moses becomes much less doubtful. Moreover, it appears that the story of Moses' sin at the rock in Kadeish is yet a third telling of the same confrontation. With that thought in mind, let us examine the incident at the rock in more detail.

The Assembly needed water. "Moses raised his hand (*YaD*), and he struck the rock with his staff twice, and abundant waters went forth." (Num 20:11.) In other words, "Moses raised <u>His YuD</u>," the hidden *yud* at the end of the name YHVH, revealing the name *Yehudi*. The book of Jeremiah tells us: "My word is like fire, declares YHVH, and like a hammer that explodes a rock." (Jer 23:29.) In short, the "staff" that struck the rock—the "hammer" that exploded the rock—was a *word*. Moses revealed the name *Yehudi*, and with that powerful word, Moses *cursed* the rock.

Significantly, the Hebrew word for "and he struck" (*vayakh*) is typically used to describe the act of inflicting a mortal blow on an enemy, and the Hebrew word for "twice" (*pa'amaim*) can also be translated "a second time." Moses had once before inflicted a mortal blow upon a "rock"—in Rephidim (Exod 17:1–7)—but that time Moses did so with YHVH's express permission, and there was no mention of punishment. In Kadeish, however, Moses inflicts a mortal blow upon a "rock" a second time, and in Kadeish, Moses acts angrily and on his own initiative, and YHVH decrees death as a punishment. We might begin to wonder if, in each case, the "rock" is actually a person.

A hint based on the metaphoric meaning of the word "water" (*mayim*) lends support to this reading. Recall that the problem of there being no water in Kadeish arose immediately after Miriam's death. The Torah states: "And Miriam died there, and she was buried there, and there was no water for the Assembly, and they convened concerning Moses and concerning Aaron." (Num 20:1–2.) According to the Babylonian Talmud, "water" here refers to "teachings," "guidance," or "counsel." (*Bava Kamma* 82a.) Miriam was a source of moral teachings and wise counsel that uplifted the members of the Assembly, helping them to overcome their doubts and to seek the higher good. Therefore, immediately after Miriam's death, the Assembly has no "water"—no moral teachings, no guidance, no wise counsel—and they turn against Moses and Aaron. YHVH then tells Moses to speak to the "rock" (a person) so it will give "its waters" (its wise counsel). But Moses instead strikes the "rock" and obtains "abundant waters" (*mayim rabim*). According to Rabbi Meir Simcha HaKohen of Dvinsk (1843–1926 C.E.), Moses' striking of the "rock" profaned the name YHVH, and the "abundant waters" that poured forth were like the dirty water that animals drink.[214] In other words, Moses struck a mortal blow upon the "rock," and

---

[214] See *Meshekh Chokhmah—Chukat.*

the Assembly's thirst for guidance and counsel was quenched, but it was quenched with teachings suitable for animals, not for people, and these base teachings were far too abundant.

The two rock-striking incidents (one at Rephidim and the other at Kadeish) are similar in several notable respects. The Israelites arrive in Rephidim after traveling in the "Wilderness of Sin" (Exod 17:1), whereas they arrive in Kadeish after traveling in the "Wilderness of Tzin" (Num 20:1). In both cases, the people have no water to drink, and they complain to Moses that he has brought them out of Egypt to die. (Exod 17:1–3; Num 20:2–5.) In both cases, Moses strikes a "rock" and produces water. (Exod 17:6; Num 20:11.) Rephidim is called "*Massah U'Merivah*" ("Test and Contention") (Exod 17:7), and Kadeish is called "*Merivah*," or, more specifically, "*Mei Merivah*" ("Waters of Contention") (Num 20:13).

Clearly, the two incidents are closely related. One possibility, perhaps the most plausible, is that in reality there were not two incidents; rather, there was one incident described in two slightly different ways in the scriptural records of the ancient Israelites. Then, when the present version of the Torah was redacted, both versions of the story were preserved, making them appear as two separate incidents. That explanation of the evidence is certainly persuasive, and it also makes sense of other episodes in the book of Exodus that repeat in the book of Numbers. These include the giving of manna and quail (Exod 16:2–35; Num 11:1–9, 11:18–20, 11:30–34), the attack by Amalek (Exod 17:8–16; Num 14:40–45), and the appointment of seventy minor judges (Exod 18:13–26, 24:1–10; Num 11:14–17, 11:24–29).

Of course, the Torah's standard chronology places the two rock-striking episodes thirty-nine years apart (see Exod 16:1, 19:1; Num 33:36–38; Deut 2:14), which implies that they were actually separate incidents. But longstanding tradition asserts that the Torah's narrative is not chronologically linear. Moreover, the forty-year period of wandering in the wilderness was

almost certainly figurative, indicating an intergenerational transfer of power, not an actual passage of forty years. (See Deut
5:3–4, 8:4, 11:2–7, 29:4; Neh 9:21.) We have already seen that
the word "forty" signifies, according to the Kabbalah, *chalav*
("milk"), because of the numeric values traditionally associated
with the letters of *CHaLaV* (*chet* = 8, *lamed* = 30, *beit* = 2).
Thus, the reference to "forty years" can signify "milk years," a
period of several years spent living the austere life of Bedouins,
eating a Bedouin diet of milk, buttermilk, yogurt, and cheese.
For this reason, the Torah describes the manna that the Israelites
ate as a cheese-like substance. (See Exod 16:31; Num 11:7–9.)
But even if the two rock-striking episodes were closer in time
than the plain text of the Torah suggests, it remains possible
that Moses really did inflict a mortal blow upon two separate
"rocks," not one.

The Hebrew word used for the first "rock," the rock in Rephidim, is *tzur*. The word *tzur* connotes a "huge unmovable rock"
or a "rock mountain," but Tzur is also *a personal name* in the
Torah; it is an alternative name for Balak, the Midianite prince
who became king over the Moabites (see Num 31:8),[215] and
Hebrew scripture tells us explicitly that Moses "struck down"
Balak (Josh 13:21).

The Hebrew word used for the second "rock," the rock in
Kadeish, is *sela*. The word *sela* refers to "rock cliff" or a "bald
rock formation." Significantly, the name Korach means "bald,"
and so the word *sela* might be an appropriate pseudonym for
him. Was perhaps the first "rock" (*tzur*) that Moses struck a
reference to Balak and the second "rock" (*sela*) a reference to
Korach?

In the book of Isaiah, we read: "A man will be... like...

---

[215] On the assertion that Tzur (the prince of Midian) is the same as Balak
(the king of Moab), see Ginzberg, *The Legends of the Jews, Volume 3*, p.
353.

a heavy rock [(*sela*)] in a land of thirst." (Isa 32:2.) This verse, hidden away in one of the later books of the Bible, is intended to disclose an important secret about Moses' sin at the rock. It informs us that the "rock" (*sela*) in Kadeish, where "there was no water" for the people (Num 20:2)—that is, the "heavy rock [(*sela*)] in a land of thirst" (Isa 32:2)—was actually no rock at all; rather, the "rock" was a *person*. Ali ibn Abi Talib, the successor to the prophet Muhammad, knew the same secret, saying: "An ignorant man is a rock from which no water flows."[216] Here, again, we are informed that the "rock from which no water flow[ed]"—the rock in Kadeish, that is—was really an ignorant man.

So let us reconsider Moses' sin at the rock, having in mind three things:

- Moses publicly invoked the secret name *Yehudi* (Num 20:11 ["Moses raised His *YuD*"]);
- Moses' sinful act was an angry curse, not a physical blow (Ps 106:32–33 ["They provoked at the Waters of Contention, and it was bad for Moses because of them, for they defied his spirit, and he pronounced with his lips."]); and
- The "rock" was really a person (Isa 32:2 ["A man will be... like... a heavy rock in a land of thirst."].

When we do, we see that the entire rock-striking episode is indistinguishable from the confrontation between Korach and Moses, a confrontation in which Moses angrily expressed the name YHVH and cursed Korach to die an unnatural death.

And if the foregoing evidence is not sufficient to establish that these two episodes are really the same, then consider Moses' final blessing to the tribe of Levi. Moses declared about that tribe: "Your *Tumim* and your *Urim* are for the man of your

---

[216] Chapman, *Maxims of Ali*, p. 25.

devotion whom you tested at Massah, [whom] you disputed at the Waters of Contention." (Deut 33:8.) The words *"Tumim"* and *"Urim"* refer to precious stones worn by the chief priest in his breastplate (see Exod 28:30; 1 Sam 14:41), and the phrase "Waters of Contention" refers, of course, to the rock in Kadeish, which was called by that name (Num 20:13). Thus, according to Moses' blessing, the incident at the rock in Kadeish involved members of the tribe of Levi contesting against Aaron, the chief priest.

Korach was a prominent Levite who contested for Aaron's position as chief priest (Num 16:10–11), and he was the leader of the specific group of rebels that challenged the leadership of Moses and Aaron, provoking Moses' angry curse. (See Num 16.) Thus, Moses' statement when blessing the Levites that they contested with Aaron, the chief priest, at the rock in Kadeish (Deut 33:8) strongly implies that Moses' curse of Korach and his sin at the rock in Kadeish are one and the same event.

The rock in Kadeish is alluded to again in an excerpt from the "Book of the Wars of YHVH" that appears in chapter 21 of the book of Numbers. The "Book of the Wars" is a lost text that may be the "book" referred to in chapter 17 of Exodus (vv. 8–14), where we read of the Israelites battling Amalek and YHVH telling Moses to write "as a remembrance in the book" that he will erase Amalek's memory. Alternatively, the "Book of the Wars" may be the missing book of the Torah that, according to tradition, is signified by the two inverted letters (each a *nun*) that appear in Numbers chapter 10 (vv. 35–36). In either case, all we now have of the "Book of the Wars" is this cryptic excerpt:

> Vaheiv in Sufah,
> And the ravines of Arnon,
> And the base of the ravines
> That stretches to dwell in Ar
> And leans to the border of Moab,

And from there toward the well.
It is the well that YHVH said to Moses:
'Gather the people,
And I shall give to them water.'
Then Israel sang this song:
'Go up to the well! Answer it!
The well—the princes dug it,
The nobles of the people, with the lawgiver,
Excavated it with their staffs.'[217]

This text uses obscure vocabulary and is difficult to trans-late, but the "well" where YHVH said "gather the people, and I shall give to them water" seems to refer to the "rock" in Kadeish where YHVH told Moses to "convene the Assembly" and "speak to the rock," causing it to "give its waters." (Num 20:8; cf. Exod 17:5–6.) The "Book of the Wars" asserts, however, that this well/rock was "dug" not only by Moses with his staff but also by "the nobles of the people… with their staffs." The significance of the latter detail is hard to interpret, but it recalls an episode that took place on the day after Moses' defeat of Korach, yet again linking the rock-striking incident in Kadeish to the Korach confrontation.

After Korach's death, the Assembly indicted Moses and Aaron for murder and convened against them in a judicial pro-ceeding. (Num 17:6–7.) Aaron's staff was then matched against the staffs of all the leaders of the tribes, each staff inscribed with a name and placed "before YHVH in the tent of the testimony." (Num 17:16–22.) Aaron's staff, which represented the tribe of Levi, "sprouted a sprout," thereby symbolically indicating YHVH's selection of that tribe. (See Num 17:23.) The story sug-gests that the challenge that Korach (the Levite) posed against Moses and Aaron evolved immediately after Korach's death

---

[217] Num 21:14–18.

into a broader challenge against Levite leadership over the other tribes. The "well," therefore, that the "nobles of the people" dug "with their staffs" appears to be a metaphoric affirmation that "water" (*i.e.*, teachings and guidance) flows from the tribe of Levi.

So let us summarize three superficially distinct episodes of the Torah:

- "[T]he son of an Egyptian man" (Moses is called "an Egyptian man" in Exod 2:19) fought with the son of Shelomit (Korach is called "Shelomit" in 1 Chron 23:18), and this son of an Egyptian man (Moses) expressed the name YHVH and cursed the son of Shelomit (Korach), bringing about (according to the chiastic structure of the text) the latter's death. (See Lev 24.)
- Moses expressed the name YHVH and angrily cursed Korach, a Levite, to die an unnatural death, and the earth then opened, killing Korach and his closest supporters. (See Num 16.)
- Moses raised the hidden *yud* of the name YHVH, thus revealing the name *Yehudi*, and then, invoking that name in a blasphemous curse (Num 15:30), Moses angrily struck down a "rock" that was no rock—a "rock" that was really a Levite man contesting against Aaron for the position of chief priest. (See Num 20, Deut 33:8.)

It is clear from the foregoing summary that all three episodes are the same, and because Moses' blasphemy resulted in Korach's death, the prescribed punishment was Moses' death. "And YHVH said to Moses: 'Ascend to this mountain of the Hebrews . . . , and you shall be gathered to your people [(*i.e.*, you shall die)] . . . because you defied [the word of] my mouth in the Wilderness of Tzin, in the strife of the Assembly, [failing] to cause me to be sanctified in the waters before their eyes; they are the Waters of Contention, Kadeish, Wilderness of Tzin." (Num 27:12–14.)

But Moses most certainly acted for a noble purpose. Korach

wanted to replace Aaron as chief priest, and he was part of an unjustified rebellion against Moses' leadership. Moreover, if we accept the dogma that Moses had prophetic powers, then Moses foresaw that Korach would be reborn as the prophet Samuel (see *Bamidbar Rabbah* 18:15) and that the descendants of Korach would be counted among the greatest seers of Judaism (Num 26:11; Pss 42, 44–49, 84–85, 87–88; 2 Chron 20:19). But regardless of what Moses' justification and foresight might have been, he committed blasphemy. Moses angrily invoked the name YHVH in its revealed form, and he publicly cursed Korach to die an unnatural death. Moses struck down the "rock" at Kadeish.

4. Benayahu the Son of Yehoyada

The *Zohar*, the leading work of the Jewish mystical tradition, confirms (1) that Moses was the "son of an Egyptian man" described in the blasphemer story, (2) that Moses' sin at the rock was an act of belligerence, and (3) that Moses was executed for that act.

At a certain point in the *Zohar*'s narrative, two men—Rabbi Abba and Rabbi Elazar—are traveling together and encounter a "donkey driver" who turns out to be the reincarnation of Rav Hamnuna Sava. The donkey driver proceeds to explicate a cryptic passage from 2 Samuel, a passage that describes Benayahu the son of Yehoyada, who was an adviser to both King David and King Solomon. First, for the sake of context, here is the relevant passage from 2 Samuel:

> And Benayahu the son of Yehoyada, the son of a living man, abundant in deeds, from *Qavtz'el*—he struck down the two altar-stones [(*ari'el*)] of Moab, and he descended and struck down the lion in the midst of the well in a day of snow. And he struck down an Egyptian man that was a man of appearance,

and in the hand of the Egyptian was a spear, and he descended upon him with a club and wrenched the spear from the hand of the Egyptian and killed him with his [own] spear. These [things] did Benayahu the son of Yehoyada, and to him was name [(*i.e.*, renown)] among the three mighty ones. From the thirty, he was glorified, and to the three, he did not come. And [King] David set him to his bidding.[218]

This passage from 2 Samuel is full of obscure allusions, but the *Zohar* asserts that the passage is not actually about an adviser to King David at all; rather, it is about the death of Moses. To connect the passage to Moses, the *Zohar* relies on the interpretive rule that references in Hebrew scripture to "an Egyptian man" signal that Moses is the person under discussion, a rule that is derived from the scene at the well in Midian when Jethro's daughters refer to Moses as "an Egyptian man" (see Exod 2:15–19). The *Zohar*, however, is a difficult text, and some readers might find its explication of the foregoing passage from 2 Samuel to be even more obscure than the passage itself. It is nonetheless worthwhile to read the *Zohar*'s explication closely. Note that the *Zohar* translation appearing here uses italics to signify quotations from scripture:

He [(Benayahu son of Yehoyada)] *slew an Egyptian, a man of... appearance* (2 Sam [23:]21). Here the mystery of the verse discloses that whenever Israel sinned [the divine aspect *Yesod*] departed, withholding from them all the goodness, all the light illumining them. *He slew an Egyptian man*—the light of that light illumining Israel. Who is it? Moses, as it is written: *They said, 'An Egyptian man rescued us'* (Exod 2:19). There [(in Egypt)] he [(Moses)] was born, there he was raised, there he rose to the highest light. *A man of* מראה

(*mar'eh*),... *appearance,*... as is said: *Man of Elohim* (Deut 33:1)—husband, as it were, of that מראה (*mar'eh*), *appear-ance,* [*husband*] *of the Presence of* YHVH, for he was worthy of conducting this [spiritual] rung on earth in any way he wished—something no other human attained. [¶] *The Egyp-tian had a spear in his hand* (2 Sam [23:21]).... With this [spear] he [(Moses, the Egyptian)] sinned at the rock, as is said: *He struck the rock with his staff twice* (Num 20:11). The Blessed Holy One said to him, "Moses, I did not give you My staff for this. By your life! From now on, it will no lon-ger be in your hand." Immediately *He went down to him with a club* (2 Sam [23:21])—with [the divine aspect of] severe judgment. *And wrenched the spear out of the Egyptian's hand* [(2 Sam 23:21)], for from that moment it was withheld from him [(Moses)] and was never again in his hand. *And killed him* [(Moses)] *with his own spear* [(2 Sam 23:21)]. Because of the sin of striking [the rock] with that staff, he died and did not enter the Holy Land, and his light was withheld from Israel.[219]

As noted, the *Zohar* is a difficult text, but this passage makes several points clear: (1) the phrase "an Egyptian man" when used in Hebrew scripture signals that Moses is the person under dis-cussion, for Moses was reared as an Egyptian and was called "an Egyptian man" by Jethro's daughters; (2) Moses was the "hus-band" of a female form of YHVH called "appearance" (see Num 12:8 [referring to YHVH as "appearance"]); (3) the metaphor of a weapon (a "spear") is appropriate for describing Moses' act of striking the "rock" in Kadeish, suggesting that the act was one of belligerence; (4) Benayahu son of Yehoyada was really a man sent by God to act as Moses' executioner, punishing Moses for his act of belligerence toward the rock; and (5) Moses did not just die—he was killed.

---

[219] *Zohar* 1:6b, translated in Matt, *The Zohar: Pritzker Edition*, vol. I, pp. 41–42.

The *Zohar*'s teaching that the scriptural phrase "Egyptian man" signifies Moses confirms our reading of the blasphemer story from Leviticus, for the blasphemer in Leviticus is called the "son of an Egyptian man" (Lev 24:10). We also know that the blasphemer in Leviticus was executed (stoned to death) for his act of blasphemy (Lev 24:23), and the *Zohar* excerpt confirms that Moses was executed for striking down the "rock" in Kadeish, an act that involved blasphemy (see Num 15:30). Thus, the *Zohar* strongly supports the connection we drew between the blasphemer story from Leviticus and Moses' sin at the rock. And the *Zohar* further informs us that from the moment of Moses' sin forward, Moses lost his spiritual power: "Moses, I did not give you My staff for this. By your life! From now on, it will no longer be in your hand."

5. The Decree of Equivalence

Classical Jewish hermeneutics, as recorded in the Babylonian Talmud, recognizes *gezeirah shavah* ("decree of equivalence") as one method for decoding the Torah. (See *Pesachim* 66a.) According to this respected principle of scriptural interpretation, a reader can identify a link or equivalence between two seemingly disparate passages of the Torah based on the catchwords or expressions the two passages have in common. Consider, in light of *gezeirah shavah*, the following chart, which places the story of Korach's confrontation with Moses side by side with the story of Moses' striking the rock in Kadeish, pointing out the literary clues that link the two stories to one another. Each column of the chart can be read vertically, but it is also important to read the chart horizontally to reveal the connections between the texts. According to the principle of *gezeirah shavah*, the many common words and expressions that appear in the two stories support the conclusion that the two stories are really one.

Korach's Confrontation with Moses	Moses' Sin at the Rock in Kadeish	Verses that Decode the Torah
*A group of "**rebels**" (Num 17:25) rises up against the leadership of Moses and Aaron. They are "**Levites**" led by Korach. (Num 16:8.)*	*A group of "**rebels**" (Num 20:10) rises up against the leadership of Moses and Aaron. Their tribe is "**Levi**." (Deut 33:8.)*	
"And Korach ... took, and [also] Dathan and Aviram ... and On ..., and they rose before Moses [with] men of the descendants of Israel—two hundred and fifty leaders of the Assembly, those summoned to the Meeting, men of name. **They convened against Moses and against Aaron**, and they said to them: '...Why do you raise yourselves above the congregation of YHVH?'" (Num 16:1–3.)	"And the descendants of Israel and the entire Assembly came to the Wilderness of Tzin in the first month, and the people resided in Kadeish, and Miriam died there, and she was buried there, and there was no water for the Assembly, and **they convened against Moses and against Aaron**." (Num 20:1–2.)	

Korach's Confrontation with Moses	Moses' Sin at the Rock in Kadeish	Verses that Decode the Torah
*YHVH's advice was to **speak to the rebels**, urging them to disperse.*	*YHVH's advice was to **speak to the Rock**, causing it to give forth its water.*	"**An ignorant man is a Rock** from which no water flows." (Ali ibn Abi Talib, successor to Mohammed) (Photo © Pierre Richer)
"**And YHVH spoke to Moses, saying**: '**Speak to the Assembly**, saying, "Ascend from around the sanctuary of Korach, Dathan, and Aviram."'" (Num 16:23–24.)	"**And YHVH spoke to Moses saying**: 'Take the staff and convene the **Assembly**—you and Aaron your brother—and you shall **speak to the Rock** before their eyes, and it will give its water, and you shall bring forth for them water from the Rock....'" (Num 20:7–8.)	"**A man will be** ... like a shadow, a heavy **Rock** in a land of thirst." (Isa 32:2.)

Korach's Confrontation with Moses	Moses' Sin at the Rock in Kadeish	Verses that Decode the Torah
*But Moses and Aaron did not just speak to Korach's Assembly; **Moses invoked the name YHVH and angrily cursed Korach to die an unnatural death.***	*But Moses and Aaron did not just speak to the Rock; "**Moses raised his hand**" and struck the rock. (Num 20:11.)*	"The soul that acts with a **raised hand** ... he is a **blasphemer of YHVH**." (Num 15:30.)
"And Moses said: 'If YHVH creates a new creation, and the soil opens its mouth and swallows them and all that is theirs, and they descend alive to the netherworld, then you will know that these men provoked YHVH.' And it was, when he finished speaking all these words, the soil that was beneath them split, and the earth opened its mouth and swallowed them..., and they... descended alive to the netherworld...." (Num 16:30–33.)	"And Moses took **the staff** from before YHVH, as he commanded him, and Moses and Aaron convened the congregation before the face of the Rock, and he said to them: 'Listen now, rebels! Out of this Rock, we shall bring forth for you water.' And Moses **raised his hand** ... ...and he struck the **Rock** with his staff twice." (Num 20:9–11.)	*This is the "**staff**" Moses used to work miracles; it bore the letters of the name YHVH (see Targum Yerushalmi on Exod 2:21), implying perhaps that the "staff" was really the name.* "The soul that acts with a **raised hand**,... he is a **blasphemer of YHVH**." (Num 15:30.) "My Word...—declares YHVH—[is] like a hammer that **explodes a rock**." (Jer 23:29.)

Korach's Confrontation with Moses	Moses' Sin at the Rock in Kadeish	Verses that Decode the Torah
"And the entire Assembly of the descendants of Israel [convened and] indicted Moses and Aaron the next day [for murder], saying: 'You caused the people of YHVH to die.'" (Num 17:6–7.)	"These are the **Waters of Contention**...." (Num 20:13.)	"They provoked at the **Waters of Contention**, and it was bad for Moses because of them, for they defied his spirit, and **he pronounced [the name] with his lips**." (Ps 106:32–33.)
*And the punishment for murder is **death**. (Lev 24:17, 21.)*	*YHVH declared a harsh punishment that included **death**. (Deut 32:50.)*	
"The one who spills the blood of man, **by man his blood will be spilled**." (Gen 9:6.)	"And YHVH said to Moses and to Aaron ..., saying: '**Aaron shall be gathered to his people**, for he shall not come to the land ..., because you **defied** [the word of] my mouth at the **Waters of Contention**.'" (Num 20:23–24.)	"They provoked at the **Waters of Contention**, and it was bad for Moses because of them, for they **defied** his spirit, and he pronounced [the name] with his lips." (Ps 106:32–33.)

Korach's Confrontation with Moses	Moses' Sin at the Rock in Kadeish	Verses that Decode the Torah
"Any man who will denigrate his god [(as Moses did when he expressed the name YHVH in anger and cursed Korach to die)], he will bear his sin.... And a man who smites any human soul **will surely die**.... Break for break, eye for eye, tooth for tooth...." (Lev 24:15–20.)	"And YHVH said to Moses: 'Ascend to this mountain of the Hebrews ..., and **you shall be gathered to your people**—also you—just as Aaron your brother was gathered, because you **defied** [the word of] my mouth in the Wilderness of Tzin, in the strife of the Assembly, [failing] to cause me to be sanctified in the waters before their eyes; they are the **Waters of Contention**, Kadeish, Wilderness of Tzin.'" (Num 27:12–14.)	"They provoked at the **Waters of Contention**, and it was bad for Moses because of them, for they **defied** his spirit, and he pronounced [the name] with his lips." (Ps 106:32–33.)

Korach's Confrontation with Moses	Moses' Sin at the Rock in Kadeish	Verses that Decode the Torah
"…And the one who smites a man shall **die**." (Lev 24:21.) "A soul that… blasphemed YHVH,… **his iniquity is upon him**." (Num 15:30–31.)	"And YHVH spoke to Moses in the bone of that day saying: 'Ascend to this mountain of the Hebrews, Mount Nebo, that is in the land of Moab…, **and die** at the mountain that you will ascend there, and be gathered to your people, in the same way as Aaron your brother **died** at Mount Hor and he was gathered to his people, because you **defied me** amidst the descendants of Israel, at the **Waters of Contention**, Kadeish, Wilderness of Tzin, because you did not sanctify me among the descendants of Israel.'" (Deut 32:48–51.)	"They provoked at the **Waters of Contention**, and it was bad for Moses because of them, for they **defied** his spirit, and he pronounced [the name] with his lips." (Ps 106:32–33.)

In summary, Moses publicly expressed the name YHVH in its unabbreviated form and angrily cursed Korach to die, thus bringing the name of God into disrepute. (Num 16.) And irrespective of his reasons for acting as he did, he had to suffer the prescribed punishment, which was his own death. The blasphemer story from Leviticus fills in the missing details: Moses was brought to judgment before the Assembly and stoned to death for his crime. (Lev 24:11–12, 24:23.)

6. "A man, the one who gathers logs on the Sabbath Day"

But what about Aaron? Was not Aaron complicit in Moses' actions in Kadeish? Was he not the one against whom Korach contested for the position of chief priest? Did he not participate as Moses' spokesman (Exod 4:15–16) in the blasphemous curse that brought Korach down to the netherworld? (See Num 16:18–35.) Did he not likewise participate when Moses inflicted a mortal blow upon the "Rock"? (See Num 20:9–11.) And with the plural form of the word "you"—"because you [(pl.)] defied [the word of] my mouth" (Num 20:24, 27:14)—does not YHVH expressly state that Aaron was Moses' accomplice? Therefore, Aaron too was charged with blasphemy, and Aaron too was convicted and sentenced to die.

Consider in this regard the rather obscure story that immediately precedes the story of Korach's rebellion: "And they found a man, the one who gathers logs (*eitzim*) on the Sabbath day. . . . And they stoned him with stones, and he died." (Num 15:32–36.) On its surface, the story reads as if it is meant to prescribe the punishment of death by stoning for one who violates the rules of the Sabbath. But does God really decree capital punishment for a mere ritual violation? The Sabbath signifies the seventh in any series, and it relates directly to God's aspect as earthly sovereign (*Malkhut*). In the Jewish tradition, to consecrate the Sabbath (the Seventh) is to honor God in a very important way, but are we really to believe that honoring the Sabbath requires that the community stone a person to death for gathering logs? As with so many other puzzling laws of the Torah, the riddle is solved when we recognize that the log-gatherer story, like the blasphemer story, is descriptive, not prescriptive.

The law of the Sabbath forbids adding wood to a fire on the Sabbath: "You will not kindle fire in any of your dwellings on the Sabbath day." (Exod 35:3.) There were, however, several important exceptions, and one of those exceptions involved the service of the temple: "And the fire on the altar, it shall burn upon it, it will not be extinguished, the priest will burn upon it logs (*eitzim*) every morning...." (Lev 6:5.) Who, then, is the only person who, at the time of the log-gatherer story in Numbers, might have been out gathering logs on the Sabbath day? Aaron, of course, the chief priest, for it was his *express duty* to kindle the fire on the altar every morning, including the Sabbath morning. In other words, the phrase "the one who gathers logs on the Sabbath day" discloses the man's *identity*, not his *crime*, and it does so in a discreet way, concealing his name to preserve his dignity.[220]

And what became of the Sabbath log-gatherer? "The entire Assembly drew him out to the outside of the camp, and they stoned him with stones, and he died, according to that which YHVH had commanded Moses." (Num 15:36.) In short, the log-gatherer—Aaron, that is—was executed, but he was not executed for fulfilling his priestly duty of gathering logs on the Sabbath; rather, he was executed for being an accomplice to Moses when Moses angrily expressed the name YHVH in its unabbreviated form and cursed Korach to die.

Indeed, the blasphemy for which the Sabbath log-gatherer was stoned to death is confirmed when the passage is read in its full context, for we then see that the story of the log-gatherer is tied directly to the short statement describing "the soul that

---

[220] The Babylonian Talmud (*Shabbat* 96b–97a) records the assertion of Rabbi Akiva ben Joseph (1st and 2nd centuries C.E.) that the Sabbath log-gatherer was Tzelophchad, who is described in Num 26:33, 27:1–11, but it also records Rabbi Yehudah ben Beseira's convincing response that Tzelophchad (a descendant of Joseph) was *not* the log-gatherer; rather, Tzelophchad was among the defiant group that "presumed to ascend" to Canaan without YHVH in their midst and that was struck down (Num 14:40–45; Deut 1:41–45).

acts with a raised hand" (*i.e.*, the blasphemer). Here is the full passage:

> The soul that acts with a raised hand [(as Moses does just a few chapters later, with Aaron standing complicitly at his side)],... he is a blasphemer of YHVH, and that soul will be cut off from among its people, for he scorned the word of YHVH and nullified his commandment. That soul will surely be cut off; his sin is upon him [(*i.e.*, the evil that follows from his inappropriate invocation of God's name will be revisited upon him)]. And the descendants of Israel were in the wilderness, and they found a man, the one who gathers logs (*eitzim*) on the Sabbath day [(*i.e.*, they found Aaron, the chief priest)]. And the ones who found him—the log-gatherer—brought him near to Moses and to Aaron and to the entire Assembly, and they put him under guard for it was not clear what he would do to him. And YHVH said to Moses, the man will surely die, all the Assembly will stone him with stones outside the camp. And the entire Assembly drew him out to the outside of the camp, and they stoned him with stones, and he died, according to that which YHVH had commanded Moses.[221]

When the passage is read as a single integrated narrative, we see that the Sabbath log-gatherer was stoned for a blasphemous curse that resulted in death, not for violating the Sabbath, and that the phrase "the one who gathers logs on the Sabbath day" serves only to identify him. It is true that the Torah states about anyone who profanes the Sabbath or does any gainful work on the Sabbath that "he will surely die" (Exod 31:14–15, 35:2), but that idiom can mean only that the violator is a mortal human being (*i.e.*, that he will die *someday*), not that he should be violently executed by the community. For example, YHVH says to Adam that on the day Adam eats from the forbidden tree, "you

---

[221] Num 15:30–36.

will surely die" (Gen 2:17), but Adam does not die on that day; rather, he becomes mortal on that day.[222]

It is also noteworthy that the passage in Numbers describing the stoning of the Sabbath log-gatherer (*i.e.*, Aaron) is strikingly similar to the passage in Leviticus describing the stoning of the blasphemer who was the "son of an Egyptian man" (*i.e.*, Moses), although the two passages are situated in different books of the Torah.

- Both passages describe the legal matter being brought to Moses. (Lev 24:11 ["and they brought it to Moses"]; Num 15:33 ["and they brought it near … to Moses"].)
- Both passages refer to placing the man under guard to clarify the will of YHVH. (Lev 24:12 ["They placed him under guard to clarify for themselves according to the mouth of YHVH."]; Num 15:34 ["They put him under guard for it was not clear what he [(YHVH)] would do to him"].)
- Both passages use a phrase indicating measure-for-measure punishment (Lev 24:15 ["he will bear his sin]; Num 15:31 ["his sin is upon him"]), suggesting (because both offenders were stoned) that both crimes involved someone's death.
- Both passages describe a similar penalty. (Lev 24:23 ["they stoned him with a stone"]; Num 15:35–36 ["they stoned him with stones"].)

Clearly, the two passages are closely related, supporting the conclusion that they both involve the same underlying criminal event.

Like the statement that the offender in the blasphemer story

---

222 The Babylonian Talmud asserts that a Sabbath violator was stoned to death during the time of Greek rule (see *Yevamot* 90b), but even if this assertion is true, it is not clear that those who assumed the right to impose that harsh punishment were properly interpreting the Torah when they did so.

(*i.e.*, Moses) was "brought... to Moses" (Lev 24:11), the statement that the Sabbath log-gatherer (*i.e.*, Aaron) was "brought
near to Moses and to Aaron and to the entire Assembly" (Num
15:33) is not to be read literally; rather, it is a formulaic way of
saying that the matter was brought to be judged at the highest
level of the judiciary. Similarly, the assertion that "they [(*i.e.*, the
entire Assembly)] stoned [the Sabbath log-gatherer] with stones"
(Num 15:35) is misleading, implying the frenzied response of an
angry mob pelting a man with stones seized from the ground.
Rashi, however, explains that the Assembly acted through an
agent.[223] In other words, the Assembly appointed an officer to
execute its judgment. The Sabbath log-gatherer (*i.e.*, Aaron) was
stoned to death, but as a consequence of a deliberative judicial
proceeding, not a mob attack.

And the Torah later gives more details about Aaron's death,
making clear that it was inflicted as punishment for the incident
at the "rock" in Kadeish, a place that was also called "Waters of
Contention" (Num 20:13). Shortly after the rock-striking incident, YHVH says to both Moses and Aaron: "Aaron shall be gathered to his people [(*i.e.*, he shall die)], for he shall not come to
the land..., because you [(pl.)] defied [the word of] my mouth at
the Waters of Contention." (Num 20:24.) In other words, Aaron
was Moses' accomplice in committing the sin at the rock, and it
was that sin—which we have identified as a blasphemous curse
(Ps 106:32–33)—that called for Aaron's death.

Moses, Aaron, and Elazar (Aaron's son) then "ascend to
Mount Hor before the eyes of the entire Assembly," and in
accord with YHVH's instructions, "Moses strip[s] Aaron of his
garments, and he dresse[s] with them Elazar his son, and Aaron
die[s] there at the head of the mountain, and Moses and Elazar
descend from the mountain." (Num 20:27–28.) The Torah does
not specify in this particular passage *how* Aaron dies, but we

---

[223] Rashi on Lev 24:14, translated in Yitzchaki, *Rashi: Commentary on
the Torah*, vol. 3, p. 313.

know that people do not typically ascend a mountain in solemn procession before the members of a governing council, remove their clothes as part of the ritual investiture of a successor, and then drop dead of natural causes. The Torah elsewhere uses the phrase "by the mouth of YHVH" to describe Aaron's death (Num 33:38), and according to tradition, the phrase "by the mouth of YHVH" is a euphemism for martyrdom.[224]

7. The Red Heifer

The book of Numbers appears on its surface to be a series of obscure, disconnected episodes, but when the links between these episodes are brought to the surface, the book becomes a dramatic tale of power politics, unjustified rebellion, and tragedy. But one odd ritual of the book remains elusive: the sacrifice of the "red heifer" (*parah adumah*), described in chapter 19. Here is the Torah's description of the red heifer sacrifice (Num 19:1–9):

> And YHVH spoke to Moses and to Aaron, saying: "This is a decree of the Torah that YHVH commanded, saying: Speak to the descendants of Israel, and they shall take to you [(sing.) (*i.e.*, to Moses)] a red heifer, perfect, [one] that [has] not in it a blemish, that has not had a yoke ascend upon it, and you shall give her to Elazar the priest. And he will draw her out to the outside of the camp. And he shall slaughter her before him. And Elazar the priest shall take from her blood with his finger and sprinkle from the blood toward the face of the Tent of the Meeting seven times, and he [(someone other than Elazar)] shall burn the heifer before his eyes—its hide and its flesh and its blood, upon its dung, he shall burn. And the priest [(Elazar)] shall take cedarwood and hyssop and crimson thread,

---

[224] See Fishbane, *The Kiss of God*, pp. 51–52, 82, 84–86.

and he shall dispatch them into the midst of the burning of the heifer. And the priest shall immerse his garments and wash his flesh in water, and, after, he may come to the camp, and the priest shall be impure until evening. And the one who burns her shall immerse his clothes in water and wash his flesh in water, and he will be impure until evening. A pure man shall gather the ash of the heifer and put it outside the camp in a pure place, and it will be for the Assembly of the descendants of Israel for a safekeeping, it is for water of separation from sin."

According to the Torah, the sacrifice of the red heifer is a powerful engine of spiritual elevation, and its ashes are the ultimate detergent, capable of cleansing the people from the stain of sin. But before we explicate the secret of this elusive ritual, let us consider, by way of background, a story from the Babylonia Talmud (*Shabbat* 31a).

A man comes to Shammai, who is the head of a prominent school in the 1st century of the Common Era. The man seeks to convert to Judaism. He asks Shammai: "How many Torahs do the Jews have?" Shammai replies: "We have two Torahs—the written Torah and the Torah of our oral tradition." The man says: "I have faith in your written Torah, but I do not have faith in your oral tradition. I wish to convert, but you must teach me only your written Torah."

Shammai dismisses the would-be convert, and so the man goes over to the school of Hillel, another prominent teacher of the time. The man asks Hillel: "How many Torahs do the Jews have?" Hillel replies: "We have two Torahs—the written Torah and the Torah of our oral tradition." The man says: "I have faith in your written Torah, but I do not have faith in your oral tradition. I wish to convert, but you must teach me only your written Torah." Hillel accepts the man as a convert.

So the man begins his studies with Hillel, and Hillel teaches him the Hebrew alphabet: *alef, beit, gimmel, dalet....* The next day the man returns to Hillel for another lesson, and Hillel again teaches him the ABCs, but this time Hillel rearranges the letters, placing them in a new sequence. The man objects: "Yesterday, you did not say it like this!" Hillel answers him: "Didn't you [need to] rely on me [yesterday when I taught you the alphabet]? [Therefore,] also rely on me [today to teach you] about the Torah of our oral tradition."

In other words, one cannot even begin to learn the written Torah without relying on the oral tradition, because the written Torah is composed of letters, and one must rely on the oral tradition just to know what those letters signify and the sequence in which they should be read. The book of Psalms validates this anagrammatic method of interpreting the Torah, saying: "The sayings of YHVH are [letter] permutation[s]." (Ps 18:31; see also 2 Sam 22:31; Ps 119:140; Prov 30:5.)[225] And we already applied this method in concluding that the divine name El Shaddai is the equivalent of the national name Israel (see pp.150–151, above).

In light of this method, let us examine the sacrifice of the red heifer. One of the oddities of this particular sacrifice is its victim. Why a "red heifer"? And does a "red heifer" even exist? At best, a heifer might be a ruddy brown, not red. Consider, however, that the Hebrew phrase *PaRaH ADuMaH* ("red heifer") contains the same letters as the phrase *ADaM Ha-PoReH* ("fruitful man" or "fertile man"). If one rereads chapter 19 of Numbers, having in mind that *the red heifer is a man*, then the entire ritual takes on a new significance.[226] It then fits perfectly into the

---

[225] Reading the Hebrew word *TZeRUPHaH* ("refined") as *TZeiRUPHaH* ("combination," "permutation," "acrostic").

[226] Of course, the Hebrew text describing the red heifer sacrifice uses feminine grammatical forms and refers to a "yoke" (*'ol*). Thus, the word "heifer" fits the text much better than the word "man." The red heifer can be understood to be a man only in an *encoded* sense, based on an anagrammatic reading of the Hebrew.

hidden subtext of the book of Numbers, constituting an encoded instruction about Aaron's execution.

In the chart that follows, the Torah's description of the red heifer sacrifice is presented in the left column, and the Torah's description of Aaron's death is presented in the middle column. The right column repeats a quote from the story of the Sabbath log-gatherer, but it also includes other verses from scripture that reveal connections between the red heifer sacrifice and Aaron's death. Again, it is critical to read the chart both horizontally and vertically. According to the hermeneutical principle of *gezeirah shavah*, the many common words and expressions that appear in these scriptural passages indicate that the passages are linked, which supports the conclusion that they describe a single event. (See next pages.)

If one reads the description of the red heifer sacrifice without knowing that it conveys encoded instructions about Aaron's impending execution, one is surprised to find that the ritual takes place "outside the camp" where executions occur (Lev 24:23; Num 15:36) instead of on the north side of the altar where whole-offering sacrifices occur (Lev 1:11). One is also surprised that a sacrificial ritual that produces ashes capable of purifying people from sin somehow makes the priest and his assistant impure. And finally, one is surprised to find that the ritual is performed by Elazar, not by Aaron. After Aaron's initiation as chief priest, Aaron performs every important ritual for the community, but here we have the most important of all rituals, the ritual that produces the ultimate medium of purification from sin, and we find Elazar, not Aaron, presiding.

The Sacrifice of the Red Heifer	The Death of Aaron	The Sabbath Log-Gatherer
"**And YHVH** spoke **to Moses and to Aaron**, saying:	"**And YHVH** said **to Moses and to Aaron** at Mount Hor on the border of the land of Adom, saying: 'Aaron shall be gathered to his people, for he shall not come to the land that I gave to the descendants of Israel, because you defied [the word of] my mouth at the Waters of Contention. **Take Aaron** and Elazar his son, and cause them to ascend Mount Hor, and strip Aaron of his garments, and	
'This is a decree of the Torah that YHVH commanded, saying: Speak to the descendants of Israel, and they shall **take** to you [(sing.)] a **red heifer**, perfect, that [has] not in it a blemish, that has not had a yoke ascend upon it, and you shall give her to **Elazar** the priest.'" (Num 19:1–3.)		*PaRaH ADuMaH ("**red heifer**") equals ADaM Ha-PoReH ("Fruitful Man").*
	cause **Elazar** his son to dress in them,...	*Note: In the red heifer ritual, **Elazar** is priest, not Aaron. Why? Because Aaron is the victim.*
" 'And he will draw her out to the **outside of the camp**.'" (Num 19:3.)		"[They] drew out [the log-gatherer] to the **outside of the camp**, and they stoned him with stones, and **he died**...." (Num 15:36.)
	...and Aaron will be gathered and will **die** there.'" (Num 20:23–26.)	

The Sacrifice of the Red Heifer	The Death of Aaron	The Sabbath Log-Gatherer
" 'And he shall **slaughter** her before him. And Elazar the priest shall take from her blood with his finger and sprinkle from the blood toward the face of the Tent of the Meeting seven times, and he [(not Elazar)] shall burn the heifer before his eyes—its hide and its flesh and its blood, upon its dung, he shall burn. And the priest shall take cedarwood and hyssop and crimson thread, and he shall dispatch them into the midst of the burning of the heifer. And the priest shall immerse his garments and wash his flesh in water, and, after, he may come to the camp, and the priest shall be impure until evening.' " (Num 19:3–7.)	"And Moses did as YHVH commanded, and they ascended to Mount Hor before the eyes of **the entire Assembly**, and Moses stripped Aaron of his garments, and he dressed Elazar his son with them, **and Aaron died there** at the head of the mountain, and Moses and Elazar descended from the mountain." (Num 20:27–28.)	"He who **slaughters** a cow slays a man." (Isa 66:3.) "And **the entire Assembly** drew out [the Sabbath log-gatherer] to the outside of the camp, and they stoned him with stones, **and he died**, according to that which YHVH had commanded Moses." (Num 15:36.)

The Sacrifice of the Red Heifer	The Death of Aaron	The Sabbath Log-Gatherer
"'And the one who burns her [(i.e., Moses)] shall immerse his clothes in water and wash his flesh in water, and he will be impure until evening. A pure man shall gather the ash of the heifer and put it **outside the camp** in a pure place, and it will be for **the Assembly** of the descendants of Israel for a safekeeping, it is for water of separation from sin.'" (Num 19:8–9.)		"And the entire **Assembly** drew out [the Sabbath log-gatherer] to the **outside of the camp**, and they stoned him with stones, and he died, according to that which YHVH had commanded Moses." (Num 15:36.)

Of course, all the oddities of the red heifer sacrifice (see p. 270, above) are neatly resolved once we recognize that Aaron is the red heifer. He is not presiding as sacrificial priest, because he is the sacrificial *victim*, being executed outside the camp for his role as an accomplice to Moses in the incident at the "rock" in Kadeish, and because the "sacrifice" is an execution, it renders the participants impure until evening, as is true of executions (Lev 22:4–7). Through the prophet Isaiah, YHVH confirms this incredible secret of the Torah, saying: "He who slaughters a cow [(*e.g.*, a red heifer)] slays a man." (Isa 66:3.) And if that clue from the book of Isaiah is not sufficient confirmation, there are also the names of Aaron's oldest sons, Avihua and Nadav, which translate as: "My father (*avi*), he is (*hua*) a freewill offering (*nedavah*)." In other words, Aaron the peacemaker (Mal 2:4–6) freely offered his own life, hoping that doing so would appease

the angry and rebellious Assembly. Aaron died as a sacrifice—
a martyr to the cause of peace.

A careful reader of the Torah will observe that the mechanics of the red heifer sacrifice closely track the mechanics of the
two bull sacrifices described in Leviticus chapter 4. All these
sacrifices use a cognate of the word *par* ("bull") to describe the
victim;[227] in all cases, the underlying sin affects the "Tent of
the Meeting" (the mobile sanctuary), and therefore the blood
is "sprinkle[d]" by the priest's "finger" "seven times" in (or
toward) the Tent of the Meeting; and in all cases, the animal
is burned completely, including its "skin" and "dung," and at
least part of this burning is done "outside the camp." This ritual
similarity is no accident. The first bull sacrifice expiates a sin
of the *chief* priest (Lev 4:2–12, 6:23, 16), and the second expiates a sin of the *full* Assembly in rendering a legal determina-
tion (Lev 4:13–21, 6:23; see also Num 15:22–26). Therefore, the
similarity of these sacrifices to the red heifer sacrifice tends to
confirm that the red heifer sacrifice, like the two bull sacrifices,
concerned either (1) some sin committed by Aaron, who was the
chief priest at the time, or (2) some oversight by the Assembly in
its resolution of a capital charge against Aaron, for that was the
only charge that the full Assembly, acting as high court (Great
Sanhedrin), would have been called upon to adjudicate. Either
way, Aaron's conduct was at issue, and either way, his willing
death expiated the sin.

A venerable tradition holds that no one knows the secret of
the red heifer sacrifice. (*BT Yoma* 14a.) In fact, it is asserted
that even King Solomon, who was famed for his knowledge of
esoteric wisdom, did not know that secret. Of course, the reason
for this tradition is that the secret of the red heifer sacrifice—the
martyrdom of Aaron—is too controversial to be admitted, and

---

[227] The addition of a *hei* (H) to render words in the red heifer sacrifice
feminine can be understood to be the addition of a letter from God's
name. See Gen 17:5; Num 13:16.

certainly if wise King Solomon could not figure it out, then the rest of us should not dare to speculate. In truth, however, there have been many people who knew the secret of the red heifer; indeed, some knew it a little too well. Tradition asserts that there have been nine red heifer sacrifices, and a tenth is yet to come. (See *Mishnah Parah* 3:5.) In other words, the holy sacrifice referred to as the "red heifer" is not just Aaron, the chief priest of Torah times; it is also many other martyrs of Jewish history.[228] And, broadly speaking, it is every martyr, including the millions who died in the Holocaust.

8. Bala'am Son of B'eor

With the death of Korach (Num 16:31–33) and the martyrdom of Aaron (Num 20:28), the leadership of the community is in crisis. Aaron had always mediated between Moses and the Israelites (Exod 4:16), and we know from the blasphemer story that Moses is "under guard" because of angrily cursing Korach

---

[228] The Babylonian Talmud asserts that the first red heifer sacrifice took place at the time of the consecration of the wilderness tabernacle just one year after the Israelites left Egypt. *Gittin* 60a–60b. In that instance of the sacrifice, the "red heifer" can be interpreted to be Aaron's eldest two sons, Avihua and Nadav, who both died mysteriously at that time. See Lev 10:1–5. Recall, in this connection, that after the sin of the golden calf, YHVH was very angry with Aaron, even "to destroy him," and that Moses prayed for Aaron. Deut 9:20. Moses' prayer can be understood as diverting upon *Aaron's sons* a heavenly decree that was initially intended for Aaron. But their deaths provided Aaron with only a temporary reprieve, and his own death sometime later (see Num 20:22–29, 33:37–39) was therefore the *second* "red heifer" sacrifice. This insight resolves a confusing passage from the book of Deuteronomy, in which Moses says that Aaron died at the time of the consecration of the tabernacle. See Deut 10:6–9; cf. Num 33:32–33. Moses was alluding to Aaron's *decreed* death, which was actualized in the death of Aaron's sons.

to die (Lev 24:12). The people are left to seek out their next "Horus" (their next good king), but everywhere they look, they find only a "Set" (a troublemaking contender). At that time of uncertainty, many Israelites attach themselves to a new prophet named Bala'am son of B'eor. We discussed Bala'am briefly in Part One, where we were examining the identity of the fierce aspect of God called "Shaddai." Bala'am was a Canaanite prophet whose historical existence is verified by the Deir 'Alla inscription, which describes him as having a nighttime vision of Shaddai's plan to punish the world on account of the subversion of the social order.

Jewish legend describes Bala'am as one of the leading prophets of Moses' time. The tradition holds that when Egypt's pharaoh first became concerned about the increasing number and power of the Israelites (see Exod 1:9), he consulted three prophets: Jethro, the priest of Midian; Job, from the land of Utz; and Bala'am son of B'eor. Legend also asserts that Bala'am and his sons were the specific wonderworkers whom the pharaoh summoned to match the wonders performed by Moses and Aaron (see Exod 7:11, 7:22, 8:7). Some Torah commentaries claim that Bala'am is the same person as "Bel'a the son of B'eor," who is listed among the "kings who reigned in the land of Adom before a king reigned over the descendants of Israel." (Gen 36:31–32.) Other commentators claim that Bala'am was a descendant of Laban, Jacob's uncle. Either way, Jewish tradition places Bala'am on the same prophetic level as Moses himself. The Torah, for example, relates Bala'am's ability to talk directly with YHVH and even to "meet" YHVH (Num 23:16), and Jewish tradition adds that Bala'am knew the brief moment in each day when God is angry (see Exod 12:29)—the moment, in other words, when curses are most effective.

The section of the book of Numbers that describes Bala'am stands out from the rest of the book because the narrative viewpoint shifts abruptly from that of Moses to that of Bala'am himself. This shift is all the more striking because it is the only such shift in the four books of the Torah that relate Moses' story. Suddenly, Moses is excluded from the narrative, and the Israelites are viewed by outsiders.

As the Torah tells the story, Balak the king of Moab decides to use Bala'am's skills as a prophet and wonderworker for political advantage against the Israelites. Jewish tradition claims that Balak was the Midianite son of Jethro and thus the brother-in-law of Moses.[229] Interestingly, the latter half of the names Bala'am and Balak can be combined to yield the name Amalek, the kingdom that battled the Israelites in Rephidim. (Exod 17:8–16.) Moreover, Balak is also called "Tzur,"[230] and if Balak is the specific Tzur ("rock") that Moses "struck down" in Rephidim (Exod 17:6), then the incident at Rephidim may be closely connected to the Bala'am episode now under discussion.

In any case, Balak the king of Moab is concerned about the increasing power of the Israelites, and he sends messengers to Bala'am the prophet, summoning him for the purpose of cursing the Israelite people. (Num 22:2–7.) Before responding, Bala'am consults with YHVH and is told not to go, so he dismisses Balak's messengers. (Num 22:7–13.) Later, however, when Balak sends a second embassy of more senior ministers, YHVH tells Bala'am to go, and Bala'am does so, although he warns the ministers that he will not be able to do anything that YHVH—whom Bala'am expressly calls "my God"—does not approve. (Num 22:14–20.)

On the way, God's anger flares against Bala'am, and an "angel of YHVH" stations itself in the path "for a *satan* [("adversary")] to him." (Num 22:22.) The fact that an "angel of YHVH" appears in the form of "Satan" to Bala'am, who is associated with the fierce aspect of God called "Shaddai," recalls to mind the book of Job in which Satan is commissioned by YHVH to afflict Job, who then refers to his afflicter as "Shaddai." Eventually,

[229] See *Zohar* 3:196b–197a, translated in Matt, *The Zohar: Pritzker Edition*, vol. IX, pp. 386–387, explicating Num 22:2.

[230] See Ginzberg, *The Legends of the Jews, Volume 3*, p. 353.

the angel permits Bala'am to proceed to his meeting with Balak, but the angel warns Bala'am that he will not be able to speak any curse or blessing that the angel does not approve. (Num 22:31–35.)

Bala'am and Balak next ascend three mountain peaks (Bamoth-Ba'al, Rosh Ha-Pisgah, and P'eor), and in each location, Bala'am builds seven altars and sacrifices seven bulls and seven rams. After each heptad of sacrifices, Bala'am—in a state of prophetic inspiration—declares the word of YHVH, and in each location, Bala'am enrages Balak by *blessing* the Israelites, instead of *cursing* them, giving a total of four beautiful and poetic blessings. Thus, in the face of an ill-intentioned scheme, YHVH's love and protection of the Israelites is definitively proved. (Num 22:41–24:25.)

There is a mystical teaching recorded in the Babylonian Talmud that a blessing can sometimes be hijacked by jealous angels, but one can guard against that possibility by concealing one's blessing in the form of a curse. (See *Moed Katan* 9b; see also *Sotah* 33a.) By that logic, Bala'am's blessing was more likely to reach its target precisely *because* it was intended as a curse and came from an enemy of the Israelite people.

Bala'am's four blessings are particularly notable not only for the beauty of their poetry, but also for the names Bala'am uses for God. Bala'am variously calls God "El," "Elyon," and "Shaddai," saying at two points that it was El (not YHVH) that took Israel out from Egypt. (Num 23:22, 24:8.) In addition, Bala'am twice uses a distinctive construct that we find frequently in the book of Job,[231] placing the names El and Shaddai in adjacent parallel statements. (Num 24:4, 24:16.) And Bala'am only rarely uses the name YHVH in these blessings. In short, the blessings of Bala'am bring to mind the El/Shaddai religion of the Israelite

---

[231] Job 8:3, 8:5, 13:3, 15:25, 22:17, 23:16, 27:2, 27:11, 27:13, 33:4, 34:10, 34:12, 35:13.

patriarchs (and of Job) more than they do the YHVH religion of Moses (the "Egyptian man").

The first mountain peak that Bala'am and Balak ascend is Bamoth-Ba'al, which means "High Places of Ba'al" and suggests a place where Ba'al was worshiped. Ba'al, we will recall, was the son of El and corresponds to Shaddai and also to Egypt's Set.

The second mountain peak that they ascend is Rosh Ha-Pisgah ("Head of the Summit"). It is the place where Moses later dies: "And Moses ascended from the plains of Moab to Mount Nebo, head of the summit [(*rosh ha-pisgah*)] that is on the face of Jericho…, and Moses, servant of YHVH, died there in the land of Moab, by the mouth of YHVH." (Deut 34:1–5; see also Deut 3:26–29.)

Interestingly, these first two mountain peaks that Bala'am and Balak ascend—Bamoth-Ba'al and Rosh Ha-Pisgah—are also locations described in chapter 21 of Numbers, which lists a few of the encampments of the Israelites in the desert.[232] There, we read that the Israelites traveled "from Nachaliel [to] Bamoth and from Bamoth [to] the valley that is in the field of Moab, Rosh Ha-Pisgah, and overlooks upon the face of the desert." (Num 21:19–20.) Apparently, therefore, Bala'am and Balak are following the Israelites through the desert in their effort to curse the Israelites.

The third mountain peak that Bala'am and Balak ascend is P'eor. There, Bala'am says about the Israelites: "The ones who bless you are blessed, and the ones who curse you are cursed" (Num 24:9), which echoes what YHVH said to Abraham several generations earlier: "I will bless those that bless you, and those that curse you I will curse" (Gen 12:3). It is also an inversion of something Balak earlier said about Bala'am: "The thing that you bless is blessed and that you curse will be cursed." (Num 22:6.) That being so, God has caused Bala'am to utter only blessings.

---

[232] A different list appears in Numbers 33.

Unable to curse the Israelites in a manner that satisfies Balak, Bala'am advises Balak to send women to seduce the Israelites (Num 31:15–16) and thus to pervert their religion. The plan apparently works, for we are told that many Israelites commit sexual improprieties (see Num 25:1) and child sacrifice (see Ps 106:28–38) at a place called "Temple of P'eor" (Deut 3:29, 4:46). The Israelites also become attached to the Lord of P'eor, thereby kindling YHVH's anger against them. (Num 25:3–5; Deut 4:3; Hosea 9:10; Ps 106:28.)

Here again, we are presented with a secret of the Torah that is based on the letter shapes of the *Ashuri* alphabet, thus dating the Torah to the 5th century B.C.E. or later. The name P'eor begins with a Hebrew letter *pei*, a letter that, when written correctly, outlines in its center a letter *beit*, so that every *pei* implies a *beit*, and every *beit* implies a *pei*:

Beit   *Pei*
  B   P

If one chooses to read the white *beit* (B) that is at the center of the black *pei* (P) at the beginning of the name P'eor, then the place where the sexual improprieties and child sacrifices of the Israelites occurred is the Temple of B'eor, and the one to whom the Israelites became attached was the Lord of B'eor. The latter title implies, of course, Bala'am himself, who is called "son of B'eor."

After this new perverse devotion spreads among the Israelites, Zimri (the son of the leader of the tribe of Simeon) brings Cozbi (the Midianite daughter of Tzur/Balak) into the Tent of the Meeting. The Tent of the Meeting was, of course, the mobile sanctuary that the Israelites consecrated in the wilderness and access to it was strictly limited to Levites. (Num 18:22–23.) Nonetheless, Zimri (the Simeonite) brings Cozbi (the Midianite) into the sanctuary in plain view of Moses and the Assembly. (Num 25:6, 25:14–15.) Moses—who has lost his spokesman Aaron and who is "under guard" (Lev 24:12)—says nothing (Num 25:6), but the righteous-minded Pinchas takes a fierce moral stand, pursuing Zimri and Cozbi into the holy Tent and killing them both, apparently while they are lying, one atop the other, in sexual congress. (Num 25:7–8.)

Pinchas was the son of Elazar, who was the son of Aaron. For his zeal, YHVH praises him and rewards him with a "covenant of peace" and a "covenant of eternal priesthood" (Num 25:10–13), although we do not know whether a more merciful response by Pinchas would have evoked even greater praise and reward.[233] The story, among other things, reaffirms Levite control of the sanctuary, and as a result of Pinchas's vengeful act, the "plague" of Bala'am—sexual impropriety and child sacrifice—comes to an end. (Num 25:8.) Later, we are briefly informed that the Israelites killed Bala'am, and Moses killed Tzur/Balak. (Num 31:8; Josh 13:21–22.)

We again read briefly about Bala'am in the book of Micah (Mic 6:5), which says: "My people, remember please what Balak king of Moab planned and what Bala'am son of B'eor answered him, from out of Shittim until Gilgal, so that you know the righteousness of YHVH." The phrase "Shittim until Gilgal" refers to the passage of the Israelites across the Jordan, into the land that YHVH promised their ancestors. (See Josh 3:1, 4:19.) Thus, the

---

[233] The word "peace" in YHVH's blessing to Pinchas (Num 25:12) is written in Torah manuscripts with a broken letter *vov*, indicating that any peace achieved through violence is a broken peace. Moreover, the broken *vov* looks like a *yud* and can be read as a *yud*, which changes the word from "peace" (*shalom*) to "pair of errors" (*shalayim*). Thus, in killing Zimri and Cozbi, Pinchas commits a "pair of errors."

book of Micah implies that it was specifically Bala'am's blessing that made that fateful crossing possible.

The book of Numbers receives its English name from the census of the Israelites that appears at the beginning of the book. (Num 1–4.) The book then proceeds to relate a tale of rebellion and tragedy, culminating in the corrupt worship practices advocated by Bala'am. After the "plague" of Bala'am, a new census is taken. (Num 26.) The tribe a Simeon, which later receives no blessing from Moses (Deut 33:6–24), has suffered the greatest loss; other tribes have grown in size. In total, there are one thousand eight hundred and twenty fewer Israelites than at the time of the previous census. Significantly, the name YHVH appears in the Torah a total of one thousand eight hundred and twenty times—once for each Israelite soul that was lost in the wilderness.

9. The War against Midian

Numbers presents the dramatic climax of a dramatic story. It is the story of a group of Israelite slaves who escape bondage in Egypt and flee into the desert, led by an Egyptian prince named Thutmose. These desert refugees form a government—the Assembly (Num 1:1–16; Deut 1:9–18)—and they accept Thutmose, whom they call Moses, as their king (Deut 33:5). They name one of their own, Aaron, as their chief priest. With Aaron as priest, they worship the Canaanite gods of their ancestors—El and Shaddai—while Moses, their Egyptian king, worships the Egyptian god Djyehudi.

Life in the desert is hard for these runaway slaves, and Korach, who aspires to be their chief priest in place of Aaron, leads a faction within the Assembly that wants to return to Egypt. He attempts to depose Aaron, and Moses and Aaron respond by striking him down with a curse, using Djyehudi's name as a weapon.

But even then, or especially then, the rebellion continues, and the Assembly convenes and formally charges Moses and Aaron with murder. (See Num 17:7.) Aaron is tried, convicted, and sentenced to death by stoning. He dies a martyr. Moses, under fierce political pressure, then resigns his position as head of the Assembly, appointing Joshua the son of Nun in his place. (Num 27:15–23.)

Joshua next leads this band of refugees in a successful, but brutal, war against Midian. (Num 31.) This genocidal war is recorded in the book of Numbers as if it were waged under Moses' direction, but its merciless violence is totally out of character for Moses, who is married to a Midianite and whose conduct and teachings demonstrate compassion, forgiveness, and fairness, not genocidal warfare. Indeed, Moses has repeatedly emphasized *nonaggression*, insisting that YHVH will use natural forces to fight on Israel's behalf and permitting the Israelites to use military force only when directly attacked. (See Exod 15:3, 17:8–13, 17:16, 23:23, 23:27–31, 33:2, 34:11; Num 14:42–45, 21:1–3, 21:14, 21:23–25, 21:33–35, 32:4; see also Josh 5:6, 24:12, 24:18; Zech 4:6; Ps 78:55; Neh 9:24–25.) But the cruel war against Midian is not just out of character for Moses, it is also typical of the violence associated with Joshua's later conquest of the land of Canaan. (See Josh 10–12.) Thus, it makes sense that Joshua, who is now head of the Assembly, was the one who directed this war. Why then does the Torah say that Moses directed it?

Joshua is, of course, Moses' student (Exod 24:13), and according to the Babylonian Talmud, when a student speaks, he or she is supposed to open with "My teacher said," especially during the lifetime of the teacher. (See *Eruvin* 63a–63b; *Yevamot* 96b–97a.) According to this rule, Joshua's instructions as leader of the Israelites would be expressed in the form "Moses said...," and therefore they would be recorded as the statements of Moses. But it might be that Joshua was the one responsible for the brutal destruction of Midian.

Two clues support this reading. The first clue is YHVH's instruction to Moses at the beginning of Numbers chapter 31: "Avenge the vengeance of the descendants of Israel against the Midianites *after* you are gathered to your people." (Num 31:2.) In other words, do it *after* you die, not before; do it through Joshua, your successor. The second clue is Elazar's brash speaking-out-of-turn concerning the spoils of the Midian war, declaring: "This is a decree of the Torah that YHVH commanded to Moses." (Num 31:21.) Since when does Elazar announce decrees of the Torah? He does not. All the general decrees of the Torah are announced by Moses.[234]

Elazar's breach of protocol is placed here as a signal to the thoughtful reader—it is a breach that hints at the new state of affairs: Joshua and Elazar now stand in the shoes of Moses and Aaron. Aaron has died, and Moses (who is "under guard") is no longer making the decisions; rather, Joshua and Elazar are doing so, but according to accepted practice, Moses is often *credited* as the speaker. According to this logic, after the investiture of Elazar into Aaron's priestly garments (Num 20:23–28) and the appointment of Joshua as the new head of the Assembly (Num 27:15–23), many of the Torah's assertions as to what "Moses said" are actually the sayings of Joshua and Elazar, the new leaders of the Israelite people.

Yet another surprising exception to Moses' characteristic compassion and nonaggression appears in Numbers chapter 33. (See Num 33:50–56.) There, Moses instructs the Israelites to drive out the inhabitants of Canaan. Previously, the Torah had emphasized that YHVH, not the Israelites, would do so. (See Exod

---

[234] There are five places in the Torah where YHVH speaks directly to Aaron alone. In Exod 4:27, it is only to tell Aaron to go meet Moses. In Lev 10:8 and Num 18:1, 18:8, and 18:20, it is to convey laws that apply only to the priests. The tradition relates that Moses actually received these laws governing the priests and that Aaron was allowed to convey them. See Lev 10:11.

23:23, 23:27–31, 33:2, 34:11.) But the revised instruction (ordering the Israelites to do so) can be explained in the same way as the genocidal war against Midian can be explained. There has been a change in leadership, and it is not actually Moses who gives this revised instruction; rather, it is Joshua, speaking in Moses' name.

The book of Numbers is about conflict, and it ends with conflict. Joshua, the scion of Ephraim, leads the Israelites in a merciless war against Midian and later moves the conquest westward, across the Jordan, occupying Canaan and defeating the Canaanite kings. (Josh 10–12.) But this victory is only temporary, for in the generations that follow, the Israelites are repeatedly thrown back into a state of servitude and oppression. (See, e.g., Judg 2:10–19, 3:7, 3:12, 4:1, 6:1, 10:6, 13:1; Ps 78:32–37, 78:56–72; Neh 9:26–31.) Such, apparently, is the fruit of conflict.

PART FIVE

The Death of Moses
A Commentary on Deuteronomy

How long shall they kill our prophets,
While we stand aside and look? Oh!
Some say it's just a part of it;
We've got to fulfill the Book.

—Bob Marley (1945–1981 c.e.)

1. "I am not a man of Deuteronomy"

When YHVH first told Moses to lead the Israelites to freedom, Moses complained that he was not a persuasive orator. He said, "*Lo ish devarim anokhi*," meaning, "I am not a man [of] words." (Exod 4:10.) But the Hebrew word *devarim*, which means "words," is also the name that Jews use for the book of Deuteronomy. Therefore, Moses' response to YHVH can be translated, "I am not a man [of] Deuteronomy."

By its own terms, Deuteronomy was written by someone living in Judah or Israel *after* the time of Moses, relating what Moses said. It begins with this opening line: "These are the words that Moses spoke ... across the Jordan in the Wilderness...." (Deut 1:1.) Most scholars assert that Deuteronomy was composed in Judah or Israel at a relatively late date, probably shortly before the Babylonian exile. Hebrew scripture informs us that during the reign of King Josiah of Judah (641–609 B.C.E.), the chief priest "found" a "book of the Torah" in the Temple. (2 Kings 22:8.) Because Deuteronomy corresponds closely to the reforms that King Josiah implemented during his reign and because it frequently uses the phrase "book of the Torah" (Deut 28:61, 29:20, 30:10, 31:26), scholars conclude that the "book of the Torah" that was "found" during King Josiah's reign was probably the central portion of the book we now call "Deuteronomy." Scholars further note that, in King Josiah's time and at his instruction (see 2 Kings 23:21–23), the festival of Passover was, for the first time, celebrated as a Jerusalem pilgrimage in accordance with the law set forth in Deuteronomy (Deut 16:1–8) and not as a local family observance in accordance with the law set forth in Exodus (Exod 12:1–20). That clue suggests that Deuteronomy was unknown before Josiah's time.

King Josiah's reforms were preceded by comparable reforms during the reign of King Hezekiah (715–686 B.C.E.), and portions of Deuteronomy may date to that earlier period. Some textual clues, such as references to a covenant sealed in the city of Shechem (Deut 11:29–30, 27:12–26), might suggest that the book was written by worshipers of YHVH living in the Northern Kingdom, in which case an early version of Deuteronomy may have been brought to Jerusalem and deposited in the temple library after the fall of the Northern Kingdom in 722 B.C.E. This early version was then revised and supplemented until the book took more or less the shape it has today.[235]

One of the leading reforms associated with both Hezekiah and Josiah was *monotheism* (2 Kings 18:4–5, 19:19, 22:17, 23:4–24), and monotheism therefore plays an important role in Deuteronomy. But this monotheism was not the syncretistic form of monotheism that we encountered in Genesis and Exodus, asserting a single divine power underlying the plurality of gods and equating Egypt's Thoth with Canaan's El. Rather, the Deuteronomic reformers asserted a chauvinistic form of monotheism that validated the Judean national god and discredited the gods of Canaan and other nations.

Thus, Deuteronomy is the location of most statements in the Torah that:

- assert the chosenness of the Israelites by God (see, e.g., Deut 4:20, 7:2–4, 7:6–8, 10:14–15);
- denounce the gods and altars of other nations (see, e.g., Deut 4:19, 4:35, 4:39, 5:7, 6:14–15, 7:1–5, 7:25–26, 11:16–17, 11:28, 12:2–3, 12:30–31, 13, 17:2–7, 29:15–20, 30:17–18, 31:18, 32:30–39);
- reject image-worship (see, e.g., Deut 4:15–18, 5:8–10, 7:5, 7:25–26, 9:12, 12:3, 16:21–22, 27:15); and
- insist on a centralized cult at a single temple (see, e.g., Deut 12:4–27, 16:1–17, 17:8–13, 18:6–8, 26:1–11, 31:10–13).

---

[235] See Coogan, *The Old Testament*, pp. 178–179, 184; Hayes, *Introduction to the Bible*, pp. 170, 178.

We encounter similar ideas in the writings of the later prophets (see, e.g., Isa 2:6–8, 2:18–21, 40:18–20, 41:6–7, 44:6–20, 45:5–7, 45:20, 46:5–9; Jer 10:3–16, 11:12, 13:9–10), which implies a date for Deuteronomy that corresponds roughly to the time of those later prophets.

Significantly, Deuteronomy's distinctive themes contradict practices and beliefs that preceded the reign of Josiah and that enjoyed the tacit approval of respected prophets (see 1 Sam 9:12–14; 1 Kings 18:32–38). Those practices and beliefs included:

- the recognition of a pantheon of gods and goddesses that met in a divine assembly (see pp. 75–78, above; see also Gen 35:4 [describing Jacob hiding gods under a goddess-tree]; Deut 16:21 [implying that goddess worship was widespread]; Jer 44:15–19 [criticizing but unable to stop pervasive goddess worship]; Hosea 14:9–10 [making encoded references to "Asherah"]; Prov 3:13–18 [same]);
- the deification of deceased souls and, perhaps, the cultic devotion to ancestors (see Exod 20:12; Deut 5:16; 1 Sam 28:13–14 [calling the deceased soul of Samuel "god" (*elohim*)]);
- the use of household gods that took the form of small figurines (see Gen 31:19, 31:30–35, 35:4; Judg 17; 1 Sam 19:13; 2 Kings 23:24; Hosea 3:4; Zech 10:2);
- the inauguration of sacred trees, obelisks, mounds, and divine images (see Gen 21:33 [Abraham plants a sacred tree], 28:16–22 [Jacob erects a stone and pours oil over it], 31:44–54 [Jacob erects a pillar and offers a sacrifice], 35:14 [Jacob erects a stone and pours oil over it]; Exod 37:6–9 [Bezalel makes the *cheruv*s for the sanctuary]; Num 21:4–9 [Moses erects a serpent on a pole]; Josh 4 [Joshua erects a circle of twelve stones in Gilgal, which becomes a place of worship], 24:26–27 [Joshua erects a stone under a goddess-tree]; Judg 8:22–27 [Gideon makes a sacred ephod], 18 [the Danites establish a temple with an idol that Micah had made]; 2 Kings 18:4–5, 23:4–24 [describing the

prevalence of sacrificial mounds, sacred stones, and Asherah trees];

- the founding of a variety of major and minor temples at which God was localized (see Gen 12:7–8, 16:7–14, 28:16–22, 33:20, 35:14; Exod 20:21–23; Deut 27:5–7; Josh 8:30–31; Judg 6:24–27, 18, 21:4; 1 Sam 14:35; 2 Sam 24:18–25; 1 Kings 18:32; Ezek 16:25; 1 Chron 16:39–40, 21:18–30);

- ritual worship without the need for a professional priesthood (see Gen 8:20–22, 12:7–8, 13:4, 13:18, 15:7–21, 26:24–25, 28:18, 35:14; Exod 20:21–23, 24:4–8; Judg 13:16–20; 17:5; 1 Sam 13:9–14 [criticizing the practice]; 2 Sam 6:17–18, 8:18, 15:7–12, 24:25; 1 Kings 3:2–4, 3:15, 8:5, 8:62–63, 9:25, 18:36–38; 2 Kings 16:12–13; 1 Chron 21:26–28);

- the influence of astrological forces (see Gen 15:5 [YHVH telling Abraham to read his fate in the stars]; Deut 4:19 [denouncing the worship of the celestial bodies, but implicitly confirming their influence]; Judg 5:20 [stating that the stars "fought from heaven"]; Amos 5:25–26 [stating that Israel worshiped Saturn (*Chiun*)]; Ps 19:1–6 [stating that "the heavens recount the glory of El"]; Job 22:12–14 [describing El as highest of the visible planets (*i.e.*, Saturn)], 38:33 [stating that the heavens dictate events on earth]; Eccles 1:9 [describing the cycles of time], 3:1–11 [stating that all events are determined by time]);

- the appearance of God on earth in human form (see, e.g., Gen 16:7–14 [as an angel], 18 [as three men]; Exod 4:16 [as Moses], 7:1 [as Moses], 14:19 [as an angel], 16:8 [as Moses], 18:19 [as Moses], 21:6 [as Moses], 22:8 [as Moses]; Num 20:16 [as an angel], 22:22–35 [as an angel]; Deut 29:1–5 [as Moses], 31:22–23 [as Moses]; Josh 5:13–15 [as leader of the army of YHVH]; Judg 2:1–4 [as an angel], 6:11–23 [as an angel], 13 [as an angel]; 1 Chron 21:16–17, 21:27 [as an angel]; see also p. 166, above);

- monastic renunciation and asceticism (see Num 6 [describing the restrictions applicable to a *nazir*]; Deut 5:27–28 [instructing the Israelites to return "to your tents"[236] but instructing Moses to remain near to YHVH, implying that Moses continued the ascetical practices prescribed in Exod 19:10–15 (see *BT Shabbat* 87a)]; Ezek 3:26, 33:22 [describing the practice of silence]);

- reincarnation (see Gen 38:8 [levirate marriage, implying reincarnation among lineal descendants], 38:26 [same]; Deut 25:5–6 [same]; Isa 26:19 [those who dwell in the dust will come back to life]; Ezek 37 [resurrection of bones]; Amos 2:4 [descendants repeat errors of ancestors]; Job 33:25 [a dying person is rejuvenated], 33:30 [a soul returns from the grave], 42:13 [implying the reincarnation of the children described in Job 1:2, 1:19]; Ruth 3–4 [levirate marriage]; Eccles 1:4 [continuity of generations], 1:9 [cycles of time]); and
- vegetarianism (see p. 201, above).

In short, the religion presented in Deuteronomy stands in stark contrast to many of the religious practices and beliefs recorded elsewhere in scripture. The values and concerns of Deuteronomy suggest a time when the tribes constituting Judah and Israel had transitioned from a pastoral to an agrarian economy and when the Judean royal house was seeking to consolidate both political and cultic power in the Judean capital.

It is true, of course, that there are scattered statements in Exodus, Leviticus, and Numbers that, like the numerous statements in Deuteronomy, are critical of foreign gods (see Exod 22:19, 23:13, 23:24, 23:33, 34:14–16) and image-worship (see Exod 20:4–6, 20:20, 32:1–10, 34:13, 34:17; Lev 19:4, 26:1; Num

---

[236] This instruction comes immediately after the theophany of YHVH at Sinai. As discussed in detail in Parts One and Two, the people are worshipers of El/Shaddai, not YHVH. Moses tells them to return "to your tents" (*Le'AHaLaYKHeM*), but according to the Kabbalah, the reader should transpose the *hei* (H) and the *lamed* (L) so that the text says return "to your God(s)" (*Le'ELoHaYKHeM*)—to El/Shaddai, in other words.

33:52). But several of these statements appear in the "Covenant Code" section of the book of Exodus (Exod 20:19–23:33), which was added in the 7th century B.C.E., about the same time as the Deuteronomic reform.[237] Moreover, these scattered statements are made in the context of praising a deity that was described as the head of a pantheon (see Exod 21:6, 22:7–8; Isa 6:8; Jer 23:18–22; Ps 82:1; Job 1:6) and that was worshiped in the form of twined *cheruvs* (see Exod 25:17–22; Num 15:37–41; Deut 22:12). Strict monotheistic iconoclasm, therefore, was not the exclusive concern of these statements. Also, the most iconoclastic story of the first four books of the Torah—the denunciation of the Israelites' worship of the golden calf (Exod 32:1–10)— can best be understood as a Judean polemic against the calf-worshiping devotional practices of the Northern Kingdom (see 1 Kings 12:28–29), not as a per se rejection of sacred images (see 1 Kings 6:23–35, 7:25, 7:29, 7:36).

Deuteronomy itself recognizes that it represents a significant revision of the Torah. It refers to itself as "the covenant... in the land of Moab," and it states that it is a new covenant designed to supplement the covenant given at Sinai. (See Deut 4:44–46, 28:69, 31:9–13, 31:24–29.) Significantly, Moses' merciless instructions concerning the war against Midian were also given in Moab (Num 31:12), as were his instructions to drive out the Canaanites and to destroy their temples and images (Num 33:50–56), and Deuteronomy echoes that scorched-earth attitude toward the Canaanites (Deut 7:1–5, 7:22–26, 12:1–3, 12:29–31, 20:16–18). Thus, it appears that the final chapters of Numbers, in which Joshua is in control and Moses announces his harshest policies, is really part of the same Moab covenant set forth in Deuteronomy. And this Moab covenant seems to reinvent Moses to suit the values of King Josiah's time.

---

[237] See Wright, *Inventing God's Law*, pp. 346–363.

Deuteronomy also offers its own internal explanation for why its teachings are inconsistent with the teachings of the other four books of the Torah. It asserts that Moses was giving a *new* set of instructions appropriate to the *new* situation the Israelites would face once they were settled in their land. In other words, Deuteronomy presents itself as Moses' prophetic anticipation of the problems that kings such as Josiah would encounter many years after Moses' death. (See, e.g., Deut 12:8–9.)

That explanation for the revisionist content of Deuteronomy is plausible, although it is perhaps a bit too convenient, as would be true of a new book of the Torah found in modern times, revising the Torah in light of modern problems and concerns. It is suspicious, for example, that in its regulations governing kings, Deuteronomy anticipates the sins of King Solomon so specifically and idiosyncratically that the authors of Deuteronomy must have had Solomon in mind.

- Compare Deut 17:15 [YHVH must choose the king] with 1 Kings 1 [Solomon not chosen by YHVH].
- Compare Deut 17:16 [the king should not import horses from Egypt] with 1 Kings 10:26–29 [Solomon imports horses from Egypt].
- Compare Deut 17:17 [the king should not have an abundance of wives or wealth] with 1 Kings 5:1–8 [describing Solomon's vast wealth], 10:14–29 [same], 11:3 [Solomon has 700 wives and 300 concubines].

Even if we assume that this close correlation between Deuteronomy and the behavior of King Solomon is attributable to Moses' prophetic foreknowledge, Solomon either never saw the book of Deuteronomy, which seems unlikely if it was a part of the Torah at that time, or he blatantly ignored it without objection, which seems equally unlikely. What is much more likely is that Deuteronomy was added to the Torah *after* Solomon's reign, as a criticism of Solomon's behavior, which the authors of Deuteronomy saw as the reason for the division of David's kingdom.[238]

Deuteronomy also rather neatly predicts events like the fall of Jerusalem and the Babylonian exile. (See Deut 4:26–28, 28:49–57, 28:64–68, 29:26–27, 30:1–10.) And despite the explanation that Deuteronomy was a new set of instructions appropriate to the new situation the Israelites would face once they were settled in their land, it seems odd that Moses would suddenly, at the end of his life, advocate a new religious attitude that he himself had never followed. Nor is it clear, as a spiritual and moral matter, why being settled in a land requires one to be less syncretistic and more iconoclastic.

Therefore, what makes much more sense is that, with the passage of time, the extreme ritual practices associated with Canaan's gods—in particular, child sacrifice (Deut 12:31)—proved to be a continuing problem for the Israelites (see 2 Kings 17:16–17).[239] Therefore, the Deuteronomic reformers felt the need to take strong steps to denounce the Canaanite religion (see, e.g., 1 Kings 18; Jer 2:8, 2:23, 7:9, 9:14, 11:9–17, 19:5, 23:13, 23:27, 32:26–35; Hosea 2, 11:2, 13:1), and they did so by rejecting the Egypt-Canaan syncretism of Genesis and Exodus. As a result, the Canaanite gods of the Israelite patriarchs

---

[238] See Coogan, *The Old Testament*, pp. 182–183; Hayes, *Introduction to the Bible*, pp. 222–224.

[239] See also Judg 11:30–40 [Jephthah sacrifices his daughter]; 2 Kings 16:3 [associating child sacrifice with the kings of Northern Kingdom]; Jer 3:20–25 [same]; Ezek 20:26 [same], 20:31 [same], 23:31–39 [same]; Hosea 13:2 [same]; Mic 6:7 [telling Israel to do good works instead of child sacrifice]; Ps 106:35–38 [saying that the Israelites indulged in Canaanite forms of worship including child sacrifice]; see also 2 Kings 21:6 [after the fall of Northern Kingdom, King Manasseh of Judah sacrifices his son], 23:10 [after the fall of Northern Kingdom, child sacrifice comes to Judah/Jerusalem]; Jer 7:30–31 [same], 19:3–5 [same], 32:30–35 [same]; Ezek 16:20–21 [same], 23:36–39 [same].

(see Gen 14:18–19; Exod 6:2–3) became the forbidden gods of the Deuteronomic reform, and the Canaanite names "El" and "Shaddai" were recast as generic terms for "God."

Prophets, of course, speak to the needs of the times and places in which they live. Before the time of Moses, the Israelites worshiped the gods of Canaan. Hence, when Moses introduced YHVH, it was important to present YHVH as a syncretistic twin to Canaan's gods, while denouncing the Canaanite practice of child sacrifice (see Lev 18:21, 20:1–5). When, however, the worship of YHVH became more established, YHVH could be presented as a superior alternative to Canaan's gods, an alternative that avoided the temptation toward child sacrifice that Canaan's gods represented. Hence, the early prophets chose to assimilate YHVH to Canaan's gods, whereas the later prophets chose to present these gods in sharp dichotomy.

As noted, Deuteronomy rejects practices and beliefs that were widespread prior to the time of Josiah and that enjoyed the tacit approval of respected prophets and kings. Thus, if we are to believe that Deuteronomy is Moses' prophetic anticipation of the problems the Israelites would face once they settled in the land of Canaan, we must explain why its teachings were so widely ignored by the Israelites during the many centuries from Moses' death until Josiah's reforms. In this context, a few points already mentioned merit further examination. Micah made a carved image and a molten image for the purpose of worshiping YHVH, and the Danites used Micah's idols as that tribe's own idols, with Moses' grandson acting as their priest. (Judg 17–18.) The people also erected altars and worship-images at "high places" throughout the land (not just in Jerusalem), and these high places were patronized by respected prophets and kings, without any apparent disapproval. (See 1 Sam 9:6–14; 1 Kings 3:2–4.) And, of course, the Israelites worshiped golden calves in Beth-El and in Dan. (1 Kings 12:28–30.) All this evidence strongly suggests that, prior to King Josiah's time, there was simply no awareness in either Judah or Israel of the book we now call Deuteronomy.

It is also significant that the prophet Hosea (8th century B.C.E.) rails against the image-worship that was prevalent in his time, but in the entire book of Hosea, the prophet never once refers to the prohibitions against such worship that appear in Deuteronomy. Is it likely that a prophet who was determined to put an end to image-worship would neglect to cite Moses' own statements against that form of worship if they were then a part of the Torah?

Also, there is the matter of the caduceus that Moses made, which the people worshiped for centuries. (Num 21:4–9; 2 Kings 18:4.) If Moses hated divine images, why then did he make one? And why did he do so just six months before he supposedly related the contents of the book of Deuteronomy, in which he condemned the practice? (See Num 21:4–9, 33:38; Deut 1:3.) And if, having made the caduceus, Moses later decided it was a bad idea and wanted it destroyed, he certainly could have destroyed it forthwith. Why instead would he preserve the caduceus but write an iconoclastic screed justifying the actions of kings, centuries later, who chose to destroy it (2 Kings 18:4)? It is no small thing to destroy an ancient image created by Moses himself, the man reputed to be the greatest of all prophets (Deut 34:10). Doing so hardly suggests respect for Moses; rather, it suggests a revisionist effort to reinvent Moses, just as Deuteronomy reinvents the Torah.

It seems therefore that the book of Deuteronomy as we now have it is best dated from the time of Josiah's reforms. But because so much of the old religion remains in evidence in the earlier books of the Torah, we must conclude that the Deuteronomic reformers could *add* more easily than they could *subtract*, and most especially, they could not delete texts that were widely loved and deeply ingrained in the consciousness of the nation. Perhaps, however, the reformers hoped that, by adding the book of Deuteronomy to the scriptural canon, and by making other supplementary emendations throughout Hebrew scripture, they could slowly change the consciousness of the nation. That is not to say that the entirety of the book of Deuteronomy is the work of a relatively late reform movement. Deuteronomy includes some very ancient material that is stylistically distinguishable from other sections of the book. It is quite possible, therefore, that the Deuteronomic reformers had in their possession some ancient texts that they combined with newer material.

Structurally, Deuteronomy includes a section at the beginning, in which Moses pleads with the Israelites just before his death, reviewing in detail the many events that transpired since Moses began leading them. Interestingly, however, it does not mention the brutal war against Midian, thus confirming, by omission, that the Midian war came *after* Moses' death, not before. (See Num 31:2.) Of course, even if the Israelites of Moses' time were only a few thousand in number, not two million, they were too numerous to be addressed as a group by a single man, and so we must assume that Moses addressed them indirectly, through their representatives in the Assembly.

This speech is followed by a law code that repeats some of the civil and religious laws that appear elsewhere in the Torah, although with important modifications. For example, a side-by-side comparison of chapter 21 of Exodus (vv. 2–11) and chapter 15 of Deuteronomy (vv. 12–18) demonstrates that the Deuteronomy law was based directly on the earlier Exodus law, but with several humanitarian emendations.[240] More important, however, the law code of Deuteronomy adds much that is new. We have already mentioned the centralization of authority, religious chauvinism, and harsh iconoclasm that characterize this new law code. In addition, this new law code is militaristic and to some degree xenophobic, authorizing wars of aggression, establishing ethical rules to govern war, and imposing a genocidal standard regarding the conquest of the land of Canaan and the surrounding territories. (Deut 20, 21:10–14.) Why would people who just escaped oppression and slavery in one land want to

---

[240] See Hayes, *Introduction to the Bible*, pp. 171–175.

conquer, oppress, and enslave the residents of another land by
military force? They would not. Rather, the new laws set forth in
Deuteronomy represent the nationalist values of an established
kingdom many centuries later.

After presenting this reformed law code, Deuteronomy
returns to Moses' speech, including a list of blessings (if the Israelites are obedient) and curses (if they are disobedient). (Deut
28.) A different set of blessings and curses appears in the book
of Leviticus. (Lev 26:3–45.) Such lists were common features
in ancient treaties of vassalage. Those who bound themselves
as vassals did so under penalty of suffering the enumerated
curses if they showed disloyalty. In the case of Deuteronomy,
the curses are remarkably similar to the curses set forth in vassal
treaties of the Assyrian king Esar-haddon (681–669 B.C.E.), suggesting that the authors of Deuteronomy (who would have been
familiar with the Assyrian vassal treaties) used those treaties as
a model.[241] One could even argue that the blessings and curses
listed in Deuteronomy were the means by which refugees of the
fallen Northern Kingdom (see 2 Chron 30:25) expressed vassalage to the king of the Southern Kingdom and, more importantly,
to the Southern Kingdom's god, YHVH. That hypothesis might
also explain the well-known *Shema* prayer, which appears in
Deuteronomy: "Hear, O Israel [(*i.e.*, Northern Kingdom)]; YHVH
is our God; YHVH is one and only."[242]

---

[241] See Coogan, *The Old Testament*, pp. 184–186. It is unlikely that Esar-
haddon would have used Deuteronomy, a religious text of a relatively
minor kingdom, as the model for his own treaties. Thus, the similarity
of Deuteronomy's chapter 28 to the Esar-haddon vassal treaties suggests
that at least chapter 28 of Deuteronomy was composed after Esar-haddon's time.

[242] A more mystical explanation of the list of curses is given, however,
in the Babylonian Talmud (see *Moed Katan* 9b), which asserts that the
curses are really blessings in disguise. According to a similar principle
found in Hebrew scripture, any curse, if accepted humbly, without reac-

Deuteronomy closes with a prophetic song, followed by Moses' blessings to the Israelite tribes. At its very end, Deuteronomy tells of Moses' death, and it lauds Moses, describing him as the greatest prophet of all time and as the "King over Jeshurun."

2. "I am not a man of words"

In form, the book of Deuteronomy presents itself as Moses' address to the Israelites just before his death. Years earlier, Moses had complained to YHVH that he was not a persuasive orator, saying, "*Lo ish devarim anokhi*," meaning, "I am not a man [of] words." (Exod 4:10.) In response, YHVH had instructed Moses to use Aaron as a spokesman, and therefore many of the statements that are attributed to Moses in Exodus, Leviticus, and Numbers come filtered through Aaron. But by the end of the book of Numbers, Aaron has died, and so in Deuteronomy we get pure Moses, and his oratorical skills, as presented in that book, prove to be nothing short of awesome. If Moses is really the one speaking in the book of Deuteronomy, then he was just being modest when he said, "I am not a man [of] words," for in Deuteronomy we encounter some of the most beautiful passages of the Torah.

But Moses' final address to the Israelites is not just a devotional speech or sermon. Our close textual analysis of the enigmatic stories from Leviticus and Numbers revealed those stories to tell a dramatic tale of rebellion against Moses and Aaron's leadership, followed by Moses' blasphemous curse of Korach and the execution of both Moses and Aaron by stoning. But the Assembly certainly did not inflict that supreme punishment without a formal hearing. In that context, the oratorical sections

---

tion, creates a channel through which one can receives blessings. See 2 Sam 16:5–12.

of Deuteronomy can be understood to represent Moses' defense of himself at his own trial for capital murder. Deuteronomy is, then, a powerful Hebrew analog to Plato's *Apologia Socratis*.

And although Moses' moving words constitute a detailed defense of his conduct, they also—and most beautifully—constitute an impassioned defense of his god, YHVH, for Moses the Egyptian knows that a cultural and spiritual divide is the real reason the Israelites distrust him. Moses therefore implores the Israelites to accept YHVH as their own, as they had briefly done in their moment of triumph after escaping Pharaoh's pursuing army at the Sea of Reeds. As we shall see, Moses' speech alternates between plural and singular forms of the word "you," suggesting that he is sometimes addressing the entire Assembly and other times only its presiding officer.

Moses says:

> You [(sing.)] were shown to know that YHVH is the gods; [there is] *nothing else besides him.* From the heavens, he caused you to hear his voice to teach you, and upon the earth he caused you to see his great fire. And you heard his words amidst the fire.... And you have known today, and you have returned [it] to your heart, that YHVH is the gods—in the heavens above and upon the earth below, *nothing else.*[243]

Here, Moses is the uncompromising nondualist, asserting that everything in this world and also the *knowing* of this world ("he caused you to hear/see"), including every deity and spiritual power, is nothing but the one and only God that Moses refers to by the name YHVH.

Moses continues:

> Here, O Israel; YHVH is our GOD, YHVH is universal. And you [(sing.)] shall love YHVH, your god, with all your heart and all

---

[243] Deut 4:35–39.

your soul and all your intensity. And these words that I command you today shall be on your heart. And you shall teach them to your children and speak about them when you sit in your house and when you go on the way and when you lie down and when you arise. And you shall bind them for a sign upon your hand, and they shall be for an ornament between your eyes. And you shall write them upon the doorposts of your house and in your gates.[244]

Moses also insists that YHVH is trustworthy to meet the needs of the people:

For YHVH, your god, is bringing you [(sing.)] to a good land, a land flowing with waters—springs and waters of the depths, coming forth in the valley and in the highland—a land of wheat and barley and grape and fig and pomegranate, a land of olive oil and date-honey, a land in which you will not eat bread with poverty, in which you will not lack anything. A land whose stones are iron and from her mountains you will chisel copper. And you will eat, and you will be satisfied, and you will bless YHVH, your god, concerning the good land that he gave to you.[245]

Moses reminds his listeners of the ways in which they repeatedly provoked and rebelled against YHVH, mentioning for example the golden calf incident: "Rebels you [(pl.)] have been against YHVH from the day I knew you!" (Deut 9:24; see also Deut 31:27.) And Moses further reminds them that YHVH had once resolved to destroy them and that he (Moses) had fasted and prayed on their behalf, allaying YHVH's anger. (Deut 9:18–19, 9:25–29, 10:10–11.) In that context, Moses again pleads with the Israelites to accept YHVH:

---

[244] Deut 6:4–9.

[245] Deut 8:7–10.

And now, Israel, [considering all that YHVH gave you,] what
does YHVH, your god, ask of you [(sing.)]? Only to respect
YHVH, your god, to go in all his ways and to love him and to
serve YHVH, your god, with all your heart and all your soul, to
guard the directives of YHVH and his decrees, which I am com-
manding you this day for your benefit. Behold! To YHVH, your
god, belong the heavens and the heavens of the heavens and
the earth and all that is in it.[246]

Moses further insists that the Israelites should humble themselves:

And you [(pl.)] will cut away the callus of your heart, and
your neck you will not stiffen anymore. For YHVH, your god,
he is the God of the gods and the Lord of the lords, the great,
strong, and awesome El, who does not exalt faces and does
not take a bribe. He does [fair] judgment for the orphan and
the widow, and he loves the stranger, to give to him bread and
garment. And you [(pl.)] shall love the stranger, for strang-
ers you were in the land of Egypt. You [(sing.)] shall fear
YHVH, your god. Him you [(sing.)] shall serve, and in him
you [(sing.)] shall cleave, and in his name you [(sing.)] shall
swear. He is your praise, and he is your god, who did for you
[(sing.)] these great and awesome things that your eyes saw.
As seventy souls, your ancestors descended toward Egypt,
and now YHVH, your god, has set you [(sing.)] like the stars of
the heavens for abundance.[247]

Moses closes his moving address by insisting that the path of
devotion to YHVH is near, not remote:

---

[246] Deut 10:12–14.

[247] Deut 10:16–22.

For this commandment that I command you [(sing.)] today is not obscure from you [(sing.)], and it is not far from you [(sing.)]. It is not in the heaven, to say, "Who will ascend among us toward heaven and retrieve it for us, and we will hear it and do it?" And it is not from across the sea, to say, "Who will cross among us to the other side of the sea to retrieve it for us, and we will hear it and do it?" For the word [(*Yehudi*, "Jew")] is very near to you [(sing.)], in your mouth and in your heart, to do it.[248]

3. The Death of Moses

I've been to the mountaintop....
I'm not fearing *any* man!

—Martin Luther King, Jr. (1929–1968 C.E.)

(a) "And he entombed him"

The Torah very clearly describes Moses' death, like that of Aaron, as a punishment for his having struck down the "rock" in Kadeish. YHVH tells Moses: "Ascend to this mountain of the Hebrews..., and you [(sing.)] shall be gathered to your people—also you [(sing.)]—just as Aaron your brother was gathered, because you [(pl.)] defied [the word of] my mouth in the Wilderness of Tzin, in the strife of the Assembly, [failing] to cause me to be sanctified in the waters before their eyes; they are the Waters of Contention, Kadeish, Wilderness of Tzin." (Num 27:12–14; see also Deut 32:49–51.) And later, the Torah says: "And Moses ascended from the plains of Moab to Mount Nebo, head of the promontory that is on the face of Jericho..., and

---

[248] Deut 30:11–14.

Moses, servant of YHVH, died there in the land of Moab, by the mouth of YHVH. And he entombed him in the valley, in the land of Moab, across from the Temple of P'eor, and no man knows his tomb until this day.... And Joshua the son of Nun was filled with the spirit of Wisdom." (Deut 34:1–9.)

As noted in regard to Aaron's death, the phrase "by the mouth of YHVH" indicates martyrdom, and the "Temple of P'eor" is, of course, the location where the Israelites committed human sacrifices (Ps 106:28–38). We know from the blasphemer story (Lev 24:10–23) and also from Moses' prophetic foretelling of his own death (Exod 17:4) that Moses died by stoning, and therefore martyrdom makes sense. But what about the statement "he entombed him"? *Who* entombed him? The Torah is brilliant in its ability to convey meaning in the subtlest of ways, and here, with only the use of the third person singular, the Torah signals that one person besides Moses was present at Moses' death and burial. Who? A pious tradition relates that YHVH was present and that YHVH buried Moses. But pious traditions are often created to obscure painful memories. Some incarnate form of YHVH had to lift the stone that took Moses' life, and some incarnate form of YHVH had to dig the pit that received his body.

As mentioned, Rashi teaches in regard to execution by stoning that the Assembly acted through an agent.[249] Given a matter as grave as the execution of an important leader of the people, would not the *head of the Assembly* be the one most likely to act as the Assembly's agent? And who was the head of the Assembly at the time Aaron died? Moses was (Num 16:3, 27:12–17), and it was Moses who accompanied Aaron up Mount Hor to his death, stripped him of his garments, and dressed his son Elazar in them (Num 20:27–28). And who was the head of the Assembly at the time Moses died? Joshua was (Num 27:15–23)—Joshua the son

[249] Rashi on Lev 24:14, translated in Yitzchaki, *Rashi: Commentary on the Torah*, vol. 3, p. 313.

of Nun, from the tribe of Ephraim (Num 13:8, 13:16). "By a prophet [(*i.e.*, by Moses)], YHVH brought Israel out from Egypt, and by a prophet they were guarded. Ephraim has angered bitterly, and his blood will be spread upon him...." (Hosea 12:14–15; see also Neh 9:26.)

(b) The Telltale Garment

Who killed poor Moses?
Goethe supposes
That the terrible son
Of a masculine Nun,
And Caleb his crony,
Whose sire is Jephone,
Together killed Moses;
So Goethe supposes!

—James Thomson (1834–1882 C.E.)[250]

As a pious young man, Johann Wolfgang von Goethe (1749–1832 C.E.) endeavored to sanctify himself in imitation of the Israelite patriarchs. He learned Hebrew and studied the Torah closely. He concluded that Joshua the son of Nun, acting with the help of his friend Caleb the son of Jephunneh, killed Moses. Goethe recorded his controversial theory in an essay entitled *Israel in der Wüste*.[251]

And Goethe was not the only student of the Hebrew Bible to have the thought that Moses was martyred in the wilderness by the Israelites whom he was leading. Sigmund Freud famously advocated a version of this theory in his book *Moses and Monotheism*. And we have already discussed the *Zohar*'s veiled assertion, based on the story of Benayahu the son of Yehoyada, that

---

[250] Thomson, *The City of Dreadful Night*, vol. I, p. 296.

[251] Goethe, *Goethe's Werke*, vol. 6, p. 172.

some man, acting at God's command, killed Moses.252 But more significant is the report of the influential Persian historian Abu Ja'far Muhammad ibn Jarir al-Tabari (839–923 C.E.), which confirms—albeit by way of a partial denial—that it was *Joshua*, in particular, who killed Moses. Al-Tabari is best known for his *History of Prophets and Kings* (*Tarikh al-Tabari*), in which he writes:

> When Moses returned [from Mount Hor] to the Children of Israel without Aaron, they said that Moses had killed Aaron, because he had envied their love for him, for Aaron was more forbearing and more lenient with them, while Moses had a certain harshness toward them.... Moses... prayed to God, Who made the bed descend so that they could see it between heaven and earth, and then they believed Moses. [¶] Then, while Moses was walking with his servant Joshua, a black wind suddenly approached. When Joshua saw it,... [h]e clung to Moses and said, "The hour is appearing while I cling to Moses, the prophet of God." But Moses withdrew himself gently from under his shirt, leaving it in Joshua's hand. When Joshua returned with the shirt, the Israelites seized him, saying, "You have killed the prophet of God!"... He said, "If you do not believe me, give me a delay of three days." Then he prayed to God, and every man who was guarding him was approached in a dream and informed that Joshua had not killed Moses; rather, "We have raised him up to Us," and they left him alone.253

In al-Tabari's account, Moses is accused of killing Aaron, and Joshua is accused of killing Moses, and in both cases, God takes responsibility for the death, thus allaying suspicion, but

---

252 See *Zohar* 1:6b, translated in Matt, *The Zohar: Pritzker Edition*, vol. I, pp. 41–42.

253 Brinner (trans.), *The History of al-Tabari*, vol. III, p. 86.

the text nonetheless leaves open the possibility that Moses and Joshua, acting as God's agents, are the ones immediately responsible. Thus, al-Tabari's account hints at the very facts it denies—by denial, it draws attention to the person who, in each case, is the most obvious suspect.

But al-Tabari's description of Moses' death—in which Joshua is left holding Moses' shirt—is also strikingly similar to the scriptural account of the death of the prophet Elijah, and the correspondence between these two accounts is even more striking when we consider that immediately after Moses' death, Joshua splits the Jordan River (see Josh 3:9–17), just as Elisha does immediately after Elijah's death. Here is the biblical account of Elijah's death:

> And Elisha said: "And may it be, please, that twofold your spirit [comes] to me." And [Elijah] said: "...[I]f you see me taken from you, it will be so for you...." ...And—behold—a rider of fire and horses of fire [appeared] and separated between the two of them, and Elijah ascended in a storm to the heavens. And Elisha saw, and he cried out: "My Father! My Father! The Rider of Israel and its Horsemen!" And he did not see him anymore.... *And he raised the cloak of Elijah that had fallen from upon him*, and he returned, and he stood upon the bank of the Jordan. And he took the cloak of Elijah that had fallen from upon him, and he struck the waters, and he said: "Where is YHVH, God of Elijah?" Even he—and he struck the waters, and it split, hither and yon, and Elisha crossed.[254]

Clearly, if we accept al-Tabari's account of Moses' death as true, then Elijah's death was a close reenactment of Moses' death. That fact, of course, raises the possibility that al-Tabari was the recipient of an oral tradition asserting that Moses' death was like

---

[254] 2 Kings 2:9–14.

that of Elijah, and al-Tabari therefore modeled his account of Moses' death on the Elijah story.

But more important, the symbolism of all these stories is clear. Moses, at Aaron's death, is left holding Aaron's "garments." (Num 20:27–28.) Joshua, at Moses' death, is left grasping Moses' "shirt." (*Tarikh al-Tabari*.) Elisha, at Elijah's death, is left carrying Elijah's "cloak." (2 Kings 2:13.) In each case, the doffed bit of clothing, like the limp body after the soul has departed, implies death at the hand of the person left holding the cloth. Likewise, during the time of the Israelite patriarchs, the sons of Jacob were left grasping Joseph's royal "coat" (Gen 37:3, 37:31–33), the limp coat implying Joseph's death at their hands. And likewise Potiphar's wife was left grasping Joseph's "garment" (Gen 39:12), the limp garment implying "the little death" (*la petite mort*) of sexual impropriety. In all these cases, the bit of cloth left in the hand betokens the deed.

(c) Metatron

Joshua the son of Nun is called "lad" (*na'ar*) in the Torah. (Exod 33:11.) But according to the Babylonian Talmud (*Yevamot* 16b), the word "lad" (*na'ar*) signifies Metatron, an angel who lived on earth as Enoch (the seventh generation from Adam) (Gen 5:16–24) and who is considered to be the highest among the angels. Metatron is also identified as the "angel" that wrestled Jacob at the Ford of Jabbok,[255] an angel we previously compared to the Egyptian storm god Set (see pp. 60–61, above). And the Babylonian Talmud also teaches (*Sanhedrin* 38b) that Metatron is the fierce angel about whom YHVH told Moses: "Behold, I send an angel before you...; beware of him and heed his voice... for he will not forgive your transgressions, *for my name is in him*." (Exod 23:20–21; see also Exod 33:2–3.)

---

[255] Ginzberg, *The Legends of the Jews, Volume 1*, pp. 384–388; Ginzberg, *The Legends of the Jews, Volume 5*, pp. 305–306.

The letters of YHVH (*yud-hei-vov-hei*) are, of course, in Joshua's name (*yud-hei-vov-shin-ayin*), and the Torah's use of the word "lad" for Joshua suggests, according to the Talmud, a link between Joshua and Metatron, the angel that does "not forgive your transgressions" (Exod 23:21). And several additional hints confirm that link. Moses, for example, suggests a connection between Joshua and Metatron when he tells Joshua: "You are the one who is vengeful for me." (Num 11:29.) And later, Joshua has a vision of a fierce angel, and Joshua immediately bows and describes himself as the fierce angel's earthly servant:

> And it was when Joshua was in Jericho that he raised his eyes, and he saw, and—behold—a man was standing opposite him with his sword drawn in his hand. Joshua... said to him, "Are you for us or for our enemies?" He said, "Not—for I am the Prince of the Legion of YHVH. Now, I have come." Joshua fell before him to the ground and prostrated and said to him, "What does my Lord speak to his servant?"[256]

Clearly, Joshua identified with the warlike "Prince of the Legion."

It is also worth noting Joshua's final words to the Israelites: "You will not be able to serve YHVH, for he is a holy god, he is a god of vengeance, *he will not forgive your transgressions* or your sins." (Josh 24:19.) Here, Joshua uses the exact phrase ("he will not forgive your transgressions") that the book of Exodus uses to describe Metatron (Exod 23:21). We know that YHVH is associated with mercy (see Exod 34:5–7; Num 14:18–20; Deut 5:9–10), so Joshua's description of YHVH as an unforgiving "god of vengeance" tells us more about Joshua than it does about YHVH; it tells us that Joshua conceives of God in a fierce form that corresponds to Metatron.

The *Zohar*, too, confirms the identity between Joshua and

---

[256] Josh 5:13–14.

Metatron, but it adds that Joshua was "defective" on account of Adam's eating from the Tree of Knowledge.[257] Therefore, when Moses hears from YHVH that Metatron will lead the people ("I send an angel before you"), he pleads that YHVH should do so directly, and YHVH agrees (Exod 33:15–17), but as we know, it is the warrior Joshua who, in the end, leads the people across the Jordan and then proceeds to conquer Canaan's kings.

In light of the connection between Joshua and God's fierce angel Metatron, it is not surprising that it was specifically Joshua who acted as Moses' executioner. But was Joshua wrong to do so? Is it fair to say that Moses was martyred? Moses had angrily invoked the name YHVH to curse Korach and others to die, and Korach and his supporters did, in fact, die. Moses' own Torah announces the law of measure-for-measure justice that applies to such cases: "Any man who will denigrate his god, he will bear his sin.... Break for break, eye for eye, tooth for tooth." (Lev 24:10–23.) Moses "denigrate[d] his god," and therefore he had to "bear his sin"—that is, the evil that flowed from his inappropriate invocation of God's name had to be revisited upon him. Therefore, "they took the one who cursed to the outside of the camp, and [acting through their agent Joshua,] they stoned him [with] a stone, and the descendants of Israel did according to what YHVH commanded to Moses." (Lev 24:23.)

But as noted, the *Zohar* informs us that Joshua (*i.e.*, Metatron) was "defective."[258] What if Joshua, despite his great righteousness, misjudged the case? What if Joshua failed to discern that the law of measure-for-measure justice is a principle of nature (like the law of karma), not a rule to be applied by civil justice systems? What if Joshua, from the tribe of Ephraim, erred when

---

[257] *Zohar* 1:53a, translated in Matt, *The Zohar: Pritzker Edition*, vol. I, pp. 294–296.

[258] *Zohar* 1:53a, translated in Matt, *The Zohar: Pritzker Edition*, vol. I, pp. 294–296.

he took Moses' life? "Ephraim has angered bitterly...." (Hosea 12:15.)

In later times, of course, the kings of the Northern Kingdom, who, like Joshua, were descendants of Ephraim (1 Kings 11:26), rebelled against the Kingdom of Judah. And the book of Psalms reminds us of YHVH's preference for Judah: "He despised the tent of Joseph, and the tribe of Ephraim he did not choose, and he chose the tribe of Judah, Mount Zion that he loves." (Ps 78:67–68.) The backstory, then, to the death of Moses is the rivalry between two tribes, two kingdoms, two religious cultures, and two deities, and Moses, the Egyptian man who led the Israelites to freedom, died as a sacrifice, a martyr to the cause of unifying a broken world. "In that day," we are assured about the future, "YHVH will be one, and his name [will be] one." (Zech 14:9.)

(d) *Yeshu ha-Notzri*

By close analysis of Leviticus and Numbers, we have discovered that Moses, the greatest prophet of all time (Deut 34:10), died as a martyr, making his story remarkably similar to that of Jesus, the great prophet-martyr of the Christian faith. But Moses and Jesus have something else in common, for Jewish tradition associates Jesus with the blasphemer described in chapter 24 of Leviticus.[259]

The author of the present book was once studying the blasphemer story with a Jewish congregation. The rabbi's sermon focused on this verse describing the blasphemer:

ונקב שם יהוה מות יומת

"And [he who] expresses the name YHVH will surely die."
(Lev 24:16.)

---

[259] Jewish tradition also sometimes likens Jesus to Bala'am son of B'eor. *BT Sanhedrin* 106b.

The rabbi asked if anyone in the congregation knew who the blasphemer was. No one spoke up, so the rabbi highlighted the initial letters of the first three words of the verse:

ונקב שם יהוה מות יומת

By taking those letters and writing them backwards, the rabbi derived the word יש״ו (*Yeshu*, or "Jesus"), asserting that the blasphemer was Jesus. But what the rabbi perhaps did not realize was that Moses, too, was the blasphemer, which of course places Jesus in very good company.

Jewish esoteric thought asserts that every major figure of history is prefigured in the Torah, and because the name of Jesus is encoded into the blasphemer story from Leviticus, some commentators have suggested a connection. Sometimes, this verse from that story is the focus of their commentary:

בן־אשה ישראלית והוא בן־איש מצרי

"The son of an Israelite woman, and he was the son of an Egyptian man." (Lev 24:10.)

Gathering the highlighted letters together, they derive the following name:

ישו המצרי

Yeshu ha-Mitzri
"Jesu[s] the Egyptian"

Jesus, of course, grew up in Egypt (Matthew 2:13–23), but notice also that the Hebrew letter *mem* (M)—the first letter of the Hebrew word *Mitzri* ("Egyptian")—looks a little bit like the letter *nun* (N) and the letter *vov* (V) combined into a single letter:

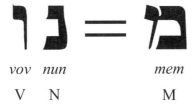

vov	nun		mem
V	N		M

Therefore, the *mem* (M) of the word *Mitzri* ("Egyptian") could, with some imagination, be read as a *nun-vov* (NV),[260] producing the word *Notzri* (נוצרי), which means "Nazarene":

מצרי = נוצרי

Notzri = Mitzri

That small adjustment yields the following name for the blasphemer:

ישו הנוצרי

Yeshu ha-Notzri
("Jesu[s] the Nazarene" or "Jesu[s] of Nazareth")

Yeshu ha-Notzri ("Jesu[s] the Nazarene") is a specific person mentioned in the Babylonian Talmud (*Sanhedrin* 43a). According to the Talmud, *Yeshu ha-Notzri* was a magician who led Jews astray. He was stoned, and then, very much like the Christian Jesus, he was hung from a wooden pole on the eve of Passover. The relevant passage from the Talmud, the context of which is a discussion of the law that applies to execution by stoning, is quoted below. The passage is long but worth considering in its entirety:

---

[260] The Hebrew letter *mem* (M) is actually drawn by joining a *kaf* (KH) and a *vov* (V), not by joining a *nun* (N) and a *vov* (V), but a *kaf* (KH) and a Sephardic-style *nun* (N) have similar shapes.

AND A HERALD PRECEDES HIM etc. This implies, only immediately before [the execution <u>must a herald precede him</u>], but not previous thereto. [In contradiction to this <u>conclusion</u>] it was taught: On the eve of the Passover Yeshu the Nazarene was hanged. For forty days before the execution took place, a herald went forth and cried, 'He is going forth to be stoned because he has practised sorcery and enticed Israel to apostasy. Anyone who can say anything in his favour, let him come forward and plead on his behalf.' But since nothing was brought forward in his favour he was hanged on the eve of the Passover!—'Ulla retorted: 'Do you suppose that he was one for whom a defence could be made? Was he not a *Mesith* [enticer], concerning whom Scripture says, *Neither shalt thou spare, neither shalt thou conceal him?* [<u>(Deut 13:9.)</u>] With Yeshu however it was different, for he was connected with the government [or royalty, i.e., influential].' [¶] Our Rabbis taught: Yeshu had five disciples, Matthai, Nakai, Nezer, Buni and Todah. When Matthai was brought [before the court] he said to them [the judges], Shall Matthai be executed? Is it not written, *Matthai* [when] *shall I come and appear before God?* [<u>(Ps 42:3.)</u>] Thereupon they retorted: Yes, Matthai shall be executed, since it is written,... *Matthai* [when] *shall* [he] *die and his name perish.* [<u>(Ps 41:6.)</u>] When Nakai was brought in he said to them: Shall Nakai be executed? Is it not written, *Naki* [the innocent] *and the righteous slay thou not?* [<u>(Exod 23:7.)</u>] Yes, was the answer, Nakai shall be executed, since it is written, *In secret places does* [<u>he</u>] *Naki* [the innocent] *slay.* [<u>(Ps 10:8.)</u>] When Nezer was brought in, he said: Shall Nezer be executed? Is it not written, *And Nezer* [a twig] *shall grow forth out of his roots.* [<u>(Isa 11:1.)</u>] Yes, they said, Nezer shall be executed, since it is written, *But thou art cast forth away from thy grave like Nezer* [an abhorred offshoot]. [<u>(Isa 14:19.)</u>] When Buni was brought in, he said: Shall Buni be executed? Is it not written, *Beni* [my son], *my first born?* [<u>(Exod 4:22.)</u>]

> Yes, they said, Buni shall be executed, since it is written, *Behold I will slay Bine-ka* [thy son] *thy first born.* [(Exod 4:23.)] And when Todah was brought in, he said to them: Shall Todah be executed? Is it not written, *A psalm for Todah* [thanksgiving]? [(Ps 100:1.)] Yes, they answered, Todah shall be executed, since it is written, *Whoso offereth the sacrifice of Todah* [thanksgiving] *honoured me.* [(Ps 50:23.)][261]

Notice that the names of *Yeshu*'s five disciples (Matthai, Nakai, Nezer, Buni, and Todah) are related to lines of scripture that use similarly spelled words (*matai* ["when"], *naki* ["innocent"], *nezer* ["offshoot"], *beni* ["my son"], and *todah* ["thanksgiving offering"]) and that the disciples are judged according to the scriptural lines in which their names appear. Notice also that the five words of scripture that the Talmud associates with the names of *Yeshu*'s five disciples can be read together as a single sentence: "When the innocent, an offshoot, my son, [is] a thanksgiving offering." Significantly, the crucifixion of Jesus is referred to in Christian sacrificial ritual as a "Eucharist," which is derived from the Greek word for "gratitude" or "thanksgiving." Thus, the early Christians understood the sacrificial death of Jesus—whom they viewed as God's offshoot and son—to be a thanksgiving offering.

We see, therefore, that the Talmud is speaking on two levels at once in its discussion of *Yeshu ha-Notzri* ("Jesus the Nazarene"). Superficially, it states the official Jewish teaching that *Yeshu ha-Notzri* was a magician who taught apostasy, was tried, condemned, and executed. More subtly, however, in listing the "names" of *Yeshu*'s five disciples, the Talmud suggests (in a veiled way) that *Yeshu ha-Notzri* ("Jesus the Nazarene") was

---

[261] *Sanhedrin* 43a, translated in Epstein (ed.), *The Babylonian Talmud, Nezikin,* vol. V, pp. 281–282 [the underscored editorial inserts are by the present author].

actually "innocent," that he was the "offshoot" and "son" of God, and that his death was a "thanksgiving offering."[262]

We saw in Part One that the ancient Egyptians, the Canaanites, and the Babylonians all believed that the living king of each generation—the righteous leader who maintained civil order, showed compassion toward the weak, and upheld justice in society—was the representative of the gods on earth. Judaism, too, once embraced the same idea. The king was God's "son" (2 Sam 7:14; Pss 2:7, 89:27–28), and he stood as a member of the Divine Council (Isa 9:1–7; Jer 23:18–22; Dan 7:9–14). The Talmud passage about *Yeshu ha-Notzri* ("Jesus the Nazarene") can be read as suggesting—albeit in code—that Jesus, in his generation, filled that role.

The book of Jeremiah confirms that, according to Jewish thought, it is possible for a human being to attain such a lofty spiritual state that he or she stands side by side with the gods of the Divine Council and receives from them a divine commission. The book of Jeremiah asks: "Who [among the so-called prophets] stood in the Council of YHVH and saw and heard his word?" (Jer 23:18.) Then, speaking as the oracle of YHVH, Jeremiah continues: "I [(YHVH)] have not sent forth prophets, but they have run forth; I have not spoken to them, but they have prophesied. *But if they stood in my Council and heard my word, [then] they would turn back my people from their ways of evil....*" (Jer 23:21–22; see also 1 Kings 22:19–23; Isa 6:1–8; Dan 7:9–14.)

Jewish tradition teaches that there is a "righteous person of the generation" (*tzadik ha-dor*) who, in each generation, fits the description set forth in Jeremiah of a human member of the Divine Council. A related teaching asserts that the "soul of the Messiah" is born in each generation, as either a man or a wom-

---

262 Prof. Schäfer presents a slightly different reading of this same passage from the Talmud in Schäfer, *Jesus in the Talmud*, pp. 75–81.

an.[263] And Jewish tradition adds that the most righteous person in a particular generation might not be a Jew.[264]

In one sense, then, it does not matter whether Moses or Jesus was the leading prophet of his generation, willingly accepting martyrdom for the sake of healing a broken world—for we are not living in the time of Moses or Jesus. We could argue about both Moses and Jesus, but if we accept that time has a circular quality (see Eccles 1:9) and that there is a righteous human being in each generation who stands in the Divine Council (see Jer 23:18–22), then the more valuable question is, who is that person today?

4. "Until the last sea"

Recall Isaac Luria's creation myth, summarized in Part One. Light sprayed from Adam's nose, mouth, ears, and eyes, and it arranged itself into ten divine potencies. But the vessels that captured the "Light"—the Heliopolitan pantheon—were not strong enough to hold it. They *shattered*. In other words, the ancient world's most sophisticated and venerable religion *shattered*, and the broken fragments of that great religion became all the diverse religious traditions.

Then more Light emanated from Adam. This new Light gathered the sparks of true religion that were scattered amidst the fragmented debris of the failed religion, and it arranged those sparks into stronger configurations that were capable of holding the Light.

---

[263] See, e.g., Ovadyah ben Avraham of Bertinoro, *Commentary on the Book of Ruth*; Hillel Rivlin, *Kol haTor* 2:2, 2:8, 2:2:4; see also Deut 18:15–22; Judg 4:4.

[264] See Zohar, "The Rabbi and the Sheikh: A Tale of 18th Century Damascus."

And according to Lurianic values, the task of gathering the last few sparks of fallen Light remains ours today. Most if not all the diverse religious traditions of the world are connected—directly or indirectly—to the ancient Egyptian religion, and scattered among the world's religions are "sparks" of the original "Light" waiting to be retrieved. Thus, all the religions of the world are valid, but they constitute pieces of a spiritual jigsaw puzzle that has yet to be fully assembled. In Luria's view, in other words, Judaism is a work in progress, and the critical pieces necessary to complete the project are to be found outside Judaism.[265]

At the end of Moses' life, YHVH sends him to the top of Mount Nebo (Rosh Ha-Pisgah) on the eastern side of the Jordan and shows him the land promised to Abraham's descendants. Moses sees every region, each named for one of the Israelite tribes, and he sees "the land of Judah *until the last sea*." (Deut 34:2.) Some English-language Bibles translate the latter phrase as "until the western sea," but the Hebrew text says "until the *last* sea" (*ad ha-yam ha-acharon*), and the same text can also be vowelized as "until the last *day*" (*ad ha-yom ha-acharon*).

The patriarch Jacob blessed his son Judah to be a "congress of nations" (Gen 49:10), and in Moses' expansive nondual vision, the land of Judah (*Yehudah*) is nothing less than all places for all time. Therefore, the real heart of the Torah is the transformation of this world that we share into a peaceful and sustainable congress of diverse cultures and nations. The reason Moses does not cross the Jordan is that Moses belongs to the world, not to a particular land. And this book is for *you who delight in all things*.

---

[265] On this interpretation of Judaism, see, e.g., Green (trans.), *Menahem Nahum of Chernobyl*, p. 95; Benamozegh, *Israel and Humanity*, pp. 72–75, 96–97.

Appendix One

Some aspects of the Kabbalah are very technical, and the texts can be difficult, but for the expert reader, they play an important role in confirming this book's assertion about the name YHVH. This appendix will delve more deeply into some Kabbalistic discussions of that name.

The *Zohar* confirms in several places that the name YHVH includes a hidden *dalet* (D), implying both *Yehudah* and *Yehudi* as unabbreviated forms of the name. One way the *Zohar* makes this point is by equating the phylactery worn on the head with the name YHVH, and the phylactery worn on the arm with the letter *dalet*, and then asserting that the two must be united. The *Zohar* identifies the head phylactery with the name YHVH based on the four excerpts from the Torah that are enclosed within its four compartments, and the *Zohar* identifies the arm phylactery with the letter *DaLeT* based on a mystical reading of the following verse from Song of Songs: "Your head upon you is like Carmel, and the locks [(Hebrew: *DaLaT*)] of your head are like purple; a king is held captive in the tresses." (Song 7:6). The *Zohar* states:

> *Tefillin* [(*i.e.*, phylacteries)] are the actual letters of the holy name. So, *Your head upon you is like Carmel*—[this is the] *tefillin* of the head.... [*And the DaLaT*], *The locks, of your head are like purple*...—[this is the] *tefillah* of the hand, who is poor [(*DaLaH*)] compared to those above.... *A king is held captive in the tresses*...—He [(God, the king)] is bound and held within those compartments [of the head phylactery], uniting with that holy name [YHVH] fittingly. [¶] So one adorned in them [(*i.e.*, the phylacteries)] is *in the image of God* (Gen 1:27). Just as the holy name is united with God, so is the holy name united with him, fittingly. *Male and female He created*

them" (ibid.)—*tefillin* of the head [(YHVH)] and *tefillah* of the hand [(*DaLeT*)]. All is one.[266]

In other words, when one wears phylacteries with the proper intention, the letters of the name YHVH (the head phylactery, male) become united with the letter *dalet* (D) (the arm phylactery, female), which yields the name *Yehudah* (YeHVDaH).

In a separate discussion of the name, the *Zohar* employs a different metaphor, comparing the letters of the name YHVH to the lights of a multicolored flame and, in that context, describing the final *hei* (H) of the name (the "blue-black light") as a union between a *dalet* (D) and the *vov* (V) of the first three letters of the name (the "white light"):

> [T]he final ה (*hei*) of the holy name is blue-black light, grasped by י-ה-ו (*yud, hei, vov*), radiant white light. [¶] Come and see: Sometimes this blue light [(*i.e.*, the final letter of YHVH)] is ד (*dalet*), sometimes ה (*hei*). When Israel does not cleave below, kindling it to be grasped by the white light [(*i.e.*, by the first three letters of YHVH)], it is ד (*dalet*). When they arouse it to join the white light, it is called ה (*hei*). How do we know? For it is written: *If there is* נערה (*na'arah), a girl, a virgin* (Deut 22:23), spelled נער (*na'ara*), without a ה (*hei*). Why? Because She has not joined a male [(*i.e.*, because She has not joined the *vov* that is the third letter of YHVH)], and wherever male and female are not found, ה (*hei*) is not found but rather ascends, leaving ד (*dalet*). Whenever She is joined to the radiant white light, She is called ה (*hei*), for all is one.[267]

---

[266] *Zohar* 1:14a, translated in Matt, *The Zohar: Pritzker Edition*, vol. I, p. 99.

[267] *Zohar* 1:51a, translated in Matt, *The Zohar: Pritzker Edition*, vol. I, pp. 284–285; 1:60a, pp. 345–346 [expressing the same idea].

This text focuses our attention on the orthographic similarity between the letters *dalet* (D) and *hei* (H). It says about the last letter of the name that when "She has not joined a male," she is a *dalet*, but when she is in union with a male, she is a *hei*. Therefore, the "male" corresponds to the pen stroke that a scribe must add to a *dalet* to transform it into a *hei*, which the text equates with the *vov* (V) that is the third letter of YHVH. In other words, when "She" (the *dalet*) joins to the male, the *vov* penetrates her, and the tip of the *vov* appears within her as a pen stroke, transforming her into a *hei*. That pen stroke takes the form of a letter *yud* (Y), which signifies *Yesod* among the *sefirot*, and which resembles a drop of semen. And, of course, by focusing our attention on the *dalet* (D) and *yud* (Y) that combine to form the final *hei* (H) of the name YHVH, the Zohar helps us to recognize that the name spells YeHVDY (*Yehudi*, or "Jew").

But the *Zohar* finds meaning not only in the *shapes* of the Hebrew letters but also in the spelled-out *names* of those letters.[268] For example, when the name of the letter *yud* (Y) is spelled out in Hebrew, it can be done so as *yud-vov-dalet*. Therefore, according to the *Zohar*, a *vov* (V) and a *dalet* (D) are subtly present as a hidden aspect of every *yud* (Y). But recall that a *vov* is also shaped like a *yud*, although elongated. (Please see the top of the next page.)

Moreover, just as a *yud* (Y) can be inserted into the lower left corner of a *dalet* (D) to form a *hei* (H), so also a tiny inverted

---

[268] The analysis of the four-letter name that appears in the next few paragraphs is drawn from several places in the *Zohar* and related texts, and in particular from the *Sifra di-Tzni'uta* and *Idra Zuta*. See *Zohar* 1:51a, translated in Matt, *The Zohar: Pritzker Edition*, vol. I, pp. 284–285; 2:123b [*Idra di-Mashkena*], 2:176b–179a [*Sifra di-Tzni'uta*], vol. V, pp. 159–161, 545–586; 3:65b, vol. VII, pp. 430–432; 3:290a–291a [*Idra Zuta*], vol. IX, pp. 789–798; see also Sperling and Simon, *The Zohar, Vol. V*, p. 57; Rosenberg, *The Anatomy of God*, pp. 145–152.

vov   yud
V   Y

vov (V) can be inserted into the lower left corner of a *dalet* (D) to form a *hei* (H). Therefore, with the seed-like *yud*, we can construct all the letters of the name YHVH. The *yud* contains, in the spelled-out form of its name, a *vov-dalet*, and when that hidden *vov-dalet* are in union, their individuality is nullified, and they appear together as a *hei*. The *yud* corresponds, among the *sefirot*, to *Chokhmah*, also called "Father" (*Abba*), and the *hei* corresponds to *Binah*, also called "Mother" (*Imma*). If this Mother—this *hei*—gives birth to the *vov* and *dalet* that it comprises, then those two letters appear individually as a "Son" and a "Daughter." In terms of the ten *sefirot*, the Son (also called "Brother" and "*Zeir Anpin*") corresponds to the hexad from *Chesed* through *Yesod*, and the Daughter (also called "Sister") corresponds to the last of the *sefirot*, *Malkhut*.

But at this stage, the Daughter (the letter *DaLeT*) is in a state of poverty (*DaLuT*), because she is separate from the Son and thus barren. Therefore, the name at this stage is *yud-hei-vov-dalet* (YHVD). The *vov* (V) (the Son) must impregnate the *dalet* (D) (the Daughter) in order to perfect her. He does so by placing a tiny *yud* (Y) (a seminal drop) within the *dalet* (D), making her, too, appear as a *hei* (H). This act has the effect of elevating the Daughter to the status of the Mother. *Malkhut* thus rises to the level of *Binah*, and the four-letter name becomes *yud-hei-vov-hei* (YHVH), which is the name as we see it in the Torah.

In other words, the name YHVH actually provides the basic structural elements of a myth involving divine actors who marry, conceive offspring, and then give birth, who suffer barrenness and poverty, and then attain their ultimate perfection. The name tells the tale of *Chokhmah/Abba* and his pregnant consort *Binah/ Imma*. *Binah* gives birth to a son called "*Zeir Anpin*" (the hexad from *Chesed* through *Yesod*) and a daughter called "*Malkhut*." Next, the son (*Zeir Anpin*) and the daughter (*Malkhut*) marry, and the daughter becomes pregnant with the son's seed.

One should not see scandal in the marriage of these siblings. In archetypal terms, the marriage of the Brother and the Sister, like the marriage of the Father and the Daughter, represents the return to unity of that which began as unity. Hence, it represents the powerful motif of separation and recombination that is central to the alchemical opus. The brother and sister who are separated at birth and later marry is, in fact, a widespread motif of folklore and myth. (Cf. *BT Gittin* 58a; see also Gen 20:12; Lev 20:17 [literal reading]; Song 5:2, 8:1–2.)

Thus, at the level of the *sefirot*, the marriage of the Brother (*Zeir Anpin*) and the Sister (*Malkhut*) is a *positive* event, and this positive event is also the secret meaning of the *Shema* prayer: *Shema, Yisrael;* YHVH *Eloheinu;* YHVH *achod* ("Hear, O Israel; YHVH is our God; YHVH is one and only"). The *Zohar* points out that when this prayer is written on a Torah scroll, the *dalet* (D) of the word *achod* ("one") is written large. Why? The oversized *dalet* (D) signifies that the word *ACHoD* can also be read as *ACH* + *dalet* (D), which means "Brother + *dalet* (D)." Thus, because the letter *dalet* (D) signifies the Sister (*Malkhut*), the word *ACHoD* ("one") can be read as a reference to the unity of the supernal Brother (*Zeir Anpin*) with the supernal Sister (*Malkhut*).

Moses Cordovero (1522–1570 C.E.), a leading Kabbalist of the 16th century, elaborates this metaphor in detail: "The secret of the Alliance [of male and female] is [the letter] *yud*." Here, the word *yud* refers to the first letter of *Yesod*, which is the last of the hexad that is collectively called "Son," "Brother," or "*Zeir*

Anpin." The members of this hexad are often associated with the various limbs of a Man, with *Chesed* and *Gevurah* constituting the right and left arms (or hands), *Tiferet* constituting the torso (or heart), *Netzach* and *Hod* constituting the right and left legs (or testicles), and *Yesod* constituting the phallus. Thus, Moses Cordovero's metaphor can be restated as follows: "The secret of the Alliance [of male and female] is [*Yesod*/phallus]."

The phallus is the organ of connection, and *Yesod* among the *sefirot* connects the "Brother" (the hexad from *Chesed* through *Yesod*, but, more broadly, the first nine *sefirot*) to the "Sister" (*Malkhut*), as Cordovero explains:

> The secret of the Alliance is [the letter] *Yud* [*Yesod*] which links the secret of [the letter] *Dalet* (d) [to the word] *Achod* ("One"), that is to say [it links] the Brother (*ach*) with the Sister (*achot*), which gives *ACHoD* ("One"), and the trunk of the *Yud* [*Yesod*] found in [the letter] *Dalet* links the Brother (*Ach*)—the nine upper *sefirot*—to [the *sefirah*] *Malkhut* [the Sister]. It is in this way that the Man will cause *Yesod* [the phallus] to penetrate into the heart of the domain of *Dalet*, in order to complete it, for [the woman] does not possess the sign [letter] of the alliance. The male completes her and this member is half included in her and half included in him....[269]

Because the letters of the name YHVH correspond to the ten *sefirot*, Cordovero's teaching can be read not only as a commentary on the *sefirot*, but also as a commentary on the letters of the name: "[T]he Man" (*i.e.*, the hexad from *Chesed* through *Yesod*), which corresponds to the letter *vov* (V) in the name YHVH, "will

---

[269] *Tefillah le-Moshe*, vol. 1, 213b, translated and quoted in Mopsik, "Union and Unity in the Kabbalah," in Goodman (ed.), *Between Jerusalem and Benares*, p. 235. The underscored editorial inserts are by the present author. See also *id.* at pp. 228–229.

cause *Yesod*," which is the lower tip of the *vov* (V), "to penetrate into the heart of the domain of *Dalet*, in order to complete it,... and this member is half included in her and half included in him...." At the top of the next page, the name YHVH is depicted vertically, showing the lower tip of the *vov* (V) (*i.e.*, *Yesod*, the phallus) penetrating the womb of a *dalet* (D) ("half included in her and half included in him") and appearing inside the *dalet* (D) as a *yud* (Y) (a drop of seed), which transforms the *dalet* (D) into a *hei* (H).

Thus, when the final *hei* (H) of God's name is seen to comprise a *dalet* (D) and a *yud* (Y), that *yud* (Y) is seen to be the graphic depiction of the *vov* (V) (the Brother) inseminating the *dalet* (D) (the Sister), linking her to him through the mystery of impregnation. Put another way, the hidden *yud* (which represents *Yesod* or the phallus) "hooks" the *dalet* to the *vov*, making the *dalet* appear as a *hei*. By union with this hidden *yud*, *Malkhut* is transformed from the barrenness of Rachel to the fertility of Leah and attains the status of *Binah*. Of course, Cordovero is also telling us that the second *hei* of the name YHVH is really a *dalet-yud*, which makes that name YeHVDY (*Yehudi*, or "Jew").

More than two centuries before Cordovero, we encounter similar ideas in *Sha'arei 'Orah* ("Gates of Light"), an extremely influential book by Joseph Gikatilla (13th century C.E.). Gikatilla begins his discussion with a statement about the Sabbath. The Torah tells us that the Sabbath is an "eternal sign" between YHVH and the Jewish people. (Exod 31:17.) But the Hebrew words that translate as "eternal sign" can also be translated as "eternal letter." Gikatilla relates this "eternal letter" to the hidden *yud* (Y) of the name YHVH:

> The secret of the word "letter"... is that the lower end of the letter *vov* [(*i.e.*, the third letter of the name YHVH)]... is known to all masters of wisdom as the small letter *yud* [(*i.e.*, *Yesod*, the last of the hexad of *sefirot* symbolized by the *vov* of the

name)] and it is known as a "little letter." It is also known as the letter of the holy covenant of circumcision [(*i.e.*, sexual morality)].[270]

Later in his book, Gikatilla brings up the same subject again, this time referring to the person "who knows the secret of the letter *yud*" (*i.e.*, the little *yud* that constitutes the lower tip of the *vov* of YHVH). Gikatilla then proceeds with the following detailed analysis of all four letters of the name YHVH (*yud-hei-vov-hei*):

[The person who knows the secret] understands how the three upper Spheres [(*i.e.*, *Keter*, *Chokhmah*, and *Binah*)] unify at the point of the [first] letter *yud* [(*i.e.*, *Keter*)] and she [(*i.e.*, *Binah*, but also the first *hei*)] also draws blessing from the inside to the letter *vov* [(*i.e.*, the hexad of *sefirot* from *Chesed*

---

[270] Weinstein (trans.), *Gates of Light*, p. 83 [Weinstein's translation has been modified slightly]. On the secret of the *vov*, see also *id.* at pp. 92–93, 243.

through *Yesod*)], and from the letter *vov*, the letter *dalet* [(*i.e.*, *Malkhut*)] receives an abundance of blessing which is the secret of the last letter *hei*.[271]

In other words, "the secret of the last letter *hei*" is that she is really a *dalet* (D) that appears as a *hei* (H) because she has been penetrated by the tip of the *vov* (V) (*i.e., Yesod*), which can be seen inside her as a little *yud* (Y) (seed). Gikatilla next quotes an obscure phrase from the book of Ezekiel: "In fourth in fifth of the month." (Ezek 1:1.) For Gikatilla, the significance of "fourth" and "fifth" is the positions of the *dalet* (D) and the *hei* (H) in the Hebrew alphabet. The *dalet* (the fourth letter of the alphabet) appears as a *hei* (the fifth letter of the alphabet) when she is in sexual union with the *vov* of the divine name, receiving within her womb the *yud* (*Yesod*) that is understood to be the tip of the *vov*.

In summary, by marriage between the Brother (*Zeir Anpin*) and the Sister (*Malkhut*), the name *yud-hei-vov* + *dalet* (God's name in a state of separation) becomes the name *yud-hei-vov-hei* (God's name as written in the Torah).

Gikatilla also explains that the name of King David's father, *YeSHaY* ("Jesse"), which is spelled *yud-shin-yud*, is really a reference to the first and second *yud*s of the name YHVH, with the holy letter *shin* (SH, or Shaddai) interposed between them. Thus, he again confirms in very plain terms that the name YHVH contains a concealed *yud* (Y) at its end, tucked inside the final *hei* (H): "Behold, according to all the Kabbalists there are two letter *yud*s [in the name YHVH], an upper *yud* which is the Sphere *Chokhmah*, and a lower *yud*... [which is the Sphere] *Yesod*"— the latter being the tip of the *vov* (V) penetrating a *dalet* (D),

---

[271] Weinstein (trans.), *Gates of Light*, p. 347 [Weinstein's translation has been modified slightly].

making her into a *hei* (H).[272] And because of these two *yud*s in
the name YHVH, Jews frequently abbreviate the name by writing
a double *yud*.

Gikatilla explains that King David corresponds to *Malkhut*
("Sovereignty"), and he became the fourth pillar of the "divine
chariot" by cleaving to the hidden *yud* (Y) (*Yesod*) of the name
YHVH, thereby conjoining *Malkhut* to *Yesod*.[273] For this reason,
YHVH says about David: "My *yud* shall be established with him"
(Ps 89:22). And, of course, if the concealed *yud* (Y) of the name
YHVH is "established"—that is, brought into full revelation—
then the name becomes YeHVDY (*Yehudi*, or "Jew").

272 Weinstein (trans.), *Gates of Light*, p. 329.

273 Weinstein (trans.), *Gates of Light*, p. 329.

Appendix Two

After the death of King Solomon, the tribes of Israel separated into two rival kingdoms, the Southern Kingdom, called "Judah," and the Northern Kingdom, called "Israel." It is important to note that Hebrew scripture reflects an unmistakable pro-Judah bias, which the book of Psalms explicitly acknowledges: "He despised the tent of Joseph, and the tribe of Ephraim he did not choose, and he chose the tribe of Judah, Mount Zion that he loves." (Ps 78:67–68.)

The Torah relates that YHVH repeatedly called the Israelites a "stiff-necked people" (Exod 32:9, 33:3–5, 34:9; Deut 9:6, 9:13, 10:16, 31:27) and finally lost patience with them (Num 14:27–35), but YHVH made an express exception for the tribe of Judah (Num 14:20–24; Josh 14:6–14), and YHVH included the tribe of Ephraim in that exception only when Aaron was present, not when YHVH was talking to Moses alone (Num 14:26, 14:30). Judah is, of course, the tribe from which the kings of the Southern Kingdom descend (Ruth 4:12–22), and Ephraim is the tribe from which the kings of the Northern Kingdom descend (1 Kings 11:26).

The Torah also records that the Israelites constantly complained to Moses, noting the following specific complaints: no water at Marah (Exod 15); no bread and meat in the Wilderness of Sin (Exod 16); no water in Rephidim (Exod 17); unspecified complaints of evil at Taberah (Num 11:1–3); no tasty foods, just manna, at Kibroth-ha-Taavah (Num 11); giants dwelling in the land that is their destination (Num 13); dangers of military attack (Num 14); inadequacy of leadership (Num 16); no water at Kadeish (Num 20); and no food or water on the journey from Mount Hor (Num 21:4–9). The Torah relates this litany of complaints by the Israelites, but the later prophets tell us that YHVH shared esoteric wisdom with "House of Jacob" (Ezek 20:5), a clear reference to Judah. In addition, the Torah very strongly condemns the worship of a golden calf (Exod 32), which not coincidently happens to be the image worshiped in the temples of the Northern Kingdom (1 Kings 12:28–30).

Later, during the time of the monarchies, the Northern Kingdom (Israel) engaged in civil war against the Southern Kingdom (Judah) for two centuries, a war in which Israel is generally described as the unjustified aggressor. (See 1 Kings 11:26–39, 12:1–24, 14:30, 15:6, 15:16–21, 15:32; 2 Kings 9:27–28, 10:12–14, 13:12, 14:8–15, 16:5–7; Isa 7:1–9; Ezek 37:15–28; 2 Chron 28:5–8.) Hebrew scripture also consistently denounces Israel's kings, saying about each of them, without exception, that he "did evil in the eyes of YHVH" (1 Kings 13:33–34, 15:26, 15:34, 16:13, 16:19, 16:25, 16:30, 22:52; 2 Kings 3:2, 10:28–31, 13:2, 13:11, 14:24, 15:9, 15:13, 15:18, 15:24, 15:28, 17:2), and employing particularly harsh terms to denounce King Ahab (1 Kings 16:30). By contrast, it praises nine of Judah's kings, saying they "did right in the eyes of YHVH" (1 Kings 11:4, 15:3–5, 15:11, 22:43, 2 Kings 12:2, 14:3, 15:3, 15:34, 18:3–4, 22:2; 2 Chron 14:2, 20:32, 24:2, 25:2, 26:4, 27:2, 29:2, 34:2), and it presents three Judean kings (King David, King Hezekiah, and King Josiah) as models of righteousness (1 Kings 11:4, 15:3–5; 2 Kings 18:3–4, 22:2; 2 Chron 29:2, 34:2). Of the Judean kings that scripture criticizes, two are denounced for their familial ties to King Ahab of Israel (2 Kings 8:18, 8:26–27; 2 Chron 21:6, 22:2–4), and most of the others postdate the fall of Israel and the absorption into Judah of refugees from that kingdom (2 Kings 21:2–16, 21:20, 23:32, 23:37, 24:9, 24:19; 2 Chron 33:2–9, 33:22, 36:5, 36:9, 36:12). Scripture repeatedly criticizes the people of the Northern Kingdom for engaging in child sacrifice (see 2 Kings 16:3, 17:16–17; Jer 3:20–25; Ezek 20:26, 20:31, 23:31–39; Hosea 13:1–2; Mic 6:7; Ps 106:35–38), and although child sacrifices also occurred in the Southern Kingdom (most prominently after the fall of the Northern Kingdom), scripture tends to blame these practices on the influence of the Northern Kingdom (see 2 Kings 16:3, 17:19, 21:2–6, 23:10; Jer 7:30–31, 19:3–5,

32:30–35; Ezek 16:20–21, 23:31–39). Finally, the prophets and the psalms repeatedly describe the Southern Kingdom (Judah) as more faithful than the Northern Kingdom (Israel), often noting the latter's transgressions. (See 1 Kings 14:7–16; 2 Kings 17:7–23, 18:3–8, 19:14–37; Ezek 20, 36; Hosea 8, 12–13; Amos 9:8–12; Pss 78, 114:1–2.)

One cannot properly interpret Hebrew scripture without appreciating its pro-Judah bias, because the numerous tales that are woven into the scriptural narrative often reflect that bias in subtle ways. Whether or not the bias is historically justified, it is the backstory that explains much of what scripture relates on its surface.

Bibliography of Cited Works

Albertz, Rainer, *The History of Israelite Religion in the Old Testament Period, Volume I: From the Beginnings to the End of the Monarchy* (Westminster/John Knox Press 1994).

Alter, Joseph S., *The Wrestler's Body: Identity and Ideology in North India* (Univ. of California Press 1992).

Assmann, Jan, *Moses the Egyptian: The Memory of Egypt in Western Monotheism* (Harvard Univ. Press 1997).

Assmann, Jan, *The Search for God in Ancient Egypt* (Cornell Univ. Press 2001).

Awn, Peter J., Satan*'s Tragedy and Redemption: Iblis in Sufi Psychology* (Brill 1983).

Baines, John, Leonard H. Lesko, and David P. Silverman, with Byron E. Shafer (ed.), *Religion in Ancient Egypt: Gods, Myths, and Personal Practice* (Cornell Univ. Press 1991).

Benamozegh, Elijah, *Israel and Humanity* (Paulist Press 1995).

Berg, Michael, and Yehuda Ashlag (trans. and eds.), *The Zohar by Rav Shimon bar Yochai: The First Ever Unabridged English Translation with Commentary* (Kabbalah Centre International 2003).

Biale, David, *Eros and the Jews: From Biblical Israel to Contemporary America* (Basic Books 1992).

Bleeker, C.J., *Hathor and Thoth: Two Key Figures of the Ancient Egyptian Religion* (Brill 1973).

Bloch, Maurice, and Jonathan Parry (eds.), *Death and the Regeneration of Life* (Cambridge Univ. Press 1982).

Bodewitz, Hendrik Wilhelm, *Jaiminiya Brahmana I, 1–65: Translation and Commentary with a Study: Agnihotra and Pranagnihotra* (E.J. Brill 1973).

Bodewitz, Hendrik Wilhelm, *The Daily Evening and Morning Offering*

(Agnihotra) According to the Brahmanas (Motilal Banarsidass 2003).

Boylan, Patrick, *Thoth: The Hermes of Egypt* (Kessinger Reprints).

Braude, William G., and Israel J. Kapstein (trans. and eds.), *Pesikta de-Rab Kahana: R. Kahana's Compilation of Discourses for Sabbaths and Festal Days* (Jewish Publication Society of America 2002).

Brinner, William M. (trans.), *The History of al-Tabari*, vol. III, *The Children of Israel* (SUNY 1987).

Brown, Shelby, *Late Carthaginian Child Sacrifice and Sacrificial Monuments in Their Mediterranean Context* (Sheffield Academic Press 1991).

Carman, John B., and Frederique Apffel Marglin (eds.), *Purity and Auspiciousness in Indian Society* (E.J. Brill 1985)

Chapman, J.A., *Maxims of Ali* (1963).

Choksy, Jamsheed, *Purity and Pollution in Zoroastrianism* (Univ. of Texas Press 1989).

Cohen, Abraham, *Everyman's Talmud: The Major Teachings of the Rabbinic Sages* (Schocken Books 1949, 1995).

Cohen, Seymour J. (trans.), *The Holy Letter: A Study in Jewish Sexual Morality* (Jason Aronson 1993).

Collier, Mark, and Bill Manley, *How to Read Egyptian Hieroglyphs: A Step-by-Step Guide to Teach Yourself* (Univ. of Calif. Press 2003).

Coogan, Michael David (trans. and ed.), *Stories from Ancient Canaan* (Westminster Press 1978).

Coogan, Michael D., *The Old Testament: A Historical and Literary Introduction to the Hebrew Scriptures* (Oxford Univ. Press 2011).

Coomaraswamy, Ananda K., "Atmayajna: Self-Sacrifice," *Harvard Journal of Asiatic Studies*, Vol. 6, No. 3/4 (February 1942).

Copenhaver, Brian P. (trans.), *Hermetica: The Greek Corpus Hermeticum and the Latin Asclepius* (Cambridge Univ. Press 1992)

Cross, Frank Moore, *Canaanite Myth and Hebrew Epic: Essays in the History of the Religion of Israel* (Harvard Univ. Press 1973).

Dalley, Stephanie (trans.), *Myths from Mesopotamia: Creation, the Flood, Gilgamesh, and Others* (Oxford University Press 2000).

Davis, Matt, "Aoccdrnig to rscheearch at Cmabrigde Uinervtisy, it deosn't mttaer in waht oredr the ltteers in a wrod are…" (Cambridge Univ. 2012)

Dimmitt, Cornelia, and J.A.B. van Buitenen, *Classical Hindu Mythology: A Reader in the Sanskrit Puranas* (Temple University Press 1978).

Doniger, Wendy, and Brian K. Smith (trans.), *The Laws of Manu* (Penguin Books 1991).

Dresner, Samuel H., *The Zaddik: The Doctrine of the Zaddik According to the Writings of Rabbi Yaakov Yosef of Polnoy* (Schocken Books 1974).

Dumont, Louis, and D. Pocock, "Pure and Impure," in Louis Dumont and D. Pocock (eds.), *Contributions to Indian Sociology* (Mouton & Co. 1959), pp. 9–39.

Edwards, Betsalel Philip, *Living Waters: The Mei HaShiloach: A Commentary on the Torah by Rabbi Mordechai Yosef of Isbitza* (Jason Aronson 2004).

Eliade, Mircea, *A History of Religious Ideas, Volume 1, From the Stone Age to the Eleusinian Mysteries* (Univ. of Chicago Press 1978).

Eliade, Mircea, *Yoga: Immortality and Freedom* (Princeton Univ. Press 1973).

Epstein, Isidore (ed.), *The Babylonian Talmud* (Soncino Press 1935).

Faulkner, Raymond O. (trans.), *The Egyptian Book of the Dead: The Book of Going Forth by Day* (Chronicle Books 1994).

Fishbane, Michael, *Kiss of God: Spiritual and Mystical Death in Judaism* (Univ. of Washington Press 1994).

Frankfort, Henri, *Kingship and the Gods: A Study of Ancient Near*

Eastern Religion as the Integration of Society and Nature (Univ. of Chicago Press 1978).

Freud, Sigmund, *Moses and Monotheism* (Vintage Books 1967).

Friedman, Richard E., *Who Wrote the Bible?* (HarperCollins 1987, 2d ed. 1997).

Fuller, C.J., *The Camphor Flame: Popular Hinduism and Society in India* (Princeton Univ. Press 1992).

Ginsburg, Elliot K. (trans. and ed.), *Sod ha-Shabbat (the Mystery of the Sabbath) from the Tolaat Yaaqov of R. Meir ibn Gabbai* (SUNY Press 1989).

Ginzberg, Louis, *The Legends of the Jews, Volume 1, From the Creation to Jacob* (Johns Hopkins Univ. Press 1998).

Ginzberg, Louis, *The Legends of the Jews, Volume 3, Moses in the Wilderness* (Johns Hopkins Univ. Press 1998).

Ginzberg, Louis, *The Legends of the Jews, Volume 5, Notes to Volumes 1 and 2, From the Creation to the Exodus* (Johns Hopkins Univ. Press 1998).

(von) Goethe, Johann Wolfgang, *Goethe's Werke: Vollstandige Ausgabe Letzter Hand*, vol. 6 (JG Cotta'sche Buchhandlung 1827).

Gonzalez, Ana M., et al., "Mitochondrial Lineage M1 Traces an Early Human Backflow to Africa," *BMC Genomics* 2007, 8:223.

Goodman, Hananya (ed.), *Between Jerusalem and Benares: Comparative Studies in Judaism and Hinduism* (SUNY Press 1994).

Gottlieb, Freema, *The Lamp of God: A Jewish Book of Light* (Jason Aronson 1996).

Graves, Robert, *The Greek Myths* (Penguin 1993).

Green, Arthur (trans.), *Hasidic Spirituality for a New Era: The Religious Writings of Hillel Zeitlin* (Paulist Press 2012).

Green, Arthur (trans.), *Menahem Nahum of Chernobyl: Upright Practices, The Light of the Eyes* (Paulist Press 1982).

Grimal, Nicolas, *A History of Ancient Egypt* (Blackwell Publishers 1992).

Hackett, Jo Ann, *The Balaam Text from Deir ʿAllā* (Harvard Semitic Monographs 31) (Scholars Press 1984).

Hallamish, Moshe, *An Introduction to the Kabbalah* (SUNY Press 1999).

Hare, Tom, *ReMembering Osiris: Number, Gender, and the Word in Ancient Egyptian Representational Systems* (Stanford Univ. Press 1999).

Hayes, Christine, *Introduction to the Bible* (Yale Univ. Press 2012).

Heesterman, J.C., *The Broken World of Sacrifice: An Essay in Ancient Indian Ritual* (Univ. of Chicago Press 1993).

Herford, R. Travers (trans. and ed.), *Pirke Aboth: The Ethics of the Talmud: Sayings of the Fathers* (Schocken Books 1969).

Hoffmeier, James K., *Israel and Egypt: The Evidence for the Authenticity of the Exodus Tradition* (Oxford Univ. Press 1996).

Horning, Erik, *Conceptions of God in Ancient Egypt: The One and the Many* (Cornell Univ. Press 1982, 1996).

Hume, Robert Ernest (trans.), *The Thirteen Principal Upanishads* (Oxford Univ. Press 1985).

Idel, Moshe, *Saturn's Jews: On the Witches' Sabbat and Sabbateanism* (Continuum 2011).

Idel, Moshe, *Studies in Ecstatic Kabbalah* (SUNY Press 1988).

Idel, Moshe, *The Mystical Experience in Abraham Abulafia* (SUNY Press 1988).

Jacobs, Louis, *Hasidic Prayer* (Schocken Books 1972).

Jacobs, Louis (comp. and trans.), *The Schocken Book of Jewish Mystical Testimonies* (Schocken Books 1976, reprint 1997).

Kaelber, Walter O., *Tapta Marga: Asceticism and Initiation in Vedic India* (SUNY Press 1989).

Kaplan, Aryeh (trans. and ed.), *Sefer Yetzirah: The Book of Creation* (Samuel Weiser 1997).

Kaplan, Aryeh (trans.), *The Bahir* (Samuel Weiser 1989).

Karo, Joseph, *Maggid Mesharim*, translated in Louis Jacobs (comp. and trans.), *The Schocken Book of Jewish Mystical Testimonies* (Schocken Books 1976, reprint 1997).

Katz, Marion Holmes, *Body of Text: The Emergence of the Sunni Law of Ritual Purity* (SUNY Press 2002).

Kilian, Rudolf, "Gen. I 2 und die Urgötter von Hermopolis" ("Gen 1:2 and the Primordial Gods from Hermopolis"), *Vetus Testamentum*, vol. 16, fasc. 4 (October 1966), pp. 420–438.

Klawans, Jonathan, *Impurity and Sin in Ancient Judaism* (Oxford Univ. Press 2000).

Kramer, Chaim, *Anatomy of the Soul* (Breslov Research Institute 1998).

Kramrisch, Stella, *The Hindu Temple* (Motilal Banarsidass 1980).

Kramrisch, Stella, *The Presence of Śiva* (Princeton Univ. Press 1994).

Krassen, Miles (trans.), *Isaiah Horowitz: The Generations of Adam* (Paulist Press 1996).

Kugel, James L., *How to Read the Bible: A Guide to Scripture Then and Now* (Free Press 2007).

Lal, B.B., "The Only Asian Expedition in threatened Nubia: Work by an India Mission at Afyeh and Tumas," *Illustrated London News*, April 20, 1963, pp. 579–581.

Leslie, Charles (ed.), *Asian Medical Systems: A Comparative Study* (Univ. of California Press 1976).

Levenson, Jon D., *The Death and Resurrection of the Beloved Son: The Transformation of Child Sacrifice in Judaism and Christianity* (Yale Univ. Press 1993).

Lichtheim, Miriam (trans. and ed.), *Ancient Egyptian Literature: A*

Book of Readings (Univ. of California Press 2006) (three volumes).

Luzzatto, Moshe Chayim, *Mesillat Yesharim: The Path of the Just* (Feldheim Publishers 1990).

Magid, Shaul, *Hasidism on the Margin: Reconciliation, Antinomianism, and Messianism in Izbica/Radzin Hasidism* (Univ. of Wisconsin Press 2003).

Mahoney, William K., *The Artful Universe: An Introduction to the Vedic Religious Imagination* (SUNY Press 1998).

Matt, Daniel C. (trans.), *The Zohar: Pritzker Edition*, vol. I (Stanford Univ. Press 2004).

Matt, Daniel C. (trans.), *The Zohar: Pritzker Edition*, vol. II (Stanford Univ. Press 2004).

Matt, Daniel C. (trans.), *The Zohar: Pritzker Edition*, vol. III (Stanford Univ. Press 2006).

Matt, Daniel C. (trans.), *The Zohar: Pritzker Edition*, vol. V (Stanford Univ. Press 2009).

Matt, Daniel C. (trans.), *The Zohar: Pritzker Edition*, vol. VI (Stanford Univ. Press 2011).

Matt, Daniel C. (trans.), *The Zohar: Pritzker Edition*, vol. VII (Stanford Univ. Press 2012).

Matt, Daniel C. (trans.), *The Zohar: Pritzker Edition*, vol. IX (Stanford Univ. Press 2016).

Meeks, Dimitri, and Christine Favard-Meeks, *Daily Life of the Egyptian Gods* (Cornell Univ. Press 1996).

Meshel, Naphtali S., *The "Grammar" of Sacrifice: A Generativist Study of the Israelite Sacrificial System in the Priestly Writings with A "Grammar" of* Σ (Oxford Univ. Press 2014).

Milgrom, Jacob, *Leviticus 1–16: A New Translation with Introduction and Commentary* (Doubleday 1991).

Milgrom, Jacob, *Leviticus 17–22: A New Translation with Introduction and Commentary* (Doubleday 2000).

Mopsik, Charles, "Union and Unity in the Kabbalah," in Hananya Goodman (ed.), *Between Jerusalem and Benares: Comparative Studies in Judaism and Hinduism* (SUNY Press 1994), pp. 232–233.

Morrison, Chanan, *Gold from the Land of Israel: A New Light on the Weekly Torah Portion from the Writings of Rabbi Abraham Isaac HaKohen Kook* (Urim Publications 2006).

Nachman of Breslov, *Likutey Moharan*.

Nachman of Breslov, *The Aleph-Bet Book (Sefer haMidot): Rabbi Nachman's Aphorisms on Jewish Living* (Breslov Research Institute 2000).

Neusner, Jacob, *A Theological Commentary to the Midrash: Volume Three: Song of Songs Rabbah* (Univ. Press of America 2001).

Neusner, Jacob, *The Idea of Purity in Ancient Judaism: The Haskell Lectures, 1972–1973* (E.J. Brill 1973).

Obeyesekere, Gananath, "The Impact of Ayurvedic Ideas on the Culture and the Individual in Sri Lanka," in Charles Leslie (ed.), *Asian Medical Systems: A Comparative Study* (Univ. of California Press 1976).

O'Flaherty, Wendy Doniger, *Hindu Myths: A Sourcebook Translated from the Sanskrit* (Penguin Books 1976).

O'Flaherty, Wendy Doniger, *Śiva: The Erotic Ascetic* (Oxford Univ. Press 1981).

O'Flaherty, Wendy Doniger, *The Origins of Evil in Hindu Mythology* (Univ. of California Press 1980).

O'Flaherty, Wendy Doniger (trans. and ed.), *The Rig Veda: An Anthology* (Penguin Books 1983).

O'Flaherty, Wendy Doniger, *Women, Androgynes, and Other Mythical Beasts* (Univ. of Chicago Press 1980).

Panikkar, Raimundo (trans. and ed.), *The Vedic Experience: Mantramanjari: An Anthology of the Vedas for Modern Man and Contemporary Celebration* (All India Books 1983).

Parker, Robert, *Miasma: Pollution and Purification in Early Greek Religion* (Clarendon Press 1983).

Parry, Jonathan P., *Death in Banaras* (Cambridge Univ. Press 1994).

Parry, Jonathan P., "Sacrificial Death and the Necrophagous Ascetic," in Maurice Bloch and Jonathan Parry (eds.), *Death and the Regeneration of Life* (Cambridge Univ. Press 1982), pp. 82–83.

Patai, Raphael, *The Messiah Texts* (Avon Books 1979).

Rawlinson, Graham E., *The Significance of Letter Position in Word Recognition*, unpublished Ph.D. dissertation, 1976, Psychology Department, University of Nottingham.

Redford, Donald B. (ed.), *The Ancient Gods Speak: A Guide to Egyptian Religion* (Oxford Univ. Press 2002).

Reinhart, A. Keven, "Impurity/ No Danger," in *History of Religions* (Univ. of Chicago Press), Vol. 30, No. 1 (August 1990), pp. 1–24.

Reuveni, Aharon, Letter, Israel State Archives (1965), translated in "Why not Judea? Zion? State of the Hebrews?" *Haaretz*, May 7, 2008.

Reznick, Leibel, *The Holy Temple Revisited* (Jason Aronson 1993).

Rosenberg, Roy A. (trans.), *The Anatomy of God* (KTAV Publishing House 1973).

Sauneron, Serge, *The Priests of Ancient Egypt* (Cornell Univ. Press 2000).

Sayce, A.H., "The Egyptian Background of Genesis 1," in *Studies Presented to F.Ll. Griffith* (Egypt Exploration Society 1932), pp. 419–423.

Schäfer, Peter, *Jesus in the Talmud* (Princeton Univ. Press 2007).

Schimmel, Annemarie, *Mystical Dimensions of Islam* (Univ. of North Carolina Press 1975).

Scholem, Gershom G., *Major Trends in Jewish Mysticism* (Schocken 1961).

Scholem, Gershom G., *On the Kabbalah and Its Symbolism* (Schocken 1969).

Scholem, Gershom G., *The Messianic Idea in Judaism: And Other Essays on Jewish Spirituality* (Schocken Books 1971).

Sela, Shlomo, *Abraham ibn Ezra and the Rise of Medieval Hebrew Science* (Brill 2003).

Shaw, Ian (ed.), *The Oxford History of Ancient Egypt* (Oxford Univ. Press 2000).

Shkolnik, A., E. Maltz, and S. Gordin, "Desert Conditions and Goat Milk Production," *Journal of Dairy Science*, Vol. 63, No. 10 (1980), pp. 1749–1754.

Simon, Maurice, and Paul P. Levertoff (trans.), *The Zohar: An English Translation, Vol. IV* (Soncino Press 1984).

Smith, Mark S., *The Early History of God: Yahweh and the Other Deities in Ancient Israel* (HarperCollins 1990).

Smith, Mark S., *The Origins of Biblical Monotheism: Israel's Polytheistic Background and the Ugaritic Texts* (Oxford Univ. Press 2001).

Sperling, Harry, Maurice Simon, and Paul P. Levertoff (trans.), *The Zohar: An English Translation, Vol. III* (Soncino Press 1984).

Sperling, Harry, and Maurice Simon (trans.), *The Zohar: An English Translation, Vol. V* (Soncino Press 1984).

Starrett, Yehoshua, *The Inner Temple* (Breslov Research Institute 2003).

Svoboda, Robert E., *Ayurveda: Life, Health and Longevity* (Penguin Books 1993).

Tachikawa, Musashi, Shrikant Bahulkar, and Madhavi Kolhatkar, *Indian Fire Ritual* (Motilal Banarsidass 2001).

Thomson, James, *The City of Dreadful Night*, vol. I (Reeves & Turner 1895).

Tuttle, Edwin H., "Dravidian and Nubian," *Journal of the American Oriental Society*, vol. 52, No. 2 (June 1932), pp. 133–144.

Vesci, Uma Marina, *Heat and Sacrifice in the Vedas* (Motilal Banarsidass 1992).

Weinstein, Avi (trans.), *Gates of Light (Sha'are Orah)* (HarperCollins 1994).

Weissman, Moshe (ed.), *The Midrash Says: The Narrative of the Weekly Torah-Portion in the Perspective of Our Sages: The Book of Sh'mos* (Benei Yakov Publications 1980).

Weissman, Moshe (ed.), *The Midrash Says: The Narrative of the Weekly Torah-Portion in the Perspective of Our Sages: The Book of Vayikra* (Benei Yakov Publications 1982).

Wiseman, Donald J. (trans. and ed.), *Chronicles of Chaldean Kings (626–556 B.C.) in The British Museum* (British Museum 1956).

Wolfson, Elliot R., "The Secret of the Garment in Nahmanides," *Da'at*, vol. 24 (1990), pp. 25–49.

Wolfson, Elliot R., *Through a Speculum That Shines: Vision and Imagination in Medieval Jewish Mysticism* (Princeton Univ. Press 1994).

Wright, David P., *Inventing God's Law: How the Covenant Code of the Bible Used and Revised the Laws of Hammurabi* (Oxford Univ. Press 2009).

Yitzchaki, Shlomo, *Rashi: Commentary on the Torah (The Sapirstein Edition)*, vol. 3 (Mesorah Publications 1999).

Zohar, Zvi, "The Rabbi and the Sheikh," *Jewish Studies Quarterly*, Vol. 16 (2009), pp. 1–32.

Index

347

352   TORAH AND NONDUALISM

Josiah (king of Judah)
  monotheistic reforms instituted
    by, 289
  Torah book found during reign
    of, 289
Judah (kingdom)
  called "Jacob", 148
  Hebrew scripture favors, 230,
    313, 331–33
  Israel refugees absorbed into,
    21–22, 300
  Israel separates from, 63, 148,
    154, 313, 332
  kings of are representatives of
    the gods, 108–10, 142
  kings of described as God's
    "son", 142, 167
  name of is pronunciation of
    YHVH, 107–11, 151–52
  secret of name YHVH known to
    people of, 148–49, 331
  universal and eternal, 320
  YHVH is god of, 151–52, 153–54
Judah (son of Jacob)
  Benjamin redeemed from prison
    by, 62
  called "congress of nations",
    108, 153, 320
  Horus comparison, 61–63
  name of is pronunciation of
    YHVH, 107–11, 151–52
  named for YHVH, 108
  sexual relations with daughter-
    in-law, 111
Judaism
  asceticism and, 292–93
  astrology and, 292, see also Sat-
    urn (planet)
  before Deuteronomic reforms,
    291–94
  Days of Awe, meaning of, 37–38
  divine images, use of, 141–46,
    291–92, 294, 297–98

God in human form and, 166,
    292, see also Divine Council:
    human member of
  iconoclastic monotheism and,
    290–91, 296–97
  oral Torah and, 268–69
  pantheon of gods and goddesses
    recognized by, 68, 75–78, 78,
    291–92
  power of words recognized by,
    141, 149, 237–38
  reincarnation and, 293
  two religions interwoven into
    one, 33–34, 42, 139, 155–57,
    229
  vegetarianism and, 201, 293
  work in progress, 320
Kadeish
  Korach's rebellion at, 234–37
  Miriam's death at, 242, 245
  Moses' sin at rock of, 242–44
  Rephidim is similar to, 245, 246,
    247
  rock of is a man, 247–48
karma (law of nature)
  Joshua and, 312
  phrase "eye for an eye" and,
    214–16, 232–34, 312
  phrase "he will bear his sin" and,
    232–34, 265, 312
  phrase "his sin is upon him" and,
    264, 265
Karna (figure in *Mahabharata*), 13
Kook, Abraham Isaac
  vegetarian sacrifices and, 201
  white spaces of Torah and, 85
Korach (cousin of Moses)
  Aaron's chief priest posi-
    tion challenged by, 234–35,
    236–37
  Moses' confrontation with, 231,
    234–37
  rock of Kadeish refers to, 247–
    48, 248–49

About the Author

JAMES H. CUMMING received his B.A. from Columbia University and his J.D. from the University of Pennsylvania Law School, graduating *magna cum laude*. He clerked at the U.S. Court of Appeals for the D.C. Circuit and has served for over twenty years as a chambers attorney at the California Supreme Court. His religious scholarship began in 1981 with Kashmiri Shaivism. In the 1990s, his studies included the leading classics of Vedanta, in particular, the *Mahabharata* and the *Upanishads*. In the 2000s, he taught himself to read Hebrew and undertook a comprehensive study of Jewish mysticism that included the multivolume *Zohar* and the leading texts of Lurianic Kabbalah. After studying Hebrew scribal techniques, he closely reread the Hebrew scriptures, applying the hermeneutical methods described in the *Sifra di-Tzni'uta*, the *Idra Rabba*, and the *Idra Zuta*. Most recently, his research has focused on Western philosophy and the monistic thought of Baruch Spinoza (1632–1677 C.E.). He lives with his wife and two sons in Berkeley, California.